MW00330446

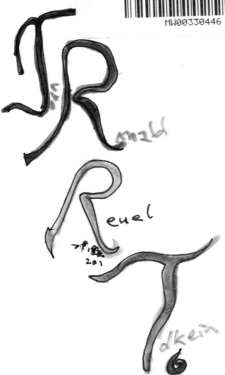

Fire

Reuel

dkein

THE RING OF WORDS

The Ring of Words

Tolkien and the *Oxford English Dictionary*

PETER GILLIVER

JEREMY MARSHALL

EDMUND WEINER

Bright is the ring of words
When the right man rings them,
Fair the fall of songs
When the singer sings them.

Robert Louis Stevenson

OXFORD
UNIVERSITY PRESS

OXFORD

UNIVERSITY PRESS

Great Clarendon Street, Oxford OX2 6DP

Oxford University Press is a department of the University of Oxford.
It furthers the University's objective of excellence in research, scholarship,
and education by publishing worldwide in

Oxford New York

Auckland Cape Town Dar es Salaam Hong Kong Karachi
Kuala Lumpur Madrid Melbourne Mexico City Nairobi
New Delhi Shanghai Taipei Toronto

With offices in

Argentina Austria Brazil Chile Czech Republic France Greece
Guatemala Hungary Italy Japan Poland Portugal Singapore
South Korea Switzerland Thailand Turkey Ukraine Vietnam

Oxford is a registered trade mark of Oxford University Press
in the UK and in certain other countries

Published in the United States
by Oxford University Press Inc., New York

© Peter Gilliver, Jeremy Marshall, Edmund Weiner

The moral rights of the authors have been asserted
Database right Oxford University Press (maker)

First published 2006

All rights reserved. No part of this publication may be reproduced,
stored in a retrieval system, or transmitted, in any form or by any means,
without the prior permission in writing of Oxford University Press,
or as expressly permitted by law, or under terms agreed with the appropriate
reprographics rights organization. Enquiries concerning reproduction
outside the scope of the above should be sent to the Rights Department,
Oxford University Press, at the address above

You must not circulate this book in any other binding or cover
and you must impose this same condition on any acquirer

British Library Cataloguing in Publication Data
Data available

Library of Congress Cataloging in Publication Data
Data available

Designed by George Hammond
Typeset by Alliance Interactive Technology
Printed in Great Britain
by Clays Ltd, Bungay, Suffolk

ISBN 0–19–861069–6   ISBN 978–0–19–861069–4

1 3 5 7 9 10 8 6 4 2

Contents

Preface

Nay, I have worried at whiles even over the tongues of Men,
but Melko take them! they shift and change, change and shift, and when
you have them are but a hard stuff whereof to labour songs or tales.
(Rúmil, in *The Book of Lost Tales*; *HME* I. 47)

The *Oxford Dictionary of National Biography* describes J. R. R. Tolkien as 'writer and philologist'. Tolkien was certainly both of these things; but for him the two activities were utterly, indissolubly linked—perhaps more so than for any other writer or philologist. Many authors before and since have taken an interest in the words they use—to do so is arguably intrinsic to being an author—and many have invented words in the course of their writing; but few writers can have found so much of their creative inspiration in the shapes and the histories of words themselves. It is in this respect that he is a uniquely 'philological' writer (a theme expounded in detail in the writings of T. A. Shippey, especially *The Road to Middle-earth*).

As lexicographers engaged in the revision of the *Oxford English Dictionary*, we share Tolkien's fascination with words. But our link with him is stronger than that: Tolkien's first job, on returning home from war service in the trenches, was as an assistant on the original Dictionary, then still incomplete. Of his time spent on the *OED* he said that he 'learned more in those two years than in any other equal period of my life'. What, then, did he learn? Of course he must have learned much about philology in the academic sense, as he investigated the origins of words like *walrus* and *warlock*, or traced the intricate ways in which words like *wan* and *wake* have changed in meaning over the centuries. In particular, he must have become intimately familiar with the *OED* itself, and with the ways of thinking which lexicographers need in order to discover and record the history of words. This would stand him in good stead professionally: he was to draw on this philological expertise throughout his academic career.

He was also a philologist in another sense: that of having a love of, indeed passionate interest in, words, which began long before he started work on the *OED*. But many people—and many writers— have a passion for words: it is, unsurprisingly, a common trait among lexicographers. What form did Tolkien's passion take? Could it be that his work on the Dictionary caused this passion to develop in a unique way? In describing his own creative processes, Tolkien often comments on how the contemplation of an individual word can be the starting point for an adventure in imagination— and contemplating individual words is precisely what lexicographers do. As workers on the same great project, we find ourselves in the unusual position of looking at language from very much the same perspective. Hence our reason for wanting to write this book: to examine Tolkien's word-hoard with a lexicographer's eye.

This book does not deal with all the words invented by Tolkien. Much has been written about the languages he invented for Middle-earth, and rightly so: the process of their creation was inextricably bound up with the evolution of Middle-earth itself. A few of the words in these invented languages do have a fascinating relationship with English, and we shall consider the most important of these. But most do not, and the *OED* has nothing to say about them. It is the vocabulary of English, the language in which Tolkien did almost all his creative writing (apart from the occasional excursion into

Old English), which is the terrain of the *OED*; and this is the terrain which we, as lexicographers of English, want to explore. In many cases Tolkien's unique perspective on language led him to choose a particular word for very precise reasons, and careful examination of such a word from a similar perspective—including consideration of how it is dealt with in the *OED*—can take us on a philological adventure which brings to light connections and resonances which may not be immediately apparent.

Tolkien's time at the *OED* seems an obvious place to start, and in Part I of this book, 'Tolkien as Lexicographer', we look at this in detail, along with his later continuing activity in the field of English lexicography. This provides a context from which to explore his skills as a craftsman with words, and this is the subject of Part II, 'Tolkien as Wordwright'. Here we examine how Tolkien's ideas about the word-hoard of English, and his contributions to it, reflect to some extent both his own lexicographical work and the influence of his predecessors and contemporaries. In the course of this survey we briefly discuss Tolkien's use of many particular words: those which appear in **bold face** are also discussed in more detail in Part III. This consists of a collection of Word Studies, arranged alphabetically, in which some of the most interesting words are individually considered. Finally, we briefly consider Tolkien's lasting influence on the English language.

Note on the *OED*

The original *OED* on which Tolkien worked was completed in 1928 (and reprinted with a one-volume Supplement in 1933). A later four-volume Supplement (1972–86) was combined with the main text to produce the *OED* (Second Edition) in 1989. Now the *OED* is undergoing a thorough revision—including documentation, bibliography, etymology, spelling, pronunciation, and definitions. This revised version, which is being published in sections in the *OED Online*, will eventually form the Third Edition. Revision started at M and at the time of publication of this book had reached partway through P. The revision is based upon the voluminous paper files and computer database created and maintained by the *OED* Department, and we have on occasion been able to refer to this material, which will in future contribute to the revision process. Words printed in SMALL CAPITALS in this book are references to entries in the *OED*.

Brief note on language names and historical texts

Old English is the language of the Anglo-Saxons, recorded from about AD 750 until 1150 in a number of regional dialects. Among its principal documents is the long alliterative poem *Beowulf*, which was a key focus of Tolkien's academic scholarship.

The interaction between Old English and the French dialect of the Norman invaders resulted in Middle English, which is conventionally regarded as lasting until about 1500. Middle English has a large literature, including the works of Geoffrey Chaucer and Langland's *Piers Plowman*. In the course of this book we shall have cause to mention the 14th-century tale in verse *Sir Gawain and the Green Knight* (which Tolkien edited with his colleague E.V. Gordon, and also translated into modern English along with *Pearl* and *Sir Orfeo*) and Laȝamon's *Brut*, a legendary history of the Britons in verse dating from the 12th or 13th century. The ancient letters thorn (þ) and edh (ð) persisted into late Middle English texts but were eventually replaced by *th*, while the letter yogh (ȝ) was generally replaced by *y* or *gh*, and the use of the letter ash (æ) as a distinct vowel was abandoned. (In an unpublished letter of 26 September 1947, partly transcribed in the *OED* files, Tolkien appears to claim that he instigated at Oxford the practice of calling this symbol by the name of the corresponding Anglo-Saxon rune.)

Old Norse was spoken by western Scandinavians in early medieval times, and by the Viking settlers in Britain. In this language were written the two collections of myth and lore known as the Eddas, and the combinations of history and adventure known as the Sagas. Written modern Icelandic is so closely similar to it that the two are sometimes treated as the same language.

Note on references

Owing to variation of page numbers in different editions, references to *The Hobbit* (1937 or 1966) are by chapter number. References to *The Lord of the Rings* (*LR*) are by chapter number within the six numbered 'books' (not the three named volumes). References to *Letters of J. R. R. Tolkien* are to the number of the letter, not the page number. *HME* stands for *The History of Middle-earth* (see Bibliography, p. 232).

Acknowledgements

The authors are grateful to those who have made valuable comments on the book at various stages of composition, especially to Elizabeth Knowles, whose encouragement sustained the project from its inception, and to Wayne Hammond, who applied his great knowledge of Tolkienian matters to a diligent reading of our draft text; also to Martin Maw and Beverley Hunt of the Oxford University Press Archives. And to our long-suffering other halves: Robin, Katie, and Clare.

Images of documents from the OUP Archives are reproduced by permission of the Secretary to the Delegates of Oxford University Press.

The letter from Tolkien to Kenneth Sisam on page 194 is reproduced by kind permission of the Tolkien Estate.

List of Illustrations

Tolkien as Lexicographer

Tolkien as Lexicographer

A philological education

THE LINK BETWEEN TOLKIEN'S interest in philology and his creative writings goes back to the very beginning. At the age of about seven, when he was making his very first attempt to write a story, his mother pointed out to him that 'one could not say "a green great dragon", but had to say "a great green dragon". I wondered why, and still do' (*Lett.* 163). This philological fact was the only thing that he could later remember about the story.

As outlined in Humphrey Carpenter's *Biography*, Tolkien arrived at the University of Oxford with a traditional school education in classics (Latin and Greek) to begin his philological training in earnest (1911–15). After initially continuing with classics, he subsequently changed to the School of English Language and Literature, and took options in comparative philology and Old Norse. While at Oxford he studied with two of the most important English lexicographers of the time: Joseph Wright, professor of comparative philology and compiler of the six-volume *English Dialect Dictionary* (which Tolkien later described as 'indispensable...I encourage people to browze in it': *Lett.* 6) and (as his tutor in Old Norse) William Craigie, one of the four Editors of the *OED*. His tutor in English Language and Literature was Kenneth Sisam, who later also became involved in the *OED*, assisting with some of the entries for words beginning with S.

In 1915 Tolkien embarked on a new lexicographical venture: the compilation of the text now known as the 'Qenya Lexicon'. He had previously begun his lifelong fascination with the invention of languages in a modest way, contributing to the development of the nonsense language Nevbosh (devised by a group of children including his cousin Mary Incledon), and then branching off to produce his own private language, Naffarin (whose surviving fragment hints at a growing aesthetic feeling for the sounds of words). These may have required simple alphabetical wordlists, but Qenya, the earliest of his Elvish languages, was an altogether more complex creation.[1] It had not only an invented vocabulary and grammar but, significantly, an invented linguistic history. The lexicon adopts a thoroughly 'philological' approach, grouping words together under their 'roots', and is therefore no mere wordlist, but aims to be a true (if entirely fictional) etymological dictionary.

It was at the end of the First World War that Tolkien's life as a lexicographer truly began. Having returned to Oxford in the hope of finding academic work, he was offered a post on the staff of the Dictionary by William Craigie, his former Old Norse tutor, although in fact he was to join Henry Bradley's team of assistants, working in the 'Dictionary Room' on the ground floor of the Old Ashmolean Building (now the Museum of the History of Science) in Broad Street, Oxford (see Fig. 1).

---

[1] The spelling *Qenya* distinguishes this early language from the later and more fully developed form known as Quenya, the High Elven tongue of *The Lord of the Rings*.

FIGURE 1. Interior of the Old Ashmolean Building, Oxford. The exact date of this photograph is unknown, but it certainly shows the Dictionary Room around the time when Tolkien worked there. Henry Bradley can be seen with an open book on his lap; William Craigie is seated on the far right, and Charles Onions is visible between them. Tolkien does not appear to have been present.

The *Oxford English Dictionary* and its staff

By 1918 the Dictionary project had been going on for over sixty years. It had its beginnings in a Committee formed in 1857 by the Philological Society of London 'to collect unregistered words in English'—words and meanings, that is, which were not recorded in two of the dictionaries considered authoritative at that time (the latest edition of Johnson's famous *Dictionary*, and another compiled by Charles Richardson). The Philological Society soon decided—apparently at the urging of Frederick Furnivall, a member of the original Committee—that it would be preferable to compile a dictionary of *all* English words, and Herbert Coleridge (another Committee member) was appointed Editor. Unfortunately Coleridge died in 1861 when the project had barely started, and although Furnivall took over, he was prevented from making much headway by various problems, not least the enormous task of collecting enough illustrative quotations to form a body of evidence on which the Dictionary could be based. A new start was made in the late 1870s, with the involvement of the Oxford University Press, and the appointment of a new Editor: James Murray. The first instalment (or 'fascicle') of the Dictionary was published in 1884; in order to accelerate production, a second Editor, Henry Bradley, was appointed in 1888, followed by William Craigie and Charles Onions as third and fourth Editor—each working on a separate alphabetical section alongside Murray. Each worked with a team of 'assistants', who helped to prepare copy for the printers, making preliminary drafts of most of the Dictionary entries. Many of the assistants worked on the Dictionary for decades, and came increasingly to be relied upon by the Editors.

For the *OED* no less than any other part of British society, the

First World War had been a difficult time. The project suffered a grievous blow with the death, on 26 July 1915, of James Murray. His assistants were transferred to Charles Onions's editorial team. In the course of the war, most of the younger and abler members of staff had gone off on active service; some had gone to do other war work, and in June 1918 even Charles Onions was summoned to the Admiralty (whither three *OED* assistants had already gone). Not all of the former staff rejoined the project after the war, so Tolkien's arrival to swell the numbers must have been particularly welcome.

In fact William Craigie had identified the need for someone with a thorough knowledge of Old and Middle English as early as 1916. As Tolkien's former undergraduate tutor he must have been well aware of his particular strengths; and many years later Tolkien gratefully acknowledged his 'kindness...to a jobless soldier in 1918'. By late November 1918 he had found rooms in Oxford for himself and his young family, although salary records kept by Oxford University Press suggest that he may not have begun work on the Dictionary until February 1919; certainly by this date he was hard at work in the Old Ashmolean. Craigie and his assistants were at this stage working on words beginning with U, among which there were relatively few of the words of Germanic origin for which Tolkien's philological skills particularly suited him; accordingly he was taken on as a member of Henry Bradley's team, who were struggling with the huge (and much more Germanic) letter W.

Bradley's four other assistants all had many years' experience of working on the Dictionary. There was the remarkable Walter Worrall, who had begun work as one of James Murray's assistants in 1885 and who would ultimately accumulate nearly fifty years of service to the Dictionary; perhaps surprisingly, he was the only one of the four with a university degree. Wilfrid Lewis, who had joined the project in 1889, was the son of an Oxford college servant, and would later go on to compile his own historical dictionary of the language of cricket. Only slightly junior to him was Henry Bayliss, a gardener's son who had started his working life as a 'Bodley boy'— one of a group of boys employed at the University's Bodleian Library to fetch books from the library stacks, who in addition to a small wage were given the opportunity to study.[2] Finally there was Bradley's own daughter Eleanor, who had worked along-side her father since 1897.

Almost all *OED* work was done on small pieces of paper, approximately 6 inches by 4 inches—the so-called 'Dictionary slip'. Not all the slips were clean pieces of paper of exactly this size: some contributors sent in quotations on more or less any similarly sized piece of paper that came to hand, and some of the editorial staff reused paper in a similar manner, using the backs of book jackets, bank statements, and even the wrappers from bars of chocolate. They also recycled the torn-up proofs of earlier *OED* fascicles and, crucially, the discarded earlier drafts of editorial material.

---

[2] Bayliss is also one of the few members of the Dictionary staff who left unmistakable evidence of a sense of humour in his work. For example, in around 1903, when the question of whether to include an entry for the recently coined word *radium* was being discussed by the Editors, Bayliss meticulously compiled a spoof entry for the word (defined as 'The unknown quantity'), with an etymology tracing it to roots in such languages as 'Prehistoric' and 'Antediluvian', and illustrated by some very dubious quotations, including one from Chaucer's 'Dustman's Tale' and another supposedly from the Diary of Samuel Pepys ('And so to bed. Found radium an excellent pick-me-up in the morning').

Editing the Dictionary

According to Humphrey Carpenter, in his first weeks Tolkien 'was given the job of researching the etymology of *warm, wash, wasp, water, wick (lamp),* and *winter.*' The extent to which Tolkien's work on these etymologies was made use of by later editors is, unfortunately, uncertain, since many of the relevant slips are missing: however, most of the etymology of *warm* at least is in Tolkien's hand, and although the completion is in Bradley's hand, it is likely that this is based on an earlier draft by Tolkien (see Fig. 2).

Probably even before this etymological research, and certainly before he began to draft entries on a substantial scale, Tolkien embarked on an ancillary task which drew upon his thorough knowledge of Old and Middle English, and whose results were made use of long after he had given up work on the Dictionary. At some stage during the collection of quotation evidence, numerous important Old and Middle English texts had been examined by readers who copied out illustrative quotations but were unable to lemmatize the words illustrated—that is, to convert the form occurring in the text (perhaps a plural or a past tense) to the form with which a dictionary entry would be headed. Tolkien was one of a small number of people who went through these slips writing in the correct lemmas, to allow the slips for each lemma to be filed together. Quotations of this type exist for words throughout the letter W.

After a little time spent in familiarizing himself with the *OED*'s working methods, Tolkien started work on the drafting of Dictionary entries. This central task seems to have been organized much as it is today: each assistant was allocated an alphabetical range by his or her Editor, and would tackle all aspects of the final text— pronunciation, variant spellings, and etymology, as well as the warm (wǭɹm) , adj.

197

[Com. Teut. : OE. wearm = OFris. warm (mod. WFris. waerm,
NFris. wāram) , MDu., Du. warm , OS. warm (MLG. war(e)m,
LG. warm) , OHG. war(a)m (MHG., G. warm) , ON. varmr
(Norw., Sw., Da. varm) Goth. warm- in warmjan 'to warm,
cherish :——— OTeut.* warmoꝥ , also *werm- (in ON. vermᵈ
wk. masc. warmᵘ , OHG. wirma , MHG. wirm(e) fem. warmᵗʰ).

The further relationship of this word is somewhat doubtful.
In spite of the difficulties attending such an etymology it is probably
to be compared with Pre-Teut. * gʷhormoꝥ, or *gʷhermoꝥ & found in
Skr. gharmá ꝥ heat, Avesta garəmō hot, Gk. θερμός hot,
L. formus warm, OPrussian gorme heat, Albanian ziarm heat,
Armenian jerm warm, derivatives of *gʷher- with a radical sense of heat.
For another possible example of initial w- in Teut. from *gʷh- or
*ĝhw- see WILD adj. Compare also the similar phonetic
phenomena in Latin whereby older gʷ- gave g- before ŭ, and
consonants, v- before other vowels (e.g. vorāre , gurges))

Small

Some scholars have referred this word to a root *wer-
found in Lith. vìrti to cook (trans.), OSl. vrěti to boil,
cook (intr.) variti to cook (trans.), varŭ hot. The primary
sense of this root, however, seems to be rather 'to well up,
bubble' than 'to be hot'; cf. Lith. versmė a spring. The
root is confined to the Balto-Slav. langs., and in them has
no derivative corresponding in sense and suffix to the Teut.
adj., which on the other view represents a widespread Indogermanic
formation.]

198

small

FIGURE 2. Dictionary slips showing Tolkien's draft of part of the etymology for *warm*, and Bradley's continuation.

division of each entry into senses and subsenses, the selection of quotations to illustrate these, and the writing of definitions. The text drafted in this way would eventually be revised by the Editor, who frequently made substantial changes such as reclassifying the senses (and rewriting the definitions accordingly), choosing different quotations, and even deciding to reject a word entirely, often because the quotation evidence was thin. Variations to this routine were made when some assistants were not competent to deal with certain aspects of particular entries, such as the etymology of a word derived from an unusual language (in some cases these were even left to be added in proof).

The raw material for the creation of Dictionary text—the quotation slips—had been accumulating for many years by the time an assistant came to work on it (over sixty years in the case of Tolkien's part of the letter W), and some preliminary work would have been done. The simple task of sorting the huge volume of material into alphabetical order could take months; the sorted slips for a particular alphabetical range would also have been posted to a 'subeditor', working far from Oxford. The work done by the subeditors varied enormously: some were capable of sorting the material for a word into its constituent subsenses, drafting definitions, compiling a list of the variant spellings, and even researching and writing the etymology—all the tasks, in other words, which might fall to an assistant like Tolkien. Others would attempt only some of these tasks; a few would attempt more than their abilities warranted. With the passage of time, and the accumulation of further quotations, the material would often need to be sent out a second time to be 're-subedited'. In the case of the early part of W, the first person to subedit the material seems to have been a Revd William Beckett of Chelmsford, who had died in 1901; the material was then re-subedited during the war by one of the most indefatigable of the Dictionary's external helpers, William Robertson Wilson, a Presbyterian minister of Dollar, Clackmannanshire (apparently known to some of his parishioners as 'Ginger-jaws' because of his red side whiskers). Even the work of the best of the subeditors, however, was more often than not reworked by the in-house assistants: their definitions are frequently written on the backs of the subeditors' discarded earlier drafts.

Tolkien's first editorial range appears to have been a short one consisting of the verb *waggle* and a couple of closely related words. This was a fairly straightforward group on which to cut his lexicographical teeth: even the most complex word, the verb *waggle* itself, would not require division into more than a few subsenses, and no words in the group were older than the 16th century. Quite what training Tolkien would have received is not at all clear: it seems most likely that once embarked on drafting proper, assistants would be expected to learn from their mistakes. This initial range of words (*waggle* to *waggly*) was evidently returned with annotations to Tolkien, who made some further corrections. At this stage Tolkien had not yet learned all the details of the Dictionary's 'house style', as can be seen from Bradley's corrections to the slip for the start of the noun *waggle* (Fig. 3a); Bradley also completely rewrote Tolkien's etymology of the verb. Tolkien's division of the verb into senses and subsenses was also revised slightly (see Fig. 3b), although this must have taken place at the proof stage: two quotations which he had grouped together as illustrating a sense 'to shake the body or any part of the body' were subsequently split up, one of them (the quotation dated 'circa 1820') being inserted in the more general sense 2a, and the other (dated 1852) identified as a distinct construction (sense 1d as published, where it is

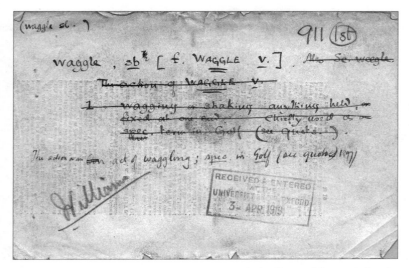

FIGURE 3a. Dictionary slip showing Tolkien's draft of part of the entry for the noun *waggle*. (The pencilled name 'Williams' is that of the compositor to whom this bundle of slips was allocated.)

described as a 'nonce' use, i.e. a one-off use of a word). Another late alteration to the entry was the addition of a new American slang sense 'to get the better of', which probably came to the Editors' attention through its inclusion in the *Century Dictionary* (published in America in 1889–91). Tolkien also wrote out two quotations for an unrelated word, *wag(g)el* 'a name for the Black-backed Gull, *Larus marinus*, in its immature state', probably through finding misfiled references to them among the evidence for *waggle*.

His next task, alphabetically, was to work on parts of the entry for the noun *wain*. It seems that only parts of this entry were assigned to Tolkien: the etymology, and the section at the end where straight-forward compounds such as *wain-house* and *wain-trees* are dealt with. (Tolkien's later use of the term *Wainriders* cannot, it seems, be traced back to his work on this entry; at least, the word is not listed

Waggle (wæ·g'l), *v.* Also 6–7 wagle, 9 *Sc.* weegle, waigle. [A frequentative of WAG *v.*; not found before the last decade of the 16th c., but possibly much older. Equivalent formations in Continental Teut. are WFris. *waggelje* to totter, Du. *waggelen* to stagger (early mod. Flem. *waeghelen*, *wagghelen*; also *trans.* to shake); (M)LG. *waggeln*, G. *wackeln* to stagger, totter (whence prob. Sw. *vakla*, Da. *vakle*); Norw., Sw. *vagla* refl. to rock, sway. Cf. ME. *wagre* WAGGER *v.*; also WIGGLE, WIGGLE-WAGGLE *vbs.*]

1. *trans.* **a.** To move (anything held or fixed at one end) to and fro with short quick motions, or with a rapid undulation; *esp.* to shake (any movable part of the body). In sports or games often (*colloq.* or *humorous*), to wield or manipulate (a bat, oar, etc.).

1594 NASHE *Unfort. Trav.* E 2 b, A third [man] wauerd & wagled his head, like a proud horse playing with his bridle.

b. *absol.* Chiefly in *Golf* (cf. WAGGLE *sb.*): To swing the club-head to and fro over the ball in the line of the intended stroke.

1897 *Outing* Aug. 423/1 On the other hand, another player, probably quite as good,.. Mr. Horace Hutchinson, waggles, and waggles, as he addresses his ball, before each shot.

c. *U.S. slang.* To get the better of, overcome. In recent Dictionaries.

d. *nonce-use.* To indicate by waggling the head.

1852 READE *Peg Woff.* xiii. 198 They all nodded and waggled assent.

2. *intr.* **a.** With *advs.* or advb. expressions denoting motion: To shake or wobble while in motion; to walk or move shakily; to waddle.

1611 COTGR., *Triballer*, to wagle, or dangle vp and downe; to goe dingle dangle, wig wag. 1625 JACKSON *Creed* v. v. 42 Apt they are not to moue many wayes, either vpward or downeward, but onely to waggle to and fro within a narrow compasse. *Ibid.* x. xxiv. 3080 Like to a Pair of Scales wl'ch never came to any Permanent Stay or constant Settling upon the right Center, but have one while wagled this way, another while that way. 1627 MAY *Lucan* v. I 3, Nor that the crow waggling along the shore Diues downe, and seemes t' anticipate a showre. 1692 R. L'ESTRANGE *Fables* ccii. 194 Why do you go Nodding, and Waggling so like a Fool, as if you were Hipshot? says the Goose to her Gosselin. 1819 W. TENNANT *Papistry Storm'd* (1827) 82 This said, the host wi' richt guid will Begoud to waigle down the hill. *c* 1820 COLMAN *Broad Grins* etc. (1872) 313 A well-fed maggot .. In some deep fruit-plate heaves, from snout to end, And works, and slips, and writhes, and waggles to ascend. 1840

FIGURE 3b. Part of the entry for *waggle* (verb) as published in the *OED* (First Edition).

among the compounds included in his draft.) The rest of the entry was evidently compiled by Bradley. Characteristically, the long etymological note contains a speculation about the ultimate derivation of the word, which Bradley felt obliged to tone down (see Fig. 4).

The work of compiling the entry for the word *waist* was similarly divided up, with Tolkien dealing with the etymology and the compounds section, although his colleague Henry Bayliss went over his work on the latter, making a few small changes to bring his text into line with house style. (The archives also contain a few Shakespeare quotations for *waist* which were copied out by Tolkien for use in the rest of the entry.) However, there are some compounds of *waist* which are significant enough to need entries of their own, and in some cases division into senses. Thus having organized the final paragraphs of the entry for the main noun, Tolkien proceeded to write full entries for *waistband* (2 senses), *waist-cloth* (3 senses), and—after considerable deliberation (surely to be expected of a future connoisseur of the garment)—*waistcoat* (see Fig. 5a). In fact Tolkien identified no fewer than four distinct varieties of garment denoted by this word, two of which he further subdivided into several subsenses, with two historical notes in small type completing the thorough description. Not all of this found its way into the published entry: inexperienced lexicographers are often prone to subdivide words into many subsenses when it may be better to use more general definitions, covering broader ranges of usage. Some of the definitions on Tolkien's rejected slips refer to uses of *waistcoat* based on evidence which has not come to light in the archives: for example, he mentions the figurative use of the word 'together with *coat* taken as a type of any idea that may be assumed or laid aside at will (e.g. a hypocritical pretence of piety)': there is no mention of

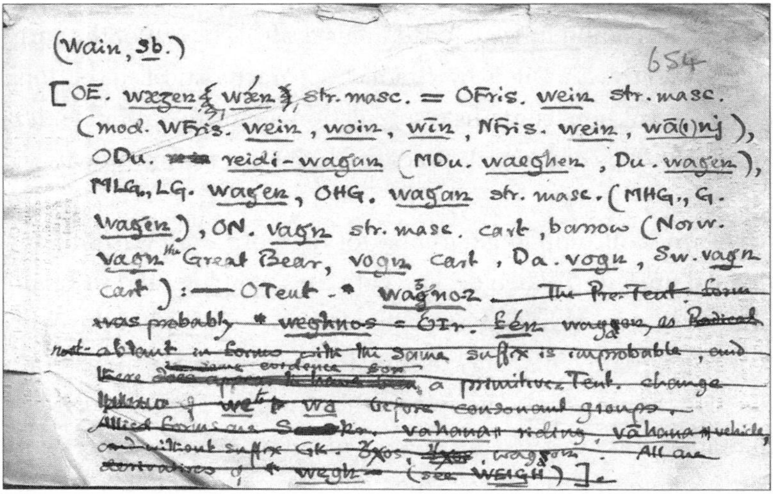

FIGURE 4a. Dictionary slips showing the draft, by Tolkien and Bradley, of the etymology of *wain*.

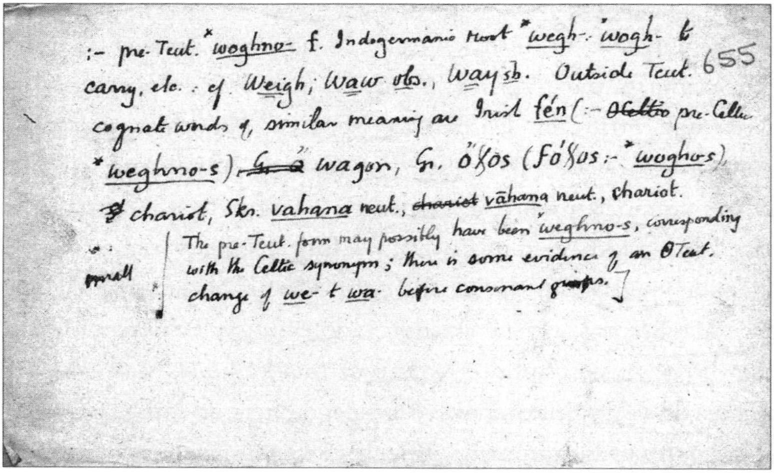

> **whene), 5–7 wane, 3– wain.** [OE. *wægen, wǽn,*
> str. masc. = OFris. *wein* str. masc. (mod. WFris.
> *wein, woin, wīn,* NFris. *wein, wā(i)nj*), OLow
> Frankish *reidi-wagan* (MDu. *waeghen,* Du. *wagen*),
> MLG., LG. *wagen,* OHG. *wagan* str. masc. (MHG.,
> G. *wagen*), ON. *vagn* str. masc. cart, barrow (Norw.
> *vagn* the Great Bear, *vogn* cart, Da. *vogn,* Sw. *vagn*
> cart) :—OTeut. **wagno-z* :—pre-Teut. **woghno-s* f.
> Indogermanic root **wegh-, *wogh-* to carry, etc. : cf.
> WEIGH, WAW *vbs.,* WAY *sb.* Outside Teut. cog-
> nate words of similar meaning are Irish *fén* (:— pre-
> Celtic **weghno-s*) wagon, Gr. ὄχος (ϝόχος :—
> **wogho-s*), chariot, Skr. *vahana* neut., *vāhana*
> neut., chariot.
>   The pre-Teut. form may possibly have been **weghno-s,*
> corresponding with the pre-Celtic form ; there is some evi-
> dence of an OTeut. change of *we-* to *wa-* before consonant
> groups.]

FIGURE 4b. Part of the entry for *wain* as published in the
OED (First Edition), showing the final version of the etymology.

this in the published entry, nor of the expression *to throw open one's
waistcoat* 'to unbosom oneself'. (Curiously, Tolkien several times
uses the spelling *waiscoat* (as in the slip in Fig. 5b)—a form which,
even more curiously, is not recorded in the published *OED* entry.
Was this Tolkien's own, rather idiosyncratic way of showing that the
t is often omitted in speech, a fact more usually indicated by 'phonetic' spellings such as *weskit*?)

After *waistcoat* follow *waisted, waist-rail,* and the like; Tolkien did
at one point consider making *waist-deep* a main entry in its own
right, with two or more subsenses, but later decided to include it in
the entry for *waist* itself, as a compound simple enough not to
require a definition. The complex word *wait* was dealt with by
Bradley, but he once again allowed Tolkien to 'mop up' the related
words, including *waiting* (along with *waiting-room* and *waiting-
woman*), *wait-a-bit* (a South African plant, whose variability of
spelling received comprehensive treatment before the simplifying

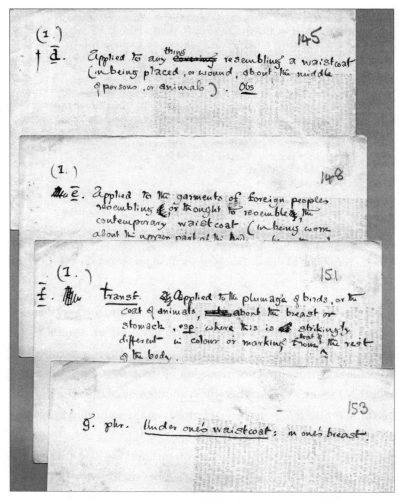

FIGURE 5a. A selection of Tolkien's definitions of *waistcoat*.

touch of Bradley's pen), and *waiter*, whose eleven senses were left much as Tolkien drafted them. In a dictionary the size of the *OED* even nonce-words can find room; however, at this stage in the project the Editors were under considerable pressure to keep the volume of text down as much as possible, and so Tolkien's original

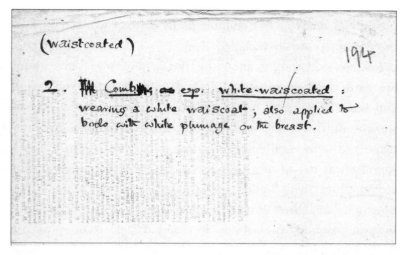

(waiscoated)

194

2. Comb. as *ep*. white-waiscoated : wearing a white waiscoat ; also applied to birds with white plumage on the breast.

FIGURE 5b. Another of Tolkien's *waistcoat* slips, showing his use of the unusual spelling *waiscoat*.

full-scale entries for *waiterage* ('the performance of a waiter's duties'), *waiterdom* ('waiters considered as a class, or collectively'), *waiterhood* ('the state or condition of a waiter'), and *waitering* ('the occupation of a waiter') were subsequently condensed into a sub-entry under *waiter*, and his definition of *waiterful* ('as much of anything as can be carried on a waiter, or tray') was omitted entirely.

With the exception of *waith* and *waive* and their cognates, the next five pages of the published Dictionary are closely based on Tolkien's work, including entries for the various kinds of *wake*—the nouns, that is: Bradley apparently considered the main verb too important or difficult for Tolkien at this stage, as he assigned the senses to be defined by the more experienced Walter Worrall, and drafted the etymology himself. (Tolkien did draft an entry for another, different verb with the same spelling—meaning 'to wander, roam' and found occasionally in Scots—but this was omitted as being too rare.) The nouns were, in any case, something of a handful, there being possibly as many as five etymologically distinct words, of which three were eventually included.

Tolkien's deliberations about the treatment of two of these nouns are worth closer examination. The first, with senses to do with vigils and wakefulness, goes back to Middle English, although it now survives only in connection with funerals (especially in Irish contexts) and some rural English merrymaking. Once again Tolkien's impulse was to say more about the history of the word and its connotations than Bradley could allow space for: a small-type note in his final draft of the published sense 3, deleted before publication, represents the last stage in a long struggle to convey a sense of the word's overtones (see Fig. 6). Earlier drafts of another sense (numbered 4b in the published entry, but originally further subdivided into two subsenses by Tolkien) show a whole succession of attempts to capture aspects of a rural English wake:

'very frequently mentioned with disapproval as characterised by riot, drunkenness, and dissolute conduct'

'a typical scene of uncultured excess or of unsophisticated simple speech'

'associated with the preservation of certain rustic sports as wrestling, single-sticks etc. ... also used as a typical scene of boorish, sometimes unsophisticated or simple, speech and manners'

'the holiday-making marked by fairs, sports and often riot and drunkenness incident to such annual local feasts'

The second etymologically distinct noun *wake* gave Tolkien problems of a different kind, to do with the arrangement of the senses. At one point he copied out the *OED* definitions of several senses of the words *rear* and *train* onto separate slips, presumably as models on

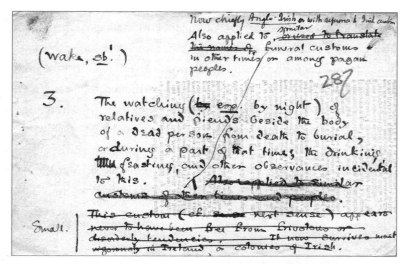

FIGURE 6. Dictionary slip showing a draft definition by Tolkien of the noun *wake*.

which to base his own treatment of the corresponding senses: indeed his final draft of the preamble to the phrase 'in the wake of' suggested that 'in these expressions WAKE is often practically synonymous with TRAIN'—a remark deleted by Bradley as not in keeping with the usually self-contained style of *OED* entries, with minimal cross-referencing. Tolkien was clearly still learning the *OED*'s ways.

Tolkien prepared entries for the plant names *wake-robin* and *wake-wort*, and another for *waldend* (a word found in *Beowulf* and meaning 'ruler'), but for the most part the words in this alphabetical range were assigned to Bayliss, Lewis, and Worrall. Tolkien's next substantial word was *wallop*: both the relatively straightforward noun, and the verb, concerning the etymology of which Tolkien provides a full five paragraphs of scholarly speculation, hardly altered at all by Bradley, who by this stage clearly had considerable confidence in him (see Fig. 7)—sufficient confidence to entrust him with the Old English word *walm* (synonymous in some senses with *wallop*, which is perhaps why Tolkien was given both to do). Incidentally, Tolkien apparently had sufficient evidence for the unpleasant expression 'the right to wallop one's own nigger' to draft a slip for it, but must have excised it from his entry at a fairly early stage, judging from the provisional sense number assigned to the definition, and no illustrative quotation for it remains in the files.

Most of the next few pages of the Dictionary is the work of others. Tolkien was not assigned a continuous range of words, but instead

Wallop (wǫˑləp), *v.* Inflected **walloped** (wǫˑləpt), **walloping.** Forms: 4–5 walop(e, 5 walloppe, 5–6 walap, wallope, 5–7 walopp(e, 9 wallup, whallup, wollup, 6– wallop [a. ONF. **waloper* = F. *galoper* (see GALLOP *v.*¹). The existence of this form is evidenced in addition to the English forms by OE. *walos* sb. pl. and the adopted form Flem. *walop(pe*, MHG. *walop, -ap* sb. MHG. *walopiren* vb., and probably by mod. Walloon (Sigart) *waloper* to rinse linen in water. Cf. Norw. (Aasen) *val(l)hoppa* vb., app. an etymologizing alteration, after Norw. *hoppa* to leap, dance.
A satisfactory origin for this word in French has not been suggested. It is probably purely echoic, or an echoic alteration of some Teut. element or elements. The Provençal form *galaupar* has suggested Teut. **ga-hlaupan* (OE. *gehléapan*, f. *ge-*Y-prefix + *hléapan* to LEAP), but the evidence for original *w-* precludes the comparison of the initial element.
In English the onomatopœic suggestion of the word has lent itself to varied extension of meanings and to a vague (usually colloq. and humorous) application to violent noisy movements, more especially since the form GALLOP ousted it from the more elevated uses (in the course of the 16th c.).
The sense 'to boil rapidly' is probably derived directly by transference from sense 1 (cf. GALLOP *v.*² to boil) in spite of the close resemblance of the word to WALL *v.*¹ + UP (cf. *well up*, and Du. *opwallen*). The relation of POTWALLOPER to POTWALLER indicates that some such association was active.
The sense 'to beat' may be ultimately due to the causative use (sense 2, and cf. F. *galoper* trans.), or may be entirely due to onomatopœic extension.]

FIGURE 7. Tolkien's etymology for *wallop* (verb) as published in the *OED* (First Edition).

worked on four individual entries, for the words *walnut, walrus, wampum,* and *wampumpeag* (the less familiar word from which *wampum* derives). *Walnut* and *walrus* were known to have unusually troublesome Germanic etymologies, which is probably why they were assigned to Tolkien. *Wampumpeag* was an etymological challenge of a rather different kind, in that it derives from an Algonquian Indian word; frustratingly, the slips for the entry are missing from the archives, but the surviving materials for *wampum* suggest that Tolkien enjoyed tackling these exotic imports from the New World. There is considerably more evidence of the struggles he had with the etymologies of *walnut* and *walrus*—which gave him such trouble that he even discussed them at home with his family. In the case of *walrus* at least six neatly written versions of the etymology (of which Fig. 8 is probably one of the earliest) precede the final printed form, all attempting to reconstruct the route by which Old Norse *rosmhvalr* or *rosmall* arrived in Dutch (from which it was borrowed into English in the 17th century) as *walrus*. Bradley was obviously pleased with the result, for when the fascicle *W–Wash* was published in October 1921, *walnut, walrus,* and *wampum* were among the few entries singled out in a prefatory note as containing 'etymological facts or suggestions not given in other dictionaries'. (For a discussion of Tolkien's entry for *walnut* see pp. 49–51.) Characteristically, Tolkien continued to puzzle over some of these etymologies long after he had left the *OED*: a notebook survives in the Bodleian Library, written while Tolkien was teaching at Leeds in the 1920s, containing many pages of notes on *walrus*—in which even more remote relatives such as Finnish *murssu* are considered—and he may have lectured on this topic at Leeds.

Tolkien seems next to have been assigned the whole of the range containing the challenging words *wan, wander,* and *wane.* Whether

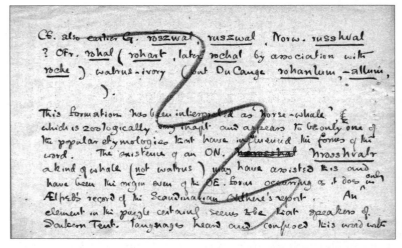

FIGURE 8. Dictionary slip showing an early draft by Tolkien of part of the etymology of *walrus*.

or not there is any truth in the suggestion, often made, that in his creative writing Tolkien brings particular enthusiasm to his descriptions of 'bad things', he certainly relished the task of working out the etymologies and sense-development of *wan* and *wane*. In particular he was intrigued that *wan*, which in Old English had meant 'dark, gloomy, black', should have come to be applied to pale or faint things: the published entry represents his final conclusions (see Fig. 9), and is once again largely unchanged by Bradley, but it does not suggest the welter of different versions Tolkien considered, some of which are barely more than strings of near-synonymous words, apparently jotted down in an attempt to clarify his thinking (e.g. 'with connot[ations] of fading foulness unnatural pallor'; 'anaemic emaciated')—a technique still used by today's lexicographers. The various versions between them contain approximately 40 'bad' adjectives and nouns, and even the final form of the entry is unusually plentiful in these. Tolkien's draft of the etymology

Wan (wǫn), *a.* Forms: 1 wan(n, won(n, 3–
wan, 3–4 won, 4–5 wane, wonn, 4–6 wann(e,
5 wonne. [OE. *wann* (*wǫnn*), dark, gloomy,
black. Not found in any of the other Teut. languages. Its original sense appears to have been
' dark in hue ', with especially frequent application to things of gloomy unpleasant associations.
Relationships to WIN *v.* (OTeut. **winnan* to strive, toil,
suffer, etc.), or to WOUND *sb.*, or WEN, present difficulties of
sense-development or form. Relationship to WANE etc. is
possible (cf. Celtic **wanno-*, OIr. *fann*, Welsh *gwan* faint,
weak, feeble), but association of the two words in later
(ME. and ModE.) periods is more probable than ultimate
connexion.
In addition to this association the application to heavenly
bodies, when obscured, or when compared to others more
bright, possibly aided the general application to pale things.
The application to the human face etc., when of unwhole-
some or unusual colour (through various emotions, disease,
or death), also provided a possible occasion of sense-change.
The senses ' livid,' ' sallow ', and ' pale, sickly ' are often
indistinguishable.]

†1. Lacking light, or lustre ; dark-hued, dusky,
gloomy, dark. *Obs.* Chiefly *poet.*
Beowulf 702 Com on wanre niht scríðan sceadugenga.
a 1000 *Boeth. Metr.* xi. 61 Hwæt, þa wonnan niht mona on-
lihteð. *c* 1230 *Hali Meid.* 43 Ant tah is betere a briht iacinct
þen a charbucle won. *a* 1300 *Signs bef. Judgm.* 43 in *E.E.P.*
(1862) 8 As fair and briȝte as þou seest ham hi worþ be-com
as blak as cole and be of hiwe durke and wan for man-is sin
þat hi sul þole. *c* 1400 *Destr. Troy* 303 So dang he þat dog
with dynt of his wappon, þat þe warlag was wete of his wan
atter. *Ibid.* 6000 Mony chivalrous Achilles choppit to dethe:
All his wedis were wete of þaire wan blode. *c* 1470 HENRY
Wallace VII. 488 In the furd weill, that was bath wan and
depe, Feyll off thaim fell. *c* 1480 HENRYSON *Cock & Fox* 62
In froist, in snaw, in wedder wan and weit. *a* 1529 SKELTON
P. Sparowe 910 With vysage wan As swarte as tan. 1591
SAVILE *Tacitus, Agricola* 244 The Ocean bringeth forth
pearle also, not orient, but duskish and wanne.

b. *esp.* in conventional application in poetry to
the sea (waves, etc.) or other waters.
The original significance was perh. that of ' dark-hued ', but
the sense often approaches, or is blended with, the next.
In more recent poetry the word is probably (exc. by conscious archaism) to be understood rather as ' grey, pale ', but
the gloomy connotation remains.
Beowulf 1374 Þonon yðeblond up astiȝeð won to wolcnum.
c 1386 CHAUCER *Knt.'s T.* 1598 Myn is the drenchyng in the
see so wan. ? *a* 1400 *Morte Arth.* 492 Wery to the wane
see they went alle att ones. *c* 1400 *Destr. Troy* 4633 The
storme.. walt vp the wilde se vppon wan hilles. *c* 1470
HENRY *Wallace* VII. 814 Her is na gait to fle yone peple can,
Bot rochis heich, and wattir depe and wan. 1501 DOUGLAS
Pal. Hon. II. liii, Ouir waters wan, throw worthie woddis
grene. 1535 STEWART *Cron. Scot.* I. 9 Quhair that tyme

FIGURE 9. Part of the entry for *wan* (adjective) as published
in the *OED* (First Edition).

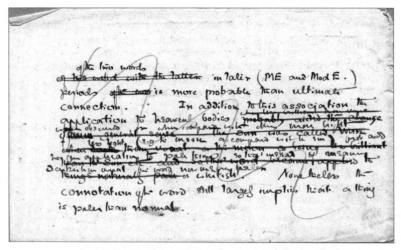

FIGURE 10. Dictionary slip showing Tolkien's draft of part of the etymology of *wan*.

(Fig. 10) is almost identical to the published version.[3] It is note-worthy that uses of *wan* in two contrasting senses occur not very far apart in 'The Lay of the Children of Húrin', a poem written at this time (lines 1058, 1860; *HME* III. 42, 69). Tolkien later cited *wan* as an example of a misused archaism (see p. 69).

The verb *wane* may not have been all Tolkien's work, although the etymology is in his handwriting (a number of the senses are defined in Bradley's hand, and no rejected versions by Tolkien are to be found): he did, however, deal with the archaic and obsolete nouns and adjective. By far the largest component of this range was the work required on the verb *wander* and its cluster of related

[3] A tiny difference is his use of the word 'connection'—which had to be corrected to 'connexion', this being the spelling which James Murray had settled on when he edited the entry for the word in 1891, and which the other editors were obliged to follow. Although Tolkien's draft shows the now more usual form, his work on the *OED* seems to have given him a lifelong preference for Murray's spelling, which occurs throughout his later writings.

words. Once again Tolkien's final versions reached the printed page with little or no alteration.

Two of Tolkien's other entries in this range reflect his awareness of the poetical qualities of words: early draft entries for the obsolete nouns *wan* 'bruise' and *wandreth* 'adversity' include a note of the other *w-* words which frequently co-occur with each of them in alliterative writing[4]—something not often commented on in *OED* definitions (and in fact deleted from *wan* by Bradley). In the case of *wandreth* Tolkien perceived in these co-occurring words (grouped as *woe/wrake/wer* and *wele/welthe/worldes* riches) a basis for distinguishing two senses, denoting respectively 'evil circumstances, affliction, misery' and 'embarrassment of circumstances, poverty': once again this was too expansive for the *OED*, and Bradley collapsed them into one definition, although a brief comment on the word's use in alliterative verse remains: 'Often alliteratively coupled with *woe* or contrasted with *weal.*' It was of course at this time, or very soon after, that Tolkien began to experiment with writing alliterative verse of his own: some of the earliest manuscript of 'The Lay of the Children of Húrin' is written on scraps of *OED* paper (see *HME* III. 3–4). Interestingly, he uses the archaic word *wanhope* early on in the poem ('the mazes of Doriath | wildered and wayworn in wanhope bound them', line 188); but he does not appear to have worked on the *OED* entry for the word, and although his attention could have been drawn to it at this time, it is at least as likely that he first encountered it in the writings of William Morris, whose use of *wanhope* in *The Wood*

---

[4] Alliterative verse—that is, verse in which the same initial letter or sound occurs in two or more accented syllables in each line—was the standard form in Old English poetry; some of the most important Middle English poems use the same device, including *Piers Plowman* and *Sir Gawain and the Green Knight*.

Beyond the World (1894) is noted in the *OED* entry. The word occasionally turns up in Tolkien's later writings (e.g. Húrin 'drowsing in wanhope': *HME* XI. 282).

Tolkien's next word was *want*—one of the 20 or so commonest verbs in English, and surely ample evidence of Bradley's willingness to let him tackle even the most significant entries more or less without intervention or correction. Of the 28 separate definitions for the verb, 19 of Tolkien's slips went to press, including those for most of the main senses, and at least two more formed the basis of revised slips by Bradley. The slips for the early part of the entry for the noun *want* are missing, but most of what remains in the manuscript is also Tolkien's largely unaltered text.

Isolated words, rather than alphabetical ranges, make up the rest of Tolkien's contribution to the *OED*; all of them have tricky Germanic etymologies, making Tolkien an obvious choice to deal with them. The first of these was *wariangle*, a name (found in Chaucer's *Canterbury Tales*) for the shrike. The popular superstition that the shrike kills nine other birds every day has led to its acquiring a number of macabre names, both in English (*murdering-bird*, *nine-killer*) and in other Germanic languages (German *Neuntöter*, a name going back to the 16th century); Tolkien concluded that behind the name *wariangle* lay a similar allusion—the first element being derived from the same Germanic word for an outlaw or murderer that inspired his later idea of the *warg* (see pp. 206–7).

After *wariangle* came the batch of slips for *warlock*, which turned out to illustrate several identically spelt words with different etymologies. The now familiar word meaning a wizard or sorcerer was once almost obsolete, but seems to have been popularized by its use in the novels of Walter Scott; unfortunately many slips for this entry are missing, but from what remains it is clear that the etymology and sense-division, and most of the definition text, are Tolkien's work. Finally there is a small group of words scattered across the letter W, all going back to Old English (and therefore requiring particularly elaborate etymologies), which are sufficiently similar in form for their early spellings to coincide, thus making it sensible for one person to work on them together. The main members of the group are *Weald, wield, wild*, and *wold*: apart from *Weald* (for which much of the material is missing, although the word itself and several derivatives were at least started by Tolkien), all of these lie in ranges edited not by Bradley but by Charles Onions, the youngest of the *OED*'s four Editors, who seems to have preferred to make his revisions by writing out a fresh slip rather than attempting to annotate it with his corrections—thus preserving frustratingly few of Tolkien's own slips. However, discarded slips for most of the entry for *wold* have survived, as has Tolkien's etymology for *wild*, and it is likely that he in fact dealt with these words in their entirety, although to judge from the example of *wold* the definitions in the printed text are probably mainly the work of Onions: very little of Tolkien's definitions of *wold*, or even of his division of it into senses, escaped alteration. The etymologies, however, are vintage Tolkien, complete with long lists of cognates in other European languages living and dead, speculations about the ulterior origins of Old Teutonic **wilþijaz* and **walþuz*, and some general remarks about the sense-development of *wold* (few of which remain in the published entry) which are unusually chatty even for Tolkien:

> The primitive meaning of this word was probably 'wild, unexplored, or untilled land; wilderness'. In early Northern Europe these senses would easily interchange with the sense 'forest'. In OE. this latter is the only evidenced meaning, and the occasional application of the

word to mountainous districts appears to be a translation of L. *saltus* (e.g. *Pireni weald*). Some of the senses that appear later in English seem more easily derivable from an original meaning 'wilderness', but this development is probably connected solely with the historical deforestation of England, which has produced districts of very varying character in place of former woodlands.

WOLD (and its different forms) appears generally speaking to have become obsolete during the 15th., or early in the 16th., century, except locally or dialectally (especially as applied as a fixed name to certain definite localities). From the seventeenth century onwards its use is largely artificial, and its senses apparently due either to the changed character of the localities where the name had become fixed, or to knowledge of the word in OE. or ME. The distinction drawn in quot[ation] 1577 (Sense 1) between the forms *Wald* and *Wold*, and so by implication between Northern and Midland or Southern usage, is not consistently borne out by the rest of the material.

Marginalia

The complete process of publishing *OED* entries—which included several rounds of extremely thorough proof-correction—took many months; so long, in fact, that Tolkien saw none of the entries he worked on in print before he left the department at the end of June 1920. In the case of *wold*, the entry did not even go for type-setting until 1926; it appeared in 1928 as part of the very last fascicle of the Dictionary to be published.

But there was one component of Tolkien's work which he would not have expected to see in print: indeed, he had no idea when it would ever come to fruition. From the moment that the first fascicle of the *OED* had been published, suggestions for how it could be revised, expanded, or updated had flowed in from all and sundry. Much of the material went into a file of slips marked 'Supplement', the idea being that once the Dictionary was complete, a supplementary volume or volumes could be issued containing the revised material—and of course the Editors themselves, and their assistants, made many contributions to this file, despite the lack of any clear plans for a supplement. But there was another way for the in-house staff to record the revisions and corrections that were needed: by writing them into one of the 'office copies' of the Dictionary, which stood on the shelves of the Old Ashmolean and which they all consulted daily. Tolkien wrote many such marginal comments in two of the office copies: one belonging to Bradley (which also contained marginalia by Worrall and some of Bradley's other assistants), and another which seems to have been Onions's copy (full of notes about Shakespeare's usages, probably written in while Onions worked on his *Shakespeare Glossary*).

The discoveries which led to notes being made for the future supplement could arise in a number of ways. Sometimes work on a word towards the end of the alphabet would cast light on words nearer the beginning, which had already been dealt with in print. Thus, for example, in the course of his struggle with the derivation of *walrus* Tolkien discovered the etymology of the obscure word *rossome* 'redness'. He wrote a slip for the 'Supplement' file suggesting that the published etymology 'Obscure' be replaced by

a. early mod. G. *roseme* :– OHG. *rosamo* rubor, lentigo, MHG. *roseme*. (See Diefenbach s.v. *Lentigo*.)

Bradley himself approved this suggestion, and wrote it into his 'office copy'; in 1933, when a corrected reissue of the Dictionary was produced to accompany the completed *Supplement*, the etymology for *rossome* was corrected—though Tolkien's version was drastically shortened to 'G. †*roseme*' to allow it to be inserted without causing the printed entry to spill over onto a new line. Another example is the entry in the *OED* for *rood-wold*: during his work on the *wild/wold* group of words Tolkien realized that the one Middle English quotation given for this supposed compound noun was in fact an instance of a variant form of the past tense of *quell* 'to kill'. (The quotation is still there: such is the scale of the current revision programme that it may be some years before the entry comes up for review.) Tolkien would also make comments on the etymologies of (mainly) Germanic words, often adducing further evidence in support of etymological hypotheses described by the *OED* as unlikely; and occasionally he would make observations on modern English, as in his suggestions for updating the definition of *brigade* ('now a subdivision (usually a 3rd or 4th part) of a "division", and consisting of 3–6 battalions')—presumably based on his own recent military experiences—and his observation that, in addition to the entry for the Middle English diminutive *-kin*, the suffix *-kins* should be included because of its modern colloquial use 'in endearing forms of address' (an entry along these lines did indeed appear in the 1933 *Supplement*).

The vast majority of Tolkien's marginal annotations arose out of work he was doing on another lexicographical project during the last few months of his time in Oxford. Kenneth Sisam, Tolkien's former English tutor, was now working for Oxford University Press (OUP) as assistant to the 'Secretary to the Delegates' (the Press's name for its chief executive). One of his publishing projects was an anthology of passages of 14th-century English for use by students. By June 1919 it had become apparent that he was not going to have the time to compile a glossary for the book as he had originally planned, and Tolkien was asked to help out. It is characteristic of Tolkien that, although he was commissioned to compile a relatively straightforward glossary—and, crucially, to do so quickly, so that it could be published as part of Sisam's volume—the project increased in size and elaborateness to the point that Sisam had to ask OUP to give Tolkien time off from his work on the *OED* to work on it, and that even then he failed to complete it before leaving for Leeds. Eventually Sisam's *Fourteenth Century Verse and Prose* was published in 1921 without a glossary, and what Tolkien called 'this mole-hill glossary (grown into a mountain by accumulated domestic distractions)' (letter to the University Printer, John Johnson, 14 February 1921, in OUP archives) was published separately in 1922 as *A Middle English Vocabulary*—Tolkien's first published book.

In the course of his work on the glossary, Tolkien came across numerous uses of words in Sisam's texts which pre-dated their first use as given in the *OED*; he wrote in the details of several dozen of these antedatings in the margins of Bradley's office copy. For example, in the *OED* the verb *hem* 'to edge or border (a garment or cloth); to decorate with a border, fringe, or the like' is recorded no earlier than 1440; Tolkien noted the phrase 'þe gurdel þat is golde-hemmed' in *Sir Gawain and the Green Knight*, which constitutes an antedating of at least 40 years. In a few cases words were antedated by over a century.

By the time work began on the Dictionary's first *Supplement*, in the late 1920s, its terms of reference were much narrower than originally anticipated: it was to to be confined to entries for words and senses which had not previously been included. Accordingly, much of the material that would have been drawn upon for a larger supplement was not used for the one-volume Supplement which eventually appeared in 1933—at which point the few remaining members of the editorial staff dispersed, and work on the *OED* ceased completely. The four-volume *Supplement to the OED*, compiled under Robert Burchfield's editorship from 1957, had a scope only slightly broader. Thus the 1989 Second Edition contains entries for *brigade* and *hem* which are unchanged as far as Tolkien's comments are concerned. Wholesale revision of the Dictionary began in the 1990s; so some of the notes made by Tolkien over 80 years ago are at last being considered and acted on, as work proceeds towards the Third Edition of the *OED*. A recent example may be found in the entry for the verb *pass*, in the specific sense defined in *OED Online* as 'To spend or use up (a period of time)', for which the date of the earliest known use was previously given as 1390; Tolkien's note (see Fig. 11) recording the

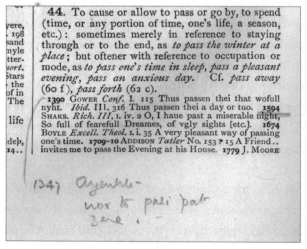

FIGURE 11. Marginal note by Tolkien about a sense of *pass* (verb), in an 'office copy' of the *OED* (First Edition).

occurrence of this sense in a work of the early 14th century (the devotional manual *Ayenbite of Inwit*) led to his quotation being added as an antedating.

The *Middle English Vocabulary*

The fact that Sisam's *Fourteenth Century Verse and Prose* had to be published in 1921 without a glossary because Tolkien had not finished compiling it might be viewed as the first great example of the 'dilatoriness' which C. S. Lewis later attributed to him, but in this case it would be entirely mistaken. On the contrary, that Tolkien completed the work for publication in 1922, at a time when he was also working on the *OED*, tutoring, and applying for and obtaining the Readership at Leeds (and moving his family there), is an astonishing achievement.

Sisam's texts amount to some 43,000 words, each of which Tolkien would have had to consider as possibly requiring explanation in the glossary. Sisam had checked all the texts against the original manuscripts, sometimes substituting his own emendations, so Tolkien could not borrow mechanically from existing editions. The glossary contains about 4,740 entries and nearly 6,800 definitions. Each of the latter is keyed to at least one place in the text where that meaning of the word occurs (the scaled-down equivalent of the quotations in the *OED*): there are almost 15,000 of these text references, every one of which would have had to be individually identified and selected. There are 1,900 cross-references, most of which are provided because Middle English has widely differing forms in different dialects for the same word. There is also a list (on similar principles) of the 236 proper names mentioned in the text. No details are available of

> **Wrþe.** *See* Worþe, *adj.*
> **Wruxled,** *pp.* in *wr. in grene,*
> **?** changed into, turned, green,
> V 123 ; but ' adorned ' is usually
> assumed here and for *wruxeled,*
> Purity 1381. [OE. *wrixl(i)an,*
> (ex)change. A sense ' adorned '
> might be derived from an (un-
> recorded) earlier sense, ' turn,
> wind round ' (? rel. to *wrēon,*
> *wrigels*), or perh. from OE.
> *wrixlan* (*blēom*), change colours,
> exhibit varied hues.]
> **Wulde.** *See* Wille, *v.*

FIGURE 12. Part of a page from *A Middle English Vocabulary* (1922) showing the entry for the rare word *wruxled*; subsequently the glossary to Tolkien and Gordon's *Sir Gawain and the Green Knight* (1925) gave a different explanation, while the *OED* (1928) merely called it 'obscure'.

the time Tolkien spent on the job, but it is difficult to imagine how it could have taken less than the equivalent of nine months' *full-time* work.[5]

Tolkien would have had to use the *OED* as a general guide and model, since there existed no reliable and detailed dictionary of Middle English at this time; the most comprehensive was that by F. H. Stratmann, issued in an English version by Henry Bradley in 1891, but regarded by everyone as eccentric in the extreme. In a prefatory note to the glossary Tolkien acknowledges his reliance on

---

[5] Shortly after the publication of the *Middle English Vocabulary*, Tolkien wrote to Elizabeth Wright, the wife of his former tutor: 'I certainly lavished an amount of time on it which is terrible to recall, and long delayed the Reader bringing curses on my head; but it was instructive' (*Lett.* 6).

the *OED*, especially for the etymologies (supplied to all entries), but it would have offered no short cut, since a modern English head-word list is completely different from a Middle English one, and the majority of the passages keyed to the glossary do not appear in *OED* quotations. In about 300 entries beginning with W, Tolkien was on his own, since this section of the *OED* had not yet been published. In the prefatory note he explains: 'this glossary does not aim at completeness, and it is not primarily a glossary of rare or "hard" words'. Instead 'I have given exceptionally full treatment to what may rightly be called the backbone of the language'. Undoubtedly it was the rigorous discipline of his *OED* service that enabled Tolkien to compile a glossary that is unparalleled for its concision, informativeness, and accuracy.

1922 and after

Tolkien remained in touch with Henry Bradley after leaving OUP, as shown by a postcard from Leeds, dated 26 June 1922, in which he quotes a riddle in Old English. (He describes it as *enigma saxonicum nuper inventum*, literally 'a recently found Saxon riddle'—although the riddle had not been found but invented; it is one of two Old English riddles which he later published in the anthology *A Northern Venture*.) While his continuing contact may well have been no more than such occasional postcards, he retained a great fondness for his former mentor. The warmth of his feelings is vividly conveyed in the obituary for Bradley (signed 'J.R.R.T.') which appeared in the *Bulletin of the Modern Humanities Research Association* in 1923: 'To see him working in the Dictionary Room at the Old Ashmolean and to work for a time under his wise and kindly hand was a privilege not at that time looked for... The memory of more recent years recalls with a sense of great loss his piled table in the Dictionary Room; and many, whether occasional visitors, or workers in that great dusty workshop, that brownest of brown studies, preserve a picture of him as he sat writing there, glimpses of him momentarily held in thought, with eyes looking into the grey shadows of the roof, pen poised in the air to descend at last and fix a sentence or a paragraph complete and rounded, without blot or erasure, on the paper before him.' The obituary ends with an alliterative verse tribute to Bradley, once again in Old English.[6]

Tolkien's work at Leeds was the start of a career which, at least as far as academia was concerned, was almost entirely devoted to philology. In addition to the *Middle English Vocabulary*, there was the edition of *Sir Gawain and the Green Knight* (1925) which he prepared with his Leeds colleague E.V. Gordon, and which includes an exceptionally extensive glossary; editions and translations of other Old and Middle English texts followed (not all published within his lifetime), and from time to time throughout his life he contributed articles and papers exploring the origin of particular English words and names. In all of this work he made constant use of the *OED*, often finding information which would in due course be of use in the revision of the Dictionary. (After returning to Oxford in 1925 as Rawlinson and Bosworth Professor of Anglo-Saxon, Tolkien renewed contact with Charles Onions, who became a fellow member of the Coalbiters, an informal club founded by Tolkien for the

---

[6] Tolkien also maintained contact with members of James Murray's family, including his daughter Rosfrith (1884–1973), who had worked alongside him in the Old Ashmolean, and his grandson Robert, who became a close friend.

reading and discussion of Norse sagas.[7] In 1933 he was unexpectedly presented with his own copy of the complete *OED*; this occasioned a letter to Kenneth Sisam expressing his 'staggerment': see p. 194.)

A particular interest in the *OED* is evident in a task undertaken by Tolkien for the English Association in the 1920s. The Association's annual survey of publications in the field, *The Year's Work in English Studies*, included a chapter on 'Philology: General Works', which Tolkien compiled for the years 1923–5. Newly published fascicles of the *OED* had, unsurprisingly, been reviewed in previous years, but Tolkien went into far more detail than the earlier reviewers in his discussions of particular entries; he evidently relished the task of scrutinizing the work of his former colleagues—and even on occasion taking issue with their conclusions. For example, in his review of the fascicle *Whisking–Wilfulness* for the 1924 volume, he discussed the word *whole* at some length, querying the absence of the Welsh word *coel* 'sign, omen' from the published etymology, and also—a little mischievously perhaps—took the opportunity to have his final say about the possible interrelatedness of the words *weald*, *wild*, and *wold*, on which he had of course himself worked.

Tolkien's discussion of *Watling Street* in the 1923 volume is particularly interesting. The *OED* might not be expected to have an entry for the name of a Roman road, but in Middle English this could also be used as an alternative name for the Milky Way. The first element of the compound has the form of a typical Old English

---

[7] The club's name derives from the Icelandic *Kolbítar*, a name given to those who stay so close to the fire in winter that they are virtually 'biting the coal'. This was not the first club with a linguistically intriguing name which Tolkien had founded: during his undergraduate days at Exeter College he had founded the 'Apolausticks'—from the word *apolaustic* 'devoted to seeking enjoyment', which, since it is extremely rare, he may well have discovered in the *OED*.

clan or family name, and Henry Bradley's etymology (he drafted the entry) discusses who these 'Wætlings' or 'Wæclings' might have been. In discussing the 'Milky Way' sense, Tolkien opined that 'the usual assumption…that it is a secondary application [of the name of the Roman road] is not so certain', and adduced various pieces of evidence in support of the idea that 'we have here an old mythological term that was first applied to the *eald enta geweorc* after the English invasion. Its original sense is probably lost for ever.' It is peculiarly characteristic of Tolkien's philological approach to imagine that behind a word's recorded senses might lie an earlier 'mythological' meaning. (On *enta geweorc* see p. 120.) The 1923 volume also contains further comment by Tolkien on the work of a former colleague: George Watson, a member of Craigie's team of assistants, whose glossary of the dialect of Roxburghshire is given a distinctly unfavourable review.

Early in 1923, when Craigie was showing signs of wanting to abandon his editorship of the Dictionary—a matter for considerable concern at OUP, especially as Bradley was now an old man (in fact he died later in the year)—Tolkien's name was mentioned as someone who might be able to take on part of the work remaining. It was not a serious suggestion: as one senior figure at the Press, R. W. Chapman, put it, 'Tolkien hasn't (yet) enough driving power—besides he has a job.' In the 1950s, when OUP was beginning to contemplate the preparation of an expanded version of the 1933 *Supplement*, the job was eventually given to Robert Burchfield—for whom Tolkien had already become an important mentor.[8] In 1951 Burchfield had begun work on an important 12th-century text,

---

[8] The editorship was also offered to Norman Davis, who was, like Burchfield, a New Zealander, and had also been taught by Tolkien.

the *Ormulum*; Tolkien, whose lectures he had attended while studying at Oxford in 1949–51, agreed to be his supervisor, and the two men met regularly to discuss Burchfield's work. Burchfield acknowledged his enormous debt to Tolkien—'the puckish fisherman who drew me into his glittering philological net'—in a tribute entitled 'My Hero' published in the *Independent* magazine in 1989.

There are also a few occasions in Tolkien's creative writing where he refers—directly or indirectly—to the *OED*. Perhaps most famous is the account in *Farmer Giles of Ham* of the 'Four Wise Clerks of Oxenford' being asked for a definition of *blunderbuss* (see p. 97). There is also a whimsical reference in 'The Notion Club Papers' (*HME* IX. 224–5) to an entry for the onomatopoeic word *doink* in 'the Third Supplement to the N.E.D.' (that is, the 'New English Dictionary', the name by which the *OED* was originally known). Of course, at the time Tolkien wrote this, during the 1940s, even the 'Second' Supplement was not being contemplated.[9]

---

[9] Ironically, Tolkien's use of the word *doink* pre-dates the earliest example currently in the *OED*'s files, from a 1960 children's story by E. W. Hildick. No entry for the word has yet been compiled.

Entries in the *OED* worked on by Tolkien

Waggle (noun & adjective), Waggly, Wain, Waist, Waistband,
Waist-cloth, Waistcoat, Waistcoated, Waistcoateer, Waisted,
Waister, Waistless, Waist-rail, Waist-tree, Wait-a-bit, Waiter,
Waitership, Waiting (noun & adjective), Waiting-maid,
Waiting-man, Waiting-room, Waiting-woman, Waitress,
Wake (noun & verb), Wake-robin, Wake-wort, Waldend,
Wallop (noun & verb), Walloper, Walloping (noun & adjective),
Walm (noun & verb), Walming, Walnut, Walrus, Wampum,
Wampumpeag, Wan (noun, adjective, & verb),
Wander (noun & verb), Wanderable, Wandered, Wanderer,
Wandering (noun & adjective), Wanderment,
Wander-year, Wandreth, Wane (noun, adjective, & verb),
Want (noun & verb), Want-louse, Wariangle,
Warlock (noun & verb), Warlockry, Warm, Weald, Wealden,
Wealding, Wield, Wild, Wold

Also (according to Humphrey Carpenter, *Biography*, p. 101):
Wasp, Water, Wick, Winter

Tolkien as Wordwright

Tolkien as Wordwright

The unique blend of philological erudition and poetic imagination...
distinguished Tolkien from other scholars.
(Alan Bliss, *Preface* to Tolkien's posthumous work *Finn and Hengest*)

What is philology?

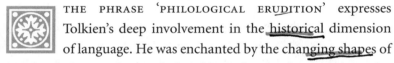

THE PHRASE 'PHILOLOGICAL ERUDITION' expresses Tolkien's deep involvement in the historical dimension of language. He was enchanted by the changing shapes of words, their growing and shrinking, the regular and irregular changes in their sounds, and their effect on each other. This was an aesthetic experience for him, and the technical framework of historical linguistics was like musical notation to a musician.

Taking the Greek roots of the word *philology* in isolation, one might suppose it to mean simply 'love of words'. To do so would be to fall into the celebrated linguistic trap called the 'etymological fallacy': the mistaken belief that a word's true or correct meaning is to be found in its oldest recorded meaning, or its meaning in another language from which it has been borrowed, or the meaning of its constituent parts—in short, its 'etymological' meaning. But in this case the etymological meaning applies as much to Tolkien's relationship with language as does the word's accepted meaning, for which we turn to the *OED*.

As the entry in *OED Online* shows, the word *philology* shifted in usage even during Tolkien's lifetime, affected by changing approaches to language study, and by different patterns of use on either side of the Atlantic. The relevant senses are:

1. Love of learning and literature; the branch of knowledge that deals with the historical, linguistic, interpretative, and critical aspects of literature; literary or classical scholarship. Now chiefly *U.S.* [*note*] By the late 19th cent. this general sense had become *rare*, but it was revived, principally in the United States, in the early 20th cent. [First example dated 1522]

3. The branch of knowledge that deals with the structure, historical development, and relationships of languages or language families; the historical study of the phonology and morphology of languages; historical linguistics. [*note*] This sense has never been current in the United States, and is increasingly rare in British use. *Linguistics* is now the more usual term for the study of the structure of language, and (often with qualifying adjective, as *historical*, *comparative*, etc.) has generally replaced *philology*. [First example dated 1716]

The *OED* records the word *linguistics* as appearing only in 1847, and it was not much used in Britain until the 20th century.

As the *OED* (Second Edition) explicitly noted, sense 3 is not truly contrasted with sense 1, but is a specialized part of it. The study of texts, whether 'literary' or not, leads naturally both 'out' to the study of the society and culture to which the texts belong, and 'in' to the study of the language in which the text is written. Tolkien and Gordon's edition of *Sir Gawain and the Green Knight*, for example, may seem specialized to those unfamiliar with such scholarly texts, but in fact it is multidisciplinary in its scope: it includes an analysis of the 14th-century dialect in which the poem is written, the verse techniques, the characteristics of characterization and narrative, the historical, fictional, and mythological sources, and the ideology and customs of the text's contemporary audience. A philologist has to be able to handle all these areas. Another notable instance is Tolkien's discussion, alongside his play *The Homecoming of Beorhtnoth*, of the single word *ofermod* in the Old English poem *The Battle of Maldon*. (*OED Online* defines it at OVERMOOD *n.*[1] as 'pride, arrogance; overconfidence' and notes that its precise meaning has been the subject of 'considerable scholarly debate'.) Philology in the *OED*'s sense 3 is, in effect, the same discipline as in sense 1, focused on the same texts and contexts, but with a different perspective, taking language as the starting point. The modern term *linguistics* is a poor substitute, implying as it does a *sole* rather than simply a *primary* focus on language. Tolkien himself said in his 'Valedictory Address to the University of Oxford': 'Philology is the foundation of humane letters' (*The Monsters and the Critics*, p. 225). He went on to say that ' "misology" is a disqualifying defect or disease' (quoted in *OED*: MISOLOGY *n.* 'hatred of learning or knowledge', here given a distinct twist as the opposite of philology).

As a little consideration will readily show, language exists on two levels. There is the level of *sounds*, of which a limited set exists in any particular language, and which may be represented by a writing system. The sound and shape of words is the most basic foundation of the aesthetic quality of poetry and expressive prose. (Tolkien, as we shall see, placed particular emphasis on the sound of language.) Then there is the level of *meanings*, which are expressed by an unlimited set of structures (primarily words, and sentences built of them) made out of the sounds of the language. The level of meaning constitutes the directly communicative quality of language, which is its primary purpose according to modern-day linguistics.

Philology is concerned with both the sound and shape of words and their meaning. And because every aspect of every language is constantly changing, philology (historical linguistics) is especially concerned with the *history* of word-forms and word meanings.

The *OED* as the focus of English philology

The *Oxford English Dictionary* is an essentially philological work, because its central concerns are the development of word-forms and word meanings. In the *OED* entry for a word with a long history in English, there is usually a list of variant spellings, which exemplify the changes of shape that the word has undergone. (These may also be further explained in the etymology section.) The structured series of definitions which comprises the main part of the entry expresses the history of the word's meanings as they have multiplied or changed through time. A block of dated illustrative quotations attached to each definition provides some literary, cultural, and historical context for each meaning; they represent a selection from the larger collection of illustrative material from which nearly everything said about the word has been deduced.

The form history and sense history of each word *before* its emergence in English is explained in the etymological section of the entry. Because this is the essential prelude to the word's story within English, the *OED* places the etymology before the series of meanings and not, as many dictionaries do, at the end of the article. Etymology is philology in its essence, for it requires the full range of philological skills: knowledge of the patterns of phonetic and grammatical change and of the interrelationships of languages; understanding of the historical and cultural context; and familiarity with the texts written in the language in question.

An etymology can truly be the unlocking of a word-hoard. A whole history of peoples and rulers, wars and trade, inventions, mysteries, beliefs, fears, and loves can spring to life from the investigation of a single word's origin. Take, for example, the etymology of WALNUT, on which Tolkien himself worked (see Fig. 13). It tells us, of course, all the related words in the Germanic languages. It also

Walnut[1] (wǭ·lnʋt). Forms: 1 walhhnutu, 4–6 walnotte, 5 wallnott, 5, 6 walnutt(e, 6–8 wall-nutt, 7 walenotte, 7–8 wallnut, 6– walnut. See also WALSH-NUT. [OE. *walhhnutu* str. fem. = WFris. *walnút* (NFris. *walnödd* from Da.), MDu. *walnote* (Kilian *walnot*), Du. *walnoot*, MLG. *wallnot, -nut*, LG. (Bremisch. Wörterb. *wallnutt*) *walnut*, G. *walnuss* (earlier *wallnuss*), ON. *valhnot* str. fem. (Norw. *valnot*, Sw. *valnöt*, Da. *valnød*). The first element is OTeut. **walχo-z* (OE. *wealh*, OHG. *walah*) 'Welshman', i. e. Celtic or Roman foreigner; see WELSH *a*.

The solitary OE. example (in a glossary *c* 1050) is the earliest known appearance of the word in any language. The word must, however, have come to England from the Continent, but there is no evidence to show whether it belonged to the primitive OE. vocabulary, or was introduced at a relatively late date. It seems to have belonged originally to the LG.-speaking district; etymologically it meant the 'nut of the Roman lands (Gaul and Italy) as distinguished from the native hazel. It is noteworthy that in the languages of these countries the word descending from L. *nux*, when used without qualification, denotes the walnut. In HG. the word appears first in the 16th c. (adapted from LG.); but MHG. had the equivalent *wälhisch nuz* (mod.G. dial. *wälsche nuss, wälschnuss*): see WALSH-NUT.

The ONF. *noix gauge, gaugue*, walnut (which survives in mod. Picard and Norman dialects) app. represents a popular L. **nux gallica*, a translation of the Teut. word.]

FIGURE 13. Etymology of *walnut* as published in the *OED* (First Edition).

tells us: (1) that the first English attestation of the word is the oldest in any Germanic language; (2) that its appearance in Old English is relatively late, and we don't know whether it goes back to much earlier times in England, or whether in 1050 it was a recent borrowing; (3) that the word is a compound whose first element originally meant 'Celtic or Roman foreigner': on the European continent this normally referred to the Romans or Romance speakers, but in Old English it was restricted to Celtic people (and is now found in the name *Wales*); (4) that in the languages descended from Latin the ordinary word for 'nut' (e.g. French *noix*), when not qualified by another word, means 'walnut' (whereas the original Germanic meaning of *nut* and its relatives was 'hazelnut'). This etymology takes us back to the time of the Roman Empire, when walnuts were relatively exotic items for the Germanic peoples, and when foreigners living to the west and south of the Germanic realms were indiscriminately called by a word which in English has become the word *Welsh*.

From the fragment of Tolkien's original draft etymology which survives in the Oxford University Press Archives (see Fig. 14) it is clear that Tolkien would have liked the *OED* entry to take the argument a step further. If the word is indeed a late arrival in Old English then it is probably what is known as a 'loan translation' from a Dutch or Low German word, in which the two elements of the compound were turned into the equivalent Old English form, ignoring the fact that the continental meaning of *walh* 'Roman' was not actually used in Old English at the time. If, on the other hand, it is an old word, then it must be very old indeed, going back to the time when even speakers of what became English, still living on the continent of Europe, used *walh* to mean 'Roman' because they had not yet moved to a land where their neighbours would be Celts. One

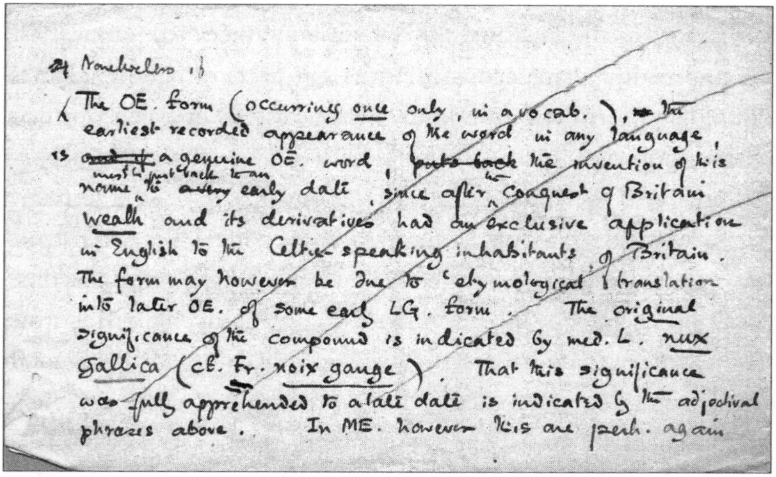
Nonetheless if
The OE. form (occurring once only, in a vocab.), the
earliest recorded appearance of the word in any language,
is a genuine OE. word, the invention of this
name must be put back to an early date, since after the conquest of Britain
wealh and its derivatives had an exclusive application
in English to the Celtic-speaking inhabitants of Britain.
The form may however be due to 'etymological' translation
into later OE. of some early LG. form. The original
significance of the compound is indicated by med. L. nux
Gallica (cf. Fr. noix gauge). That this significance
was fully apprehended to a late date is indicated by the adjectival
phrases above. In ME. however this was perh. again

FIGURE 14. Dictionary slip showing Tolkien's draft of part of the etymology of *walnut.*

can see in this draft Tolkien's characteristic impulse to imagine his way back into the depths of time.

The various meanings and uses listed in the entry for *walnut* also paint a vivid cultural picture. Apart from the unsurprising information that the word is also applied to the tree, to other similar species, and to the tree's wood, it tells us that walnuts were often eaten with wine after dinner; that an essential oil is obtained from the nut; that the wood was the material for gunstocks; and that walnut juice was (reputedly) used by Gypsies as a brown stain for the skin.

Tolkien as philologist: the reconstructive impulse

If the essential part of philology is etymology, the fundamental process in etymology is *reconstruction.* Palaeontologists with a knowledge of the anatomy and physiology of related species, living and extinct, can reconstruct missing parts of a fossil animal. Philologists, working from known relationships between words in related languages, do something similar. Two distinct processes are involved: the uncovering of relationships of shared ancestry between existing words (called *cognates*), and the reconstruction of the probable (though strictly hypothetical) form of their common ancestor—a word in the common source language from which later cognate languages have descended—or the likely form of a word in a surviving language from which it has been lost. Taking *OED* entries on which Tolkien worked, we can see this process resulting in the reconstructed 'pre-Teutonic' form of WAIN (**woghno-s*: the asterisk is conventionally used to mark reconstructed forms), the prehistoric Old Norse form of WAKE *n.*[2] (**vaku*), and the reconstructed Old Northern French form of WALLOP (**waloper*).

Trying to make sense of an enigmatic word-form requires the exercise of linguistic skills, but this very activity leads the researcher into a wider realm of history or of legend (imagined history): it calls upon the interplay of the imagination with the known facts. The reconstruction of word-forms goes hand in hand with the imaginative recreation of the lost world in which they are supposed to have been used—the recreation, in Tom Shippey's memorable phrase, of an 'asterisk-reality'.

Tolkien's education, his work on the *OED*, and his subsequent research place him squarely in the great British tradition of philological study. More unusually, though, he took the opportunity to practise the same philological techniques by applying them to his own private languages, the most substantial result being the immensely detailed 'Etymologies' of the Elvish tongues (published in *HME* V). Though everything in them is invented, they use exactly the same apparatus—reconstruction of forms in lost languages, postulation of cross-influences from related languages, replacement by loanwords—that appear in etymological discussions in the *OED* and similar works of real-world comparative linguistics. Discussing Tolkien's 'historical-philological' essays on the Elvish languages, written from around 1967 onwards, Christopher Tolkien says: 'Almost all of this work was etymological in its inspiration, which accounts for its extremely discursive nature; for in no study does one thing lead to another more rapidly than in etymology, which also of its nature leads out of itself in the attempt to find explanations beyond the purely linguistic evolution of forms' (introduction to 'Late Writings' in *HME* XII. 294). Tolkien's fascination with the interrelationship of language and history is exemplified in his reaction to a lecture by his son Christopher: 'I suddenly realized that I am a *pure* philologist. I like history, and am moved by it, but its finest moments for me are those in which it throws light on words and names!' (*Lett.* 205, 21 February 1958).

The particular languages out of which Tolkien's art grows are chiefly those in which the legends, epics, lays, and romances of the early medieval North have been handed down. They include Welsh and Finnish; but central among them are the Germanic languages, especially Old English and Old Norse, but also Old Saxon, Old Frisian, and Old High German. When Tolkien discovered Gothic, the most ancient Germanic language, he began to use the reconstructive techniques of philology to invent non-existent Gothic words to fill the gaps in its limited vocabulary. These were derived on philological principles from the analogy of words in other Germanic languages. This paved the way for all his adaptation of 'real' languages (principally the Germanic ones), of the kind that we trace in this book.

The shape of words

Apart from the pleasure of its previous development and relationships, for Tolkien a word had an aesthetic pleasure in itself:

> Being a philologist, getting a large part of any aesthetic pleasure that I am capable of from the *form* of words (and especially from the *fresh association* of word-form with word-sense), I have always best enjoyed things in a foreign language, or one so remote as to feel like it (such as Anglo-Saxon). (*Lett.* 142, 2 December 1953)

This pleasure must often have consisted of a suggestiveness, a flavour bringing other things to mind, because part of the power of Tolkien's linguistic creativity seems to lie in the fact that his created words have the same, or a similar, aesthetic effect on his readers as they did on him. Sometimes it is possible to pin down such effects: for example, when we can point to curiously appropriate resemblances to other words (in the same language or in another). Examples might be *hobbit*, with the various redolences suggested by Tolkien of *hobbledehoy, rabbit,* and the character *Babbitt*[1]; or *Arkenstone*, with its hints of *ark* in the sense of a place where something mysterious is kept, or the antediluvian *Ark* of Noah (and,

---

[1] Tolkien acknowledged in a letter to W. H. Auden (quoted in Carpenter's *Biography*) that Sinclair Lewis's 1922 novel *Babbitt* may have been 'an unconscious source-book'; and he told an interviewer that he may have associated the word *hobbit* with the name of its self-satisfied bourgeois hero, George Babbitt.

perhaps, the *arch-of-words* such as *archaic*); *Númenor*, with its hint of *numinous*; or *Gil-galad*, which for some readers combines the ancient feel of *Gilgamesh* with the Arthurian chivalrousness of *Galahad*. In other cases the associations are more elusive; but in all his word-creation Tolkien was at pains to find the right shape, to find 'a relationship, sound plus sense, that satisfies, that is when made *durable*' ('The Notion Club Papers': *HME* IX. 240).[2]

Tolkien upheld the importance of the sound of words as an independent value in language. Of an invented language, he wrote:

> It remained unfreed from the purely *communicative* aspect of language—the one that seems usually supposed to be the real germ and original impulse of language. But I doubt this exceedingly; as much as one doubts a poet's sole object, even primary one, being to talk in a special way to other people. The communication factor has been very powerful in directing the development of language; but the more individual and personal factor—pleasure in articulate sound, and in the symbolic use of it, independent of communication though constantly in fact entangled with it—must not be forgotten for a moment.
>
> ('A Secret Vice' in *The Monsters and the Critics*, p. 208)

This is an unusual and controversial view in the context of modern linguistics, in which the communicative aspect of language is seen as dominant.

---

[2] Tolkien's appreciation that this aesthetic response to language was widespread, but that it also varied from individual to individual, is strikingly illustrated by his account of the Elvish ceremony of *Essecilmë* or 'Name-choosing' (*HME* X. 214–15), which would only take place when a child had developed *'lámatyávë*...individual pleasure in the sounds and forms of words'—a propensity which the Elves considered more important as a mark of individuality even than facial features.

It was especially the shape and sound of words in particular languages that attracted him, as he tells us in the essay 'English and Welsh', where the fullest exposition of his views on 'the basic pleasure in the phonetic elements of a language and in the style of their patterns' can be found. His aesthetic response to Welsh had begun when, as a schoolboy, he had been fascinated by the Welsh place names seen on coal-trucks on the railway line. At Oxford he discovered Finnish, another language which he found entrancingly beautiful. Both languages were to provide a major fountainhead of inspiration for his own invented languages.

Old English did not have such an overwhelming effect on Tolkien: he once described it as 'that pleasing but not "delectable" language' (*Lett.* 297, 1967). But even in Old English a single word could sometimes evoke a powerful response. The consequences of his encounter with a single word—*Earendel*—can hardly be overstated. He never forgot reading the word in an Old English poem from the manuscript known as the Exeter Book in 1913: 'I felt a curious thrill...as if something had stirred in me, half wakened from sleep. There was something very remote and strange and beautiful behind those words, if I could grasp it, far beyond ancient English' (quoted in Carpenter, *Biography*, p. 64). Having learned that the word—or its equivalent in other Germanic languages, including Old Norse and Lombardic—could denote both a star and the name of a mariner, in 1914 Tolkien wrote a poem in which the ship of Earendel leaped into the heavens, and so created the first character in his whole legendarium. The name *Eärendil*, as it later became, acquired an Elvish etymology; but the mariner's connections with our own world remained—the name *Wingelot* which Tolkien later gave to his boat was derived from *Guingelot*, the boat belonging to the seafaring giant Wada or Wade of Germanic mythology (whose links to Eärendil are discussed by Christopher Tolkien in *HME* III. 142–3 and XII. 371).

The word as leaf

These little lexicographical chases open up vista after vista and one complication after another.

(Tolkien, in *The Year's Work in English Studies*, vol. VI. (1925) ii. 35)

A lexicographer's work requires each word to be scrutinized as an individual, looking at all the evidence illustrating its use and history and being prepared to follow its various aspects down whatever path they may lead. Tolkien's natural tendency—at times amounting to a compulsion—to do exactly this stood him in good stead throughout his professional life as a philologist, but it also had a profound effect on his creative writing: painstaking consideration of an individual word would often be the precursor to the unlocking of his imagination, and the development of a new facet of his created world.

In Tolkien's parable *Leaf by Niggle*, the character Niggle is often supposed to be a representation of Tolkien himself; he was

the sort of painter who can paint leaves better than trees. He used to spend a long time on a single leaf, trying to catch its shape, and its sheen, and the glistening of dewdrops on its edges. Yet he wanted to paint a whole tree, with all of its leaves in the same style, and all of them different.

There was one picture in particular which bothered him. It had begun with a leaf caught in the wind, and it became a tree; and the tree grew, sending out innumerable branches, and thrusting out the most fantastic roots... Then all round the Tree, and behind it, and through the gaps in the leaves and boughs, a country began to open out; and there were glimpses of a forest marching over the land, and of mountains tipped with snow. Niggle lost interest in his other pictures; or else he took them and tacked them on to the edges of his great picture.

The applicability of Niggle's situation to Tolkien's is striking: he could become just as compulsively fascinated by a word as Niggle could by a leaf. A word could 'ramify' and put down roots, even when—perhaps especially when—the state of knowledge of its place in the language was incomplete, and needed to be reconstructed, or at least imagined.

The most dramatic example of Tolkien's imaginative response to a single word is surely his creation of the Ents from the single, almost unknown Old English word *ent* (see the Word Study, pp. 119–21). His own comments highlight the process by which word met idea:

> As usually with me they grew rather out of their name than the other way about. I always felt that something ought to be done about the peculiar A[nglo-] Saxon word *ent* for a 'giant' or mighty person of long ago—to whom all old works were ascribed. If it had a slightly philosophical tone (though in ordinary philology it is 'quite unconnected with any present participle of the verb to be') that also interested me. (*Lett*. 157, 27 November 1954)

> And I like Ents now because they do not seem to have anything to do with me. I daresay something had been going on in the 'unconscious' for some time, and that accounts for my feeling throughout, especially when stuck, that I was not inventing but reporting (imperfectly) and had at times to wait till 'what really happened' came through. But looking back analytically I should say that Ents are composed of philology, literature, and life. They owe their name to the *eald enta geweorc* of Anglo-Saxon, and their connexion

> with stone. Their part in the story is due, I think, to my bitter dis-
> appointment and disgust from schooldays with the shabby use made
> in Shakespeare of the coming of 'Great Birnam wood to high
> Dunsinane hill': I longed to devise a setting in which the trees
> might really march to war. (*Lett.* 163, 7 June 1955)

Of course Tolkien's imagination responded to many stimuli besides
words, as his reference to Shakespeare makes clear. But some of the
most important imaginative developments can be traced back to a
thought about a word.

Perhaps the simplest linguistic thought which a word may prompt
is that it does not mean exactly what it 'ought' to mean: a mismatch
between its obvious form and its established meaning. Often there is
a touch of humour to be found in such a mismatch, as in the case of
the 'Bounders', the body of hobbits who 'beat the bounds' of the
Shire. This furnishes a pun (which Tolkien, in his 'Guide to the
Names in *LR*', calls a 'slender jest') between the almost forgotten
sense 'one who sets out or marks bounds' (*OED*: BOUNDER *n.*[1]) and
the well-known though dated slang term for 'a person of objection-
able manners or anti-social behaviour' (*OED*: BOUNDER *n.*[2]). (Such
puns are of course not peculiar to Tolkien.) More creatively, Tolkien
would sometimes use the word in its 'apparent' sense, using the
context to make this meaning so obvious that its more established
meaning could be ignored. His imagination would take flight from
the notion that *lockhole* might really be a hole in which people were
locked up, or that *waybread* might really be a kind of bread for a
journey. In this way he subverts the 'etymological fallacy' by creating
a context in which the 'wrong' explanation of a word's form turns
out actually to be the 'true' one.

A similar process, but with some sophisticated philological under-
pinning, underlies Tolkien's use of the phrase *Cracks of Doom* to

denote the volcanic fissures in the crater of Orodruin. Tolkien observed of this name that its modern sense is

> derived from Macbeth IV. i. 117, in which the *cracke of Doome* means 'the announcement of the Last Day', by a crack or peal of thunder: so it is commonly supposed, but it may mean 'the sound of the last trump', since *crack* could be applied to the sudden sound of horns or trumpets (as it is in *Sir Gawain and the Green Knight*, lines 116, 1166).
>
> ('Guide to the Names in *LR*')

Tolkien's interpretation of the Shakespearean phrase in a way which links it to the traditional image of the Last Trump (the angels' trumpet which is to announce the Day of Judgement) is a classic example of textual philology, an insight informed by his own intimate knowledge of the language of *Sir Gawain*. The two different kinds of sound are both covered in the *OED* entry for CRACK *n.*: 'a sudden sharp and loud noise as of something breaking or bursting... Formerly applied also to the roar of a cannon, of a trumpet, and of thunder'. But having dealt philologically with the word 'crack', Tolkien's creative imagination at some point came up with a quite different interpretation of the phrase. He realized that the 'sound' senses of *crack* could be replaced with a third, even more familiar sense (*OED* sense 7a: 'a fissure or opening...'); this immediately suggests that 'crack of doom' might actually be a topographical term—the name of a place, a great and ominous fissure in the earth (or, as it ultimately became, a rent in the side of a volcano called Mount Doom). As with *ent*, 'something had been going on in the unconscious', and ultimately a new meaning 'came through': and again his restless imagination insisted on creating a story (a little piece of 'asterisk-reality') to explain where or how such a meaning could come about.

With a word of Old English origin such as *wapentake*, an extra step was required. The Old English form *wæpentake* contains *wæpen* (weapon) and *take*—though these elements are no longer present in the Old English *meaning* of the word—and so, as well as giving it a 'new' meaning, he also gives it the modern spelling **weapontake**. This (relatively trivial) example illustrates a distinctively philological strand in Tolkien's word-creation: one of his imaginative responses to old or obsolete words was to ask himself, 'How would this word look if it had survived to the present day, and what might it now mean?' Using the same techniques which enabled him to reconstruct 'missing' Gothic words (see p. 53), he could craft a 'missing' modern English word from the ancient word which could have been its ancestor. This is both a scholarly process—the development of the 'later' form of the word must 'work' philologically—and a creative one—the revived word must fit into the imagined context where it is to be used (the 'great picture' has to be adapted to accommodate the new 'leaf'). As a philologist Tolkien was able to see this potential in many words whose form is opaque to the ordinary reader. Thus from Old English models he devised **Arkenstone, Dernhelm, ent, mathom,** and **smial,** as well as place names such as *Emnet*—not to mention the entire set of names for the months of the Shire calendar, 'evolved' from the obsolete Old English names (see *LR* Appendix D and *HME* XII. 122ff.). From Old English also come such compounds as *Elfsheen* (a byname of Morwen, *The Silmarillion*, p. 155; Old English *ælfsciene* 'beautiful as a fairy'). Using Middle English patterns, he came up with **dwimmerlaik, Easterling, elven, Mannish, sigaldry,** and **Westernesse**; and he adapted Old Norse forms to produce **daymeal, Elvenhome,** Oakenshield, **Over-heaven** (Old Norse *upphiminn*), and **warg.** Even when he adopted existing words, such as *farthing*, *flet*, and *halfling*, he often gave them a new (usually etymologically inspired) twist.

Philology and archaism

Although Tolkien was voted 'Author of the Century' by a 20th-century readership, his writing has deep roots in the 19th century. His scholarship grew out of a philological tradition which developed in the late 19th century; but this was deeply interconnected with a literary tradition, and Tolkien's literary work can be seen in the light of this too. It is reflected in the variety of types of language which he used in writing—especially in the formal and archaic language which permeates the early writings in *The History of Middle-earth* (and those posthumously published in *The Silmarillion*, once described by a bewildered reader as 'like the Old Testament'). It also emerges during the progress of the story not only in *The Lord of the Rings* but also in *The Hobbit*, as we move from the Edwardian comfort of Bag End to the caves of the Misty Mountains and beyond. In the following discussion, we show how Tolkien adapted the vocabulary and diction of his predecessors to his own creative purpose.

Language, folklore, and the medieval revival

Like most of the arts in northern Europe from the late 18th century, literature in English was affected by the rediscovery of the medieval. 'Dark-age' epic and medieval romance were revived and imitated, in an attempt to reincorporate them into national mythologies. Riding the crest of this wave was Sir Walter Scott (1771–1832), whose poems and especially (from 1814 onwards) outstandingly popular historical novels made the 'medieval', the 'Gothic', the 'Celtic' (especially all things Scottish), and the 'romantic' into a predominant theme of British culture (later transferred into the visual arts by the Pre-Raphaelites). The ancient Scandinavian world was particularly important to the revival, because the Norse literature of Iceland was believed to have preserved the myths and legends of the Germanic heroic age in the purest form (while other literatures had been christianized by clerical and monastic writers). It deeply interested Andrew Lang (1844–1912), whose fairy-tale collections, beginning with the *Blue Fairy Book* in 1889, include retellings of folk tales from Northern and many other traditions—including a version of the tale of Sigurd and the dragon Fafnir (in the *Red Fairy Book*) which inspired the seven-year-old Tolkien (see p. 3). There was also considerable interest in *Beowulf.* Sharon Turner's partial translation of 1805 was followed by over a dozen other versions over the next century, some in prose, some in metrical verse, and a few in an alliterative form imitating the Old English original (e.g. James Garnett's of 1882).

The revival of medieval literature and legend was accompanied and strengthened by a new interest in contemporary folklore. The Finnish epic, the *Kalevala*, compiled by Elias Lönnrot (1835) and one of the main inspirations for H. W. Longfellow's epic poem *Hiawatha* (1855), was based on poems from the folk tradition, and so stands on the border between heroic legend and folklore. All over Europe, popular literature was carefully collected (and imitated), in the belief that the surviving traditions of the ordinary, rural population were 'purer' and more 'authentic' than the sophisticated, rationalized products of urban civilization. Bishop Thomas Percy collected English ballads in his celebrated *Reliques of Ancient*

English Poetry (1765) while, in the early 19th century, Walter Scott and others collected Scots ballads. As the romanticized cult of childhood grew, legends were transformed into tales for the entertainment and edification of children, and a new influx of tales from Scandinavia, Germany, and elsewhere was added to the inherited stock of British fairy tales.

Since interest in folklore and legend meant dealing with the language—whether ancient or regional dialect—in which they were recorded, the new developments both drew upon and fuelled the new linguistic science of philology. (In Germany, the philological discoveries in the great historical dictionary compiled by the Grimm brothers were founded on their research in folklore and their collection of folk tales that lay behind.) Throughout northern Europe there was a feeling that philological research had stepped in just in time to save each nation's linguistic heritage from being lost. This encouraged the view that old words were somehow more 'authentic' than current words. 'Root' words, thought to be preserved in regional dialect as well as in medieval literature, seemed closer to the true soul of the nation than the Latinate language of learning. There was an urge to revive old words, either unchanged or with the spelling (and by implication the pronunciation) adapted to a more modern form. Some in England felt that Germanic compounds (even if newly minted, like *foreword*, coined by George Dasent in 1842 according to the *OED*) were more 'authentic' than loanwords (such as *preface*). William Barnes even tried to replace established Latin and French borrowings with coinages from Anglo-Saxon roots, with results that often now seem ludicrous (e.g. *push-wainling* for *perambulator*, quoted in the *OED* from his *Outline of English Speech-craft* (1878)). He also wrote poems in Dorset dialect (from 1884), as

Tennyson did in Lincolnshire dialect (e.g. 'Northern Farmer, Old Style', 1864), while many authors (notably George MacDonald) introduced chunks of dialect into their novels.

'Period' prose

As both medieval literature and contemporary folklore became read and translated, it prompted a novel development: the use of 'period' language in prose. Its first chief exponent was Sir Walter Scott, whose historical novels 'almost created that historical sense which we now all take for granted' (C. S. Lewis, 'Sir Walter Scott' in *They Asked for a Paper* (1962) 103). He made use of a large stock of Scots expressions hitherto unknown in England, and others which had fallen completely out of use. (Some of his revivals actually achieved general currency again: few who use words like *foray, hostel*, and *smoulder* would imagine that they had been disused for centuries before being revived by Scott.) But in addition, he frequently used a kind of hybrid English—part contemporary, part pseudo-medieval—to give (apparent) verisimilitude to the dialogue:

> 'Body of me…I should know that voice! And is it thou, in thy bodily person, Harry Gow? Nay, beshrew me if thou passest this door with dry lips. What, man, curfew has not rung yet, and if it had, it were no reason why it should part father and son.'
> (*The Fair Maid of Perth*, chapter ii)

This 'period' prose has many features in common with conventional poetic diction, a stylized literary dialect which had developed from around the time of Edmund Spenser (?1552–1599). The distinctive features of this archaic style include the old forms of the 2nd and 3rd person singular in the present tense of verbs (*thou hast, she doth,* etc.); old irregular past tense forms (*spake, brake, clomb*); contractions (*o'er, e'er, 'gan, 'neath*); the use of *do* (*the birds do sing*); the inversion of verb and subject, verb and object, or noun and adjective (*then felt I, the amorous clouds dividing, such music sweet*); and the prevalence of words and meanings not used in ordinary speech (*ere, oft, perchance, right glad, sore afraid, unto, wot, yea*)—characteristics of the language of Shakespeare's time or even earlier. Despite a shift by the Romantics and their successors towards more ordinary language in poetry, this form of poetic diction persisted even into the 20th century, where a strand of it runs through the whole of Tolkien's output in verse, from student poems ('From the many-willow'd margin of the immemorial Thames, | Standing in a vale outcarven in a world-forgotten day', 1913) to the songs in *The Lord of the Rings* ('For lost of yore was Nimrodel | And in the mountains strayed', *LR* II. vi).

However, 'period' prose was marked by a more deliberate and often quite academic use of archaic and dialect vocabulary. Scott's technique was taken up and adapted by many other writers, both in the newly fashionable novels and romances set in Saxon, later medieval, or early modern times (frequently featuring adventures and deeds of courage, and most now regarded as practically unreadable), and in translations and retellings of old legends, sagas, and romances. (The tradition of using the vocabulary of a bygone era to enhance the 'period' feel of stories with a historical setting continues today—often with the aid of the *OED*, which offers writers a handy source of reliably dated words. The Aubrey-Maturin novels of Patrick O'Brian, for example, are richly loaded with authentic vocabulary of the Napoleonic era.)

Many of these would have been familiar to Tolkien from his early reading, including Lord Macaulay's *Lays of Ancient Rome* (1842)

('And out spake strong Herminius; | Of Titian blood was he: | "I will abide on thy left side, | And keep the bridge with thee"', from 'Horatius') and the works of George Dasent (1817–96), who translated both Scandinavian folk tales (*Popular Tales from the Norse*, 1858) and Icelandic literary works such as Njal's Saga (1861). (Tolkien identified Dasent's fairy tale *Soria Moria Castle* as the source of the name *Moria*—though not its meaning in Middle-earth: *Lett*. 297.) Two other authors whose themes and words are found in Tolkien's writings are Edward Bulwer-Lytton and Charles Kingsley. Whether Tolkien read Lytton is unclear, but it seems likely that he read Kingsley's *Hereward the Wake* (1865), judging from thematic similarities and distinctive verbal echoes such as *horse-boy* ('the cursed horse-boys'; *LR* III. iii) and *ruffling* ('you ruffling young fool'; *HME* VIII. 285); see also the Word Studies on **orc** and **springle-ring**. A similar archaic style was also adopted by the authors of adventure stories with present-day but exotic settings, notably Henry Rider Haggard, whose *She* (1887) Tolkien acknowledged as having 'interested me as much as anything' in his boyhood.

It became accepted practice to revive obsolete words from Malory, Chaucer, and less well-known medieval writers. This seems warranted when referring to historic institutions or obsolete customs, and to avoid anachronistic resonances (which Tolkien criticized in his essay 'On Translating Beowulf', citing the use of terms such as *notable* and *subaltern* by other translators such as Clark Hall). But the practice often went far beyond this, using 'special' words where current words would have been perfectly adequate, simply to signal the pre-modern setting of the story. Here, for example, are some examples from Dasent's translation *The Story of Burnt Njal*, in which the light sprinkling of archaism makes the old forms stick out incongruously:

> There was a bad harvest that year in the land, yet Gunnhillda gave Hrut as much meal as he chose to have; and now he busks him to sail out to Iceland…
>
> He said, 'Ill luck is the end of ill redes, and now I see how it has all gone… Let us now gather folk and follow him up thither north.'…
>
> Swan said, 'Go thou out with me, there won't be need of much.' So they went out both of them, and Swan took a goatskin and wrapped it about his own head, and said, 'Become mist and fog, become fright and wonder mickle to all those who seek thee.'

Here, the mainstream of the narrative, and much of the dialogue, is in plain modern English, reflecting the fairly racy style of the Old Norse original. But here and there are rocky shoals of archaism ('ill redes', 'go thou out', 'he busks him', 'wonder mickle'), which result in a rather turbulent narrative flow.

Some of Dasent's archaisms represent a distortion of peculiarly philological origin, a variety of the 'etymological fallacy'. In uncovering the etymology of English words, philologists identified 'cognate' words in other Germanic languages, but this encouraged the fallacy that, because word A in English is cognate to word B in another language, or word A in modern English is descended from word B in Old or Middle English, then we can use A to translate B. So it is that an obscure word like *mickle* is used to translate Old English *micel* or Old Norse *mikill* (meaning 'great'). Tolkien attacks both gratuitous archaism and the etymological fallacy in his essay 'On Translating Beowulf' (*The Monsters and the Critics*, pp. 55–6):

> Words should not be used merely because they are 'old' or obsolete. The words chosen, however remote they may be from colloquial speech or ephemeral suggestions, must be words that remain in

literary use, especially in the use of verse, among educated people…
They must need no gloss. The fact that a word was still used by
Chaucer, or Shakespeare, or even later, gives it no claim, if it has
in our time perished from literary use. Still less is translation from
Beowulf a fitting occasion for the exhumation of dead words from
Saxon or Norse graves…To render *leode* 'freemen, people' by *leeds*
(favoured by William Morris) fails both to translate the Old English and to recall *leeds* to life…Different, though related, is the
etymological fallacy. A large number of the words used in *Beowulf*
have descended to our own day. But etymological descent is of all
guides to a fit choice of words the most untrustworthy: *wann* is not
'wan' but 'dark'; *mod* is not 'mood' but 'spirit' or 'pride'; *burg* is not a
'borough' but a 'strong place'; an *ealdor* is not an 'alderman' but a
'prince'.

The evolution of archaism from Morris to Tolkien

The love of the medieval, the fascination with the ancient heroic
North, and the reverence for 'authentic' vocabulary are all combined in the figure of William Morris (1834–96), and his late prose
romances, especially *The House of the Wolfings* (1889) and *The Roots
of the Mountains* (1889), influenced Tolkien considerably. In the
spring of 1914 he used some prize money awarded to him by Exeter
College to buy several of Morris's works; the following October he
wrote to his fiancée:

> I am trying to turn one of the stories [from the Kalevala]—which is
> really a very great story and most tragic—into a short story some-
> what on the lines of Morris' romances with chunks of poetry in
> between. (*Lett.* 1)

and after nearly half a century of creative effort he was still acknowledging his debt to Morris:

> The Dead Marshes and the approaches to the Morannon owe some-
> thing to Northern France after the Battle of the Somme. They owe
> more to William Morris and his Huns and Romans, as in *The House
> of the Wolfings* or *The Roots of the Mountains.*
> (*Lett.* 226, 31 December 1960)

By contrast with Dasent, Morris is an unabashed and profligate
archaizer. He creates a dialect of his own, with a syntax resembling
that of the King James Bible, and a vocabulary as close to Middle
English as he can get without complete obscurity (or, sometimes,
despite achieving complete obscurity). In the following (fairly
typical) passage we can see many of the familiar characteristics
of earlier archaizing writers, including period grammar and genuinely archaic words and idioms (examples of these features are
italicized).

> So in no long while *were they come* over against the *stead* [=place] of
> the Erings, and thereabouts were no beasts *a-field*, and no women, for
> all the *neat* [=cattle] were driven into the *garth* [=yard] of the House;
> but *all they* who were not war-fit were standing without doors look-
> ing down the Mark towards the *reek* [=smoke] of the Bearing dwell-
> ings, and these also sent a cry of welcome toward the host of
> their kindred. But along the river-bank came to meet the host an
> armed band of two old men, two youths who were their sons, and
> twelve thralls who were armed with long spears; and all these were
> *a-horseback*: so they fell in with their kindred and the host *made no
> stay* for them, but pressed on over-running the meadow. And still
> went up that column of smoke, and thicker and blacker it grew a-top,
> and ruddier amidmost.
>
> So came they by the abode of the Geddings, and there also the neat
> and sheep were close in the home-garth: but armed men were lying
> or standing about the river bank, talking or singing merrily *none
> otherwise than* though deep peace were on the land; and when they

saw the *faring* [=departure] of the host they sprang to their feet with a shout and *gat* to their horses at once.

(*The House of the Wolfings*, chapter xx)

Some of what looks like archaic language, though, is not genuinely old usage: progressive tenses like *were standing*, for example, and idioms like *fell in with* (not recorded before the late 16th century). Morris is also anachronistic in introducing words which never existed in older English, but seem to fit the style, such as *war-fit* and the adverbs *a-top* (first recorded 1658 in the *OED*) and *amidmost*. Even *river bank* is probably post-medieval.

The thematic influences of Morris's romances on Tolkien's tales have often been commented on, and his linguistic influence is also pervasive, particularly in the early writing, which can be strongly reminiscent of Morris, not only in the grammar but also in the use of particular words. However, it is noticeable how in the 1930s, after the 'Lays of Beleriand' had been set aside, Tolkien's style evolved. For example, a direct comparison of any number of passages in the published *Silmarillion* with the earlier drafts in *HME* shows how Tolkien worked to eliminate some of the more extreme archaisms. Thus where the earliest 'Silmarillion' describes Valmar as standing 'amidmost of the plain [of Valinor]' (*HME* IV. 80), the 1977 text has 'in the midst of the plain'; 'earth-dolven iron' (*HME* IV. 125) becomes 'earth-delved iron'; where Elwing 'let build for her a white tower' (*HME* V. 327) we later read 'there was built for her'.

The evolution of Tolkien's style was not simply a move away from Morris. He retained some of Morris's words; some he invested with a more specific significance (see several of the Word Studies), and others he subtly altered. A good example of the latter is *shieldmaiden* (twice used by Éowyn to describe herself), which Tolkien uses in preference to Morris's *shield-may*. Both forms are modelled on an

Old Norse word, *skjaldmær*, the second element of which corresponds to English *may* (*OED*: MAY *n.*³)—a word which Tolkien evidently found too archaic for his purposes, substituting *maiden* as being more comprehensible to the modern reader. More generally, Tolkien retains archaic diction as one of a number of linguistic registers, from the colloquial to the elevated. Tom Shippey has singled out the Council of Elrond, with its multiplicity of voices, as an exceptional illustration of Tolkien's ability to deploy this range of registers to indicate the differing cultural associations of the various speakers (*Author of the Century*, p. 69). In many parts of *The Hobbit*, the tone, as Tolkien later acknowledged with some regret, is that of an adult talking down to children; but only in parts—as the tale progresses the voice of the mature Tolkien begins to emerge.

> There indeed lay Thorin Oakenshield, wounded with many wounds, and his rent armour and notched axe were cast upon the floor. He looked up as Bilbo came beside him.
>
> 'Farewell, good thief,' he said. 'I go now to the halls of waiting to sit beside my fathers, until the world is renewed. Since I leave now all gold and silver, and go where it is of little worth, I wish to part in friendship from you, and I would take back my words and deeds at the Gate.'
>
> Bilbo knelt on one knee filled with sorrow. 'Farewell, King under the Mountain!' he said. 'This is a bitter adventure, if it must end so; and not a mountain of gold can amend it.' (chapter xviii)

The language here is not everyday modern English; it uses, for example, a simple rhetorical repetition (*wounded with many wounds*), *rent* rather than *torn, cast* rather than *thrown, farewell* rather than *goodbye*, the simple present rather than the progressive

(*I go now*), *I would* for *I want to*, *end so* rather than *end like this*, and the inverted construction *not a mountain of gold can amend it*. The effect is elevated and solemn, achieved without the use of any grating archaism.

We can easily see how far Tolkien had come in the years between the early legends and lays and *The Lord of the Rings* by contrasting the description of the hall of the Wolfings by William Morris with that of Meduseld by Tolkien. Both authors imagine the interior of an ancient Germanic mead-hall.

> As to the house within, two rows of pillars went down it endlong, fashioned of the mightiest trees that might be found, and each one fairly wrought with base and chapiter, and wreaths and knots, and fighting men and dragons; so that it was like a church of later days that has a nave and aisles: windows there were above the aisles, and a passage underneath the said windows in their roofs. In the aisles were the sleeping-places of the Folk, and down the nave under the crown of the roof were three hearths for the fires, and above each hearth a luffer or smoke-bearer to draw the smoke up when the fires were lighted. Forsooth on a bright winter afternoon it was strange to see the three columns of smoke going wavering up to the dimness of the mighty roof, and one maybe smitten athwart by the sunbeams. As for the timber of the roof itself and its framing, so exceeding great and high it was, that the tale tells how that none might see the fashion of it from the hall-floor unless he were to raise aloft a blazing faggot on a long pole: since no lack of timber was there among the men of the Mark.
>
> At the end of the hall anigh the Man's-door was the dais, and a table thereon set thwartwise of the hall; and in front of the dais was the noblest and greatest of the hearths; (but of the others one was in the very midmost, and another in the Woman's-Chamber) and round about the dais, along the gable-wall, and hung from pillar to pillar were woven cloths pictured with images of ancient tales and the deeds

of the Wolfings, and the deeds of the Gods from whence they came.
(Morris, *The House of the Wolfings*, chapter i)

The hall was long and wide and filled with shadows and half lights; mighty pillars upheld its lofty roof. But here and there bright sunbeams fell in glimmering shafts from the eastern windows, high under the deep eaves. Through the louver in the roof, above the thin wisps of issuing smoke, the sky showed pale and blue. As their eyes changed, the travellers perceived that the floor was paved with stones of many hues; branching runes and strange devices intertwined beneath their feet. They saw now that the pillars were richly carved, gleaming dully with gold and half-seen colours. Many woven cloths were hung upon the walls, and over their wide spaces marched figures of ancient legend, some dim with years, some darkling in the shade. But upon one form the sunlight fell: a young man upon a white horse. He was blowing a great horn, and his yellow hair was flying in the wind. The horse's head was lifted, and its nostrils were wide and red as it neighed, smelling battle afar. Foaming water, green and white, rushed and curled about its knees…Now the four companions went forward, past the clear wood-fire burning upon the long hearth in the midst of the hall. Then they halted. At the far end of the house, beyond the hearth and facing north towards the doors, was a dais with three steps; and in the middle of the dais was a great gilded chair. (Tolkien, *LR* iii. vi)

What the mature Tolkien achieved is reflected in a discussion of diction in his essay 'On Translating Beowulf':

This sort of thing—the building up of a poetic language out of words and forms archaic and dialectal or used in special senses—may be regretted or disliked. There is nonetheless a case for it: the development of a form of language familiar in meaning and yet freed from trivial associations, and filled with the memory of good and evil, is an achievement, and its possessors are richer than those who have no such tradition…But, whether you regret it or not, you will misrepresent the first and most salient characteristic of the style and flavour of the author, if in translating *Beowulf,* you deliberately eschew the traditional literary and poetic diction which we now possess in favour of the current and trivial...The things we are here dealing with are serious, moving, and full of 'high sentence'—if we have the patience and solidity to endure them for a while. We are being at once wisely aware of our own frivolity and just to the solemn temper of the original, if we avoid *hitting* and *whacking* and prefer 'striking' and 'smiting'. (*The Monsters and the Critics*, p. 55)

In *The Lord of the Rings,* even more than in *The Hobbit,* Tolkien skilfully matches the style of diction to the context. In passages relating to the Shire, he writes plain modern English, free of archaism; but as the tale passes to events 'full of "high sentence"', he brings into play this formal diction, restrained but evocative in its careful use of archaism. Théoden's speech, in particular, is marked by words of Old English provenance such as *leechcraft* (*LR* iii. vi) and *elsewhither* (*LR* iii. x). In 'The Passing of the Grey Company' (*LR* v. ii), archaisms are found both in the speech of 'heroic' characters (Éowyn says she 'can ride and wield *blade*'; for Gimli the Paths of the Dead have 'a *fell* name') and in descriptive passages (Éowyn is 'still as a figure *carven* in stone', the horse Arod '*suffered* himself to be led', Gimli is '*wroth* with himself'). Even as the narrative leads back to the homeland of the hobbits in 'The Scouring of the Shire' (*LR* vi. viii), something of this heroic atmosphere clings to the returning characters, and can on occasion burst through, as when Pippin is provoked by the insolence of one of Saruman's ruffians:

The silver and *sable* of Gondor gleamed on him as he rode forward. 'I am a messenger of the King...You are a ruffian and a fool. Down on your knees in the road and ask pardon, or I will set this *troll's bane* in you!' The sword glinted in the *westering* sun.

In this form of diction, those archaic words which do appear do so without jarring, often through the philological technique of updating which was mentioned earlier: not simply lifting ancient words out of their context, but adapting them to the forms that they would have had in modern English had they been in continued use till now.

The flight of the leprawns

Along with this refinement of Tolkien's diction in general went a reassessment of some of the key vocabulary of the earliest tales and verses. As Christopher Tolkien writes:

> Likewise, all the 'elfin' diminutiveness soon disappeared. The idea of the Cottage of the Children was already in being in 1915, as the poem *You and Me* shows; and it was in the same year, indeed on the same days of April, that *Goblin Feet* (or *Cumaþ þá Nihtielfas*) was written, concerning which my father said in 1971: 'I wish the unhappy little thing, representing all that I came (so soon after) to fervently dislike, could be buried for ever'. (*HME* I. 32)

The powerful and sinister fairies of folklore, though still glimpsed in the tales told by writers such as Hans Christian Andersen (whose work Tolkien later claimed to dislike intensely), and still lurking in the little people of Shakespeare's dramas and Christina Rossetti's poems, had become sentimentalized for the nursery, and the *glamoury* of sorcery became merely the 'glamour' of fairy glitter. As Tolkien's conception developed, it was to the dark tales of the Kalevala and the Norse myths that he turned for inspiration. So it was that the *gnome* vanished almost entirely from Middle-earth, along with the *fay* and the *fairy* (though these were to reappear to magical effect in the quite separate world of *Smith of Wootton*

Major), not to mention the 'brownies…, pixies, leprawns, and what else are they not called' that originally accompanied the Valar on their arrival in Arda (*HME* I. 66; *leprawn*, incidentally, seems to be Tolkien's own peculiar adaptation of *leprechaun*). *Goblin* was largely displaced by *orc*, though *elf* and *dwarf* were too deeply embedded to be removed. (Tolkien did express some regrets about having to retain *elf*: see p. 116.)

So Tolkien did indeed achieve what he described in his essay 'On Translating Beowulf': 'a form of language familiar in meaning and yet freed from trivial associations, and filled with the memory of good and evil'. The major works are rich in literary vocabulary which is neither current nor knowingly archaizing, carefully deployed to achieve an effect of dignity and elevation.

Compound words and colloquialisms

We have already mentioned Tolkien's deployment of a range of linguistic registers in distinguishing characters and contexts or constructing an elevated or colloquial style. Some of these registers involve distinctive vocabulary such as dialect and slang, jocular wordplay, and the particularly liberal use of compound words.

Dialect and slang

Anyone who has learned to speak English in a particular region will have picked up some of the dialect vocabulary which characterizes that region, and may use it without realizing its regional character. Even Tolkien, thorough student of dialect though he was, might occasionally do so—or at least, he might use a dialect word without apparently intending anything by it. Thus the list of the fireworks set off at Bilbo's party includes ***backarappers*** (a word from Warwickshire dialect), and Tolkien's early children's story *Roverandom* mentions *bob-owlers* (another Warwickshire word, referring to a kind of large moth). However, there are far more instances in *The Hobbit* and *The Lord of the Rings* of deliberate use of dialect words: *gaffers* and *gammers*, *mithered*, ***ninnyhammer***, *taters*, *varmint*; also *go for*, in 'they're gone for robbers' (*LR* VI. vii; *OED*: FOR *prep.*, sense 8b). These occur mainly in the speech of hobbits, who are represented as similar in many ways to the folk of the pre-industrial English countryside, and in their place names, which use words such as *hay* (*OED*: HAY *n.*², 'a hedge') and *marish*.

Since it is often in the nature of regional dialects to change more slowly than mainstream or literary forms of language, many of these usages also have an archaic feel to them. A straightforward example is ***north-away***; a rather subtler one is the use of *by* in 'The Prancing Pony by Barliman Butterbur', this being a sense of the word (*OED*: BY *prep.*, sense 33d: 'kept or managed by') which had fallen out of general use but which survived in the formulaic context of an inn sign. In another technique for avoiding the modern associations of familiar words, imparting a sense of distance from an old and traditional semi-rural culture, Tolkien adopts variant forms (by-forms) of modern words, such as ***gladden, nasturtian, oliphaunt***, and ***shirriff***.

Non-standard or colloquial usage is not associated only with hobbits: the speech of the orcs is coloured by the urban slang of London and the south of England, perhaps recalling the working-class soldiers of Tolkien's army days: 'The cursed horsebreeders will hear of us by morning. Now we'll have to *leg it* double quick' (*LR* III. iii). Many slang expressions quickly fall out of use; Tolkien's use of the adjective *peaching*, for example ('you cursed peaching sneakthief!', *LR* vi. ii; *OED*: peach *v.*, sense 2 'to inform against an accomplice'), is a relatively late survival.

Comic polysyllables and wordplay

Tolkien delighted in certain kinds of jocular wordplay. He seems to have enjoyed extending ordinary words by adding a suffix which did not quite 'fit', as for example with *staggerment*, a word of which he was particularly fond. Another example is *bogosity* (writing to Donald Swann in 1968 about his appearance in a BBC documentary, he comments on 'the complete "bogosity" of the whole performance': *Lett.* 301). He had a particular weakness for such forms of verbal whimsy when he was consciously writing for children, as in *The Father Christmas Letters* where, for example, Polar Bear calls Ilbereth a 'thinnuous elf' (a pun on *fatuous*), or *Roverandom* with its list of musical flowers ('the rhymeroyals and the pennywhistles, the tintrumpets and the creamhorns (a very pale cream)'), perhaps recalling the food-like insects of Lewis Carroll's Wonderland. The same rather avuncular vein runs through both *The Hobbit* (see Word Study on **confusticate and bebother**) and the early drafts of the opening of its sequel (*HME* VI. 11ff.), where we find *flabbergastation*, *grabsome*, and *vanishment*. Such coinages were weeded out as it became clear that *The Lord of the Rings* was to be more serious in intent. *It took over thank you,*

Compounds

Anyone who searches for 'Tolkien' in the electronic form of the *OED* will notice that his works are cited in illustration of a surprisingly large number of compound terms. Many of those cited in the *OED* (e.g. *night-speech, riding-pony*) are not especially striking in themselves, though some are more clearly characteristic of Tolkien's settings (*spell-enslaved, war-beacon*); a few may even have been first used by Tolkien (*beggar-beard, herb-master, oathkeeper, windwrithen*), no earlier examples yet having been located by the *OED*'s researchers.

Such compounds are of course a common feature of many kinds of poetry, and are particularly frequent in alliterative verse in the *Beowulf* tradition; the fact that practically every one of Tolkien's ventures into alliterative form is full of apparently newly coined compounds simply reflects the constraints placed upon any writer by this mode of composition. Tolkien makes liberal use of such compounds even when not writing alliteratively: the relatively plain prose of *The Hobbit* has many of them (*dragon-guarded*, **elf-friend**, *mountain-roots*), sometimes in clusters:

> All the while the *forest-gloom* got heavier and the *forest-silence* deeper. There was no wind that evening to bring even a *sea-sighing* into the branches of the trees. (chapter vi)

Tolkien is of course not unique in this: the formation of compounds has been a constant process throughout the history of English. But some varieties of compound are particularly characteristic of earlier periods of English (and of language intended to evoke these periods): a fact of which Tolkien was acutely aware. An example of a category of compound to which he seems to have been particularly attracted is illustrated by the words *curiousminded, quiet-footed, spell-enslaved*. The choice of a compound in preference to the more explicit 'with quiet feet', 'enslaved by a spell', etc., is sometimes dictated by the metre of a poem; it can also impart a poetic or 'high' feel to a prose description. In a number of cases he re-formed a compound on a model from Old English (*march-ward*) or Middle English (*lore-master*: see p. 227), or even Old Norse (*Elvenhome*).

   The starting point for the inclusion of a word in the *OED* is generally the fact of its having been noticed by one of the Dictionary's 'readers', the group of people who scan texts of all kinds in the search for vocabulary which needs to be recorded. When Robert Burchfield was setting up the 'reading programme' to gather such evidence for the *Supplement to the OED*, he selected both *The Hobbit* and *The Lord of the Rings* to be 'read' in this way. It is not known who read *The Hobbit*, but *The Lord of the Rings* was assigned to Roland Auty, a schoolmaster who had been contributing to various Oxford dictionary projects since the 1930s, and who was particularly assiduous in noting the compounds he encountered. The constraints of space and time (under which lexicographers labour constantly) meant that by no means all of the compounds noted made their way into the Supplement; for example, although there are over thirty quotations for '*elven-*' compounds among the materials collected for the Supplement, a note-on-a-slip from Burchfield advises the lexicographer working on the entry to 'select 3 exx. only'. In the event four compounds (*elven-kin, elvenking, elven-tongue, elven-wise*) were included.

Philologists as authors

There have always been writers who took great care over the distinctive language they devised to convey their ideas; but Tolkien's particular awareness of language, his 'philological' approach, was to some extent a consequence of his having received philological training of a kind which was not available to authors of earlier generations. The *OED*, similarly, could hardly have emerged before it did: it was arguably only in the later 19th century that philological scholarship in England advanced to the point where such a dictionary could be contemplated. But is Tolkien unique? Were there any other authors of his generation who, having received similar philological training, brought this to play on their creative writing?

Tolkien's was the first generation of authors who were in a position to consult the *OED* as a source of words. Thomas Hardy may have been one of the first to do this—although his relationship with the Dictionary was rather more complicated: he supposedly told Robert Graves of an occasion when he consulted the *OED* to check a dialect word he was planning to use, only to find that the only quotation given in the entry was from his own novel *Under the Greenwood Tree* (1872). Another early example is James Joyce, whose delight in plundering the *OED* (and many other sources) for interesting words is well known. But—notwithstanding the interesting parallels drawn by Tom Shippey between the two writers in *Tolkien: Author of the Century*—Joyce's engagement with the English language, while enormously creative, was very different from Tolkien's. (A later author who also engaged closely with the *OED*, and who knew Tolkien well, is W. H. Auden, who publicly admitted that it was an ambition of his to be recorded in the *OED* as the coiner of a word.)

Another author deeply influenced by the *OED* was E. R. Eddison, one of the most significant fantasists to precede Tolkien in constructing detailed imaginary worlds. Tolkien had read his work ('in spite of his peculiarly bad nomenclature and personal philosophy';

Lett. 294), especially liking *The Worm Ouroboros* (1922), and met the author in Oxford when he visited the Inklings (the literary circle which gathered around C. S. Lewis, of whom Tolkien was one) in 1943. However, Eddison did not have a philological training, and Tolkien cites him (*Lett.* 144) as a gifted narrator who (like most) lacked regard for the problems of language raised by a secondary world. His writing makes it clear that he was a voracious reader and a literary jackdaw: his fantasies are embellished with quotations (even entire poems) taken from English and Scots literature of the Renaissance and later periods, and his vocabulary is full of dense and obscure archaisms lifted from these sources. In particular, in many places he probably used the *OED* itself as a source of vocabulary: rare words in his text occasionally appear in the *OED*'s illustrative quotations in a closely similar context. For example, the adjective *sexly* 'characteristic of one's sex' appeared in the First Edition of the *OED* illustrated by a single quotation from an account of a speech by Queen Elizabeth I, in which she refers to her 'sexly weaknesse'; this has now been supplemented by a quotation from Eddison's posthumously published *The Mezentian Gate* (1958), in which a woman's 'sexly weakness' is also mentioned. (Interestingly, one word—the verb *witwanton*—shown in the *OED* (Second Edition) as having been revived by both Joyce and Eddison, cannot have been plundered directly from the *OED* (First Edition). In 1922, the year in which both *Ulysses* and *The Worm Ouroboros* appeared, the *OED* fascicles for all but the first part of W (*W–wash*)—as well as most of the letter U—had yet to be published. *Wit* and its compounds did not appear until 1928, in the very last fascicle of all.)

Among the Inklings, the lawyer and philosopher Owen Barfield had a deep interest in the roots and development of language, and his possible influence on Tolkien is penetratingly analysed by Verlyn Flieger in her book *Splintered Light*; but Barfield's fictional oeuvre is slight and does not share the philological roots of Tolkien's. Of more interest, unsurprisingly, is C. S. Lewis himself, who—though not strictly a philologist but a literary scholar, whose *Studies in Words* (1960) Tolkien gave a distinctly cool reception (*Lett.* 224)—was, like Tolkien, professionally concerned with the English language, and with English words as subjects of study. The two men discussed their creative writing in detail; it is well known that some Elvish names which Lewis heard during Tolkien's reading of his manuscripts appeared as echoes in his 'Cosmic Trilogy' (references to Atlantis as *Numinor*, the names Tor and Tinidril in *Perelandra*, and the name *eldil* given to the creatures of light which represent angels in Lewis's cosmology: see Tolkien's *Lett.* 227, 276, 294). A rather different example is *hross* (the name of one of the species inhabiting the planet Malacandra in *Out of the Silent Planet*), of which Lewis wrote in a letter in 1939: '*Hross* is taken from the root wh. appears in *walruss*, *rosmarine* (in Spenser) and (possibly) *horshwæl* in K[ing] Aelfred's version of *Orosius*' (*Collected Letters of C. S. Lewis*, ed. W. Hooper (2004), p. 204). This strongly suggests that he had been discussing the etymology of *walrus* with Tolkien (see p. 23).

But the languages of Malacandra were of course intended to be utterly distinct from those of Earth. Of rather more interest for our purposes is the world of Narnia: a world which, like Middle-earth, is distinct from but very similar to our own, and even has points of connection with it (though in Tolkien's world the connections became more tenuous as his conception developed). Lewis's use of language to convey both similarity and difference is in some respects very like Tolkien's. The name 'Aslan's How', for example, which is given in *Prince Caspian* (ch. vii) to the great mound where

Aslan sacrificed himself in *The Lion, the Witch and the Wardrobe*, is reminiscent of 'Snowmane's Howe' where Théoden's horse was buried—both being revivals of an old English word for 'mound' or 'barrow', recorded in the *OED* (HOW, HOWE *n.*²) as surviving only in Scotland and northern England.

More striking is the list of some of the more unpleasant creatures ranged on the side of the evil Witch in chapter xiv of *The Lion, the Witch and the Wardrobe*, which includes 'Cruels and Hags and In-cubuses, Wraiths, Horrors, Efreets, Sprites, Orknies, Wooses, and Ettins'. Here 'Orknies' is clearly a modernization of Old English *orcneas*, a kind of evil spirit, the first element of which is the same word that inspired Tolkien's *orc*. Taken alone this could con-ceivably be coincidence: after all, both Lewis and Tolkien knew the line from *Beowulf* in which *orcneas* occurs. But the same line also mentions *eotenas*: one of two obsolete words for 'giant' which Tolkien adapted for use in *The Lord of the Rings*, in the place name *Ettenmoors* (see the Word Study on ent and etten). This is too similar to Lewis's place name *Ettinsmoor* (the abode of giants in *The Silver Chair*) to be a coincidence. In this context it seems prob-able that 'Wooses' is an echo of Tolkien's *Woses* (see p. 222). Another conceivable echo is seen in the resemblance between Lewis's *Nikabrik* (the name of a dwarf in *Prince Caspian*) and *Neeker-breekers*, Sam's onomatopoeic name for the insects of the Midge-water Marshes.

Of course Lewis was just as capable as Hardy, Joyce, or Auden of encountering a word in the *OED* and deciding to reuse it. However, in at least some cases, it seems likely that Tolkien, rather than the *OED*, may have been the source of Lewis's borrowing.

The uniqueness of Tolkien's involvement, as an imaginative writer, with the English language lies in his capacity to work from within the actual or potential development of any given word. In this intimate and active involvement with the histories of words, we can imagine Tolkien, perhaps, as an Ent in the forest of language, waking up old words that had fallen asleep—or, in the case of words taken from Old Norse, encouraging transplants to put down roots in new soil.

Having surveyed many of the sources of Tolkien's English language, and the linguistic techniques which he adopted in his writing, we turn in the third section of this book to look in more detail at some individual words which, to a greater or lesser extent, illustrate his use of these sources or techniques, or have a particular story to tell.

ᚹᛖᚱᚪᛞᛗᛋ ᛫ ᚦᛁᛋᚠ ᛫
ᚹᛖᚱᛞᚻᚪᚱᛞ ᛫ ᚪᛁᛝᛏᛁ

o my word

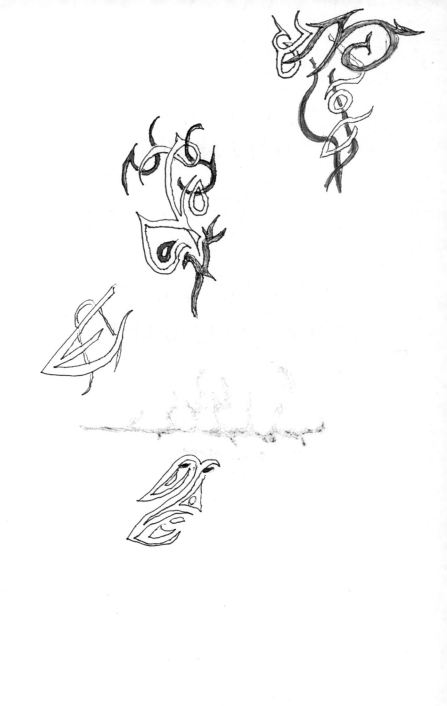

Word Studies

✢ amidmost ✢

Tolkien's description of the topography of Mordor (*LR* IV. iii) refers to 'the mournful plains of Lithlad and of Gorgoroth, and the bitter inland sea of Nûrnen amidmost'. Here is a rare survival into Tolkien's later writing of one of the archaic-sounding words which he seems to have picked up from William Morris; in his earlier writing the word occurs frequently (e.g. 'amidmost of the garden stood a white cottage': *HME* I. 18).

Morris's use of *amidmost*, as both adverb and preposition, is the earliest recorded in the *OED*; it is thus a 'pseudo-archaism', as distinct from the many genuine archaisms revived by Morris (and Tolkien) from Old and Middle English. By contrast, *midmost* (also used by Tolkien; e.g. *HME* I. 17) does go back to Old English as an adjective—although Morris's use of it as a preposition ('midmost the hall', quoted by the *OED* from *Jason* (1867)) is another pseudo-archaism.

✢ Arkenstone ✢

The name of the Arkenstone, the great white gem which surpasses everything else in Smaug's hoard (*Hobbit*, ch. xii), is one of many extinct Old English words which Tolkien revived: though he did not simply lift Old English words from their context, but fitted them into their new surroundings by giving them modernized spellings. These spellings reflect the patterns of change and pronunciation which can be seen in those words which did survive into modern English, so that they have linguistic authenticity, representing the spellings that the extinct words would have had if they had survived in continuous use through the centuries.

The Old English word was *eorcnanstan* 'precious stone' (*eorcnan* = 'precious', *stan* = 'stone'; other spellings include *eorcanstan, eorclanstan,* and *ercnanstan*). In the 10th-century *Rushworth Gospels* Christ says *Ne geweorþaþ ercnanstanas eowre beforan swinum* 'Do not cast your pearls before swine'. The authenticity of Tolkien's modernized form can be seen by comparing it with a word which actually did survive in uninterrupted use: modern English *hearken* (or *harken*: Tolkien preferred this less common spelling, which the *OED* describes as 'more regular and of earlier standing'). This is derived from Old English *heorcnian*, in which the last three letters, *-ian*, are an inflectional ending that regularly disappears before modern times, as the *-an* of *eorcnan* would have done. The change of *eor-* to *ar-* is also quite regular, and results in the first syllable having both a familiar shape and a hint of power and mystery, reminiscent either of *ark* as a place where something is kept safe and hidden, or of the *Ark* in which Noah sailed in a distant mythical age.

At about the time when *The Hobbit* was written (in the early or mid 1930s), Tolkien was also working on an Old English version of the 'Annals of Valinor', and used the Old English word *eorclanstanas* to refer to the Silmarils (*HME* IV. 282). So, although the Arkenstone has no obvious link to the wider history or mythology of Middle-earth, its name does make a hidden connection with the tales of the Elder Days.

But what does 'arken-' mean? The first part of *eorcnanstan* is probably related to a similar element in obsolete personal names, such as that of St Erconwald, Anglo-Saxon bishop of London (died 693), and of Erkenbrand, lord of Westfold in *The Two Towers* (*LR* III. vii), and to words in Old High German and Gothic meaning 'genuine'; descending ultimately from an Indo-European root meaning, appropriately enough, 'shining, white'.

✤ attercop and Shelob ✤

> Attercop! Attercop!
> Won't you stop,
> Stop your spinning and look for me?

So sings Bilbo in chapter viii of *The Hobbit*, to lead the giant spiders away from the dwarves whom they have caught in their webs. The word occurs earlier in the poem 'Errantry' (1933), in which the 'merry passenger', on his travels,

> tarried for a little while
> in little isles, and plundered them;
> and webs of all the Attercops
> he shattered them and sundered them.

The *OED* lists **attercop** as a regional dialect word for 'spider' with a long history. Like many of Tolkien's revivals, it is first attested in Old English, in an 11th-century medical treatise: *Wiþ attor-coppan bite* (for the bite of a spider); in a later medieval text we read *An atturcoppe cum owte...and bote hem by the nekkus...at II. of hem weron deed* (a spider came out and bit them in the neck so that two of them died)—an incident reminiscent of the episode in *The Hobbit*. Tolkien had encountered the word when still an undergraduate, while he was making notes on the 13th-century poem 'The Owl and the Nightingale'. It is derived from Old English *attor* 'poison' and *-coppa*, which probably itself means 'spider'. Although *cop* and its variant form *cob* are not recorded as separate words until much later (*OED*: COP *n.*[3] and COB *n.*[4]), the familiar compound word *cobweb* dates back to the early 1300s.

The form *cob* is also used by Bilbo in his second taunt song:

> Lazy Lob and crazy Cob
> are weaving webs to wind me.

Here it is paired with *lob* (or *lop*), yet another word for 'spider' in Old and Middle English (*OED*: LOB *n.*[1] and LOP *n.*[1]). *Lob* famously reappears in *The Lord of the Rings* in the name of the monster **Shelob**. As Tolkien remarks,

> It is of course only 'she + lob' (= spider), but written as one, it seems
> to be quite noisome. (*Lett.* 70, to Christopher Tolkien, 21 May 1944)

Attercop was at one time also applied to 'a venomous malignant person' (*OED*), so Bilbo's use in a song of taunting insult is appropriate.

❧ backarapper ❧

> There was also a generous distribution of squibs, crackers,
> backarappers, sparklers, torches, dwarf-candles, elf-fountains,
> goblin-barkers and thunder-claps. (*LR* I. i)

This word is not listed in the *OED*, but it is recorded (in the spelling *backrapper*) as Warwickshire dialect in G. F. Northall's *Warwickshire Word-book* (1896). He defines it as 'a firework so folded that the charges in the folds detonate in succession' (like the type called a 'jumping jack'). It seems quite possible that it is a word that Tolkien picked up in his childhood, in Sarehole in Warwickshire. Although he could have discovered it later in the course of reading about dialect, the extra syllable suggests that the word may have been learned from spoken use. The name is of obscure origin, though it appears to contain the element *rap* 'to make a sharp sound' (found also in *rip-rap*, another kind of small firework which produced repeated small explosions).

✦ bane ✦

This word is now used in English only in a greatly weakened sense: 'that which causes ruin, or is pernicious to well-being; the agent or instrument of ruin or woe' (*OED*: BANE *n.*[1], sense 4). It is often heard in the expressions 'the bane of one's life' or 'the bane of one's existence'.

In Old English the word meant 'a slayer or murderer; one who causes the death or destruction of another' (*OED* sense 1). Thus the Anglo-Saxon Chronicle for 755 records the vow of the loyal followers of Cynewulf, king of Wessex, that *hie næfre his banan folgian noldon* (under no circumstances would they wish to be followers of his killer). Almost the last occurrence of real (rather than revived) use of this meaning reported by the *OED* is this from Yorkshire in 1682: 'The jury found the horse the bane.'

Two senses of Middle English origin (*OED* senses 2b and 3) are: 'poison', which is found in the names of a number of poisonous plants or substances, such as fleabane, henbane, ratsbane, and wolfbane; and 'murder, death, destruction', as in Macbeth's fateful vaunt 'I will not be affraid of Death and Bane, Till Birname Forrest come to Dunsinane'.

Tolkien uses the word *bane* a number of times in *The Lord of the Rings*. Most importantly, the Ring is frequently referred to as 'Isildur's Bane'. This refers to a tradition that Isildur's death was caused by something that betrayed him to his enemies, though its exact identity was unknown. The mystery is well conveyed by the unfamiliarity of the word. The name 'Durin's Bane' is used by Gimli for the Balrog which had slain the last King Durin of Moria; and the epitaph for King Théoden's horse runs:

> Faithful servant yet master's bane,
> Lightfoot's foal, swift Snowmane (*LR* v.vi)

—because he had crushed Théoden in his fall.

✦ bee-hunter and skin-changer ✦

> Bear bee-hunter, boar the fighter.
> (*LR* III. iv, as quoted in the *OED*)

This line comes from Treebeard's roll of living creatures, which is in alliterative verse, and so requires the invention or adoption of poetic compounds beginning with the right letter of the alphabet, just as Old English alliterative verse did. Calling the bear a 'bee-hunter' is not surprising, in view of its well-known liking for honey. But as with so many of Tolkien's expressions, there is a cache of historical and linguistic scholarship hidden beneath.

The key can be found in R. W. Chambers's *Beowulf: an Introduction* (third edition, 1963). Chambers observes (p. 365) that the obvious interpretation of the name *Beowulf* is 'wolf (or foe) of the bee'.

Many who accepted this interpretation nevertheless could not see a reason for the hero to have this name, but Chambers asserts that 'bee-foe' simply means 'bear': 'The bear has got a name, or nickname, in many northern languages from his habit of raiding the hives for honey.' That Tolkien had assimilated this idea is clear from the Elvish word for bear, *megli*, which in origin is a compound word meaning 'honey-eater' (under LIS- in 'The Etymologies': *HME* V. 369). The bear, in the legends of Scandinavian, Finnish, Sami (Lapp), and Slavonic peoples, is regarded with awe and thought to have human understanding and enormous strength; hence 'bear' is an excellent name for an epic hero. ' "Bee-hunter" ', writes Chambers, 'is then a satisfactory explanation of *Beowulf*.' (Chambers's book was first published in 1921; Tolkien's own lecture on 'Beowulf: the Monsters and the Critics' was given in 1936, when *The Hobbit* was in the making.)

Chambers also points out that the Old Norse word for 'bear', *björn* (which is ultimately related to 'bear') seems to have an exact cognate in the Old English word *beorn*. In Old English, this word meant not 'bear', but 'a warrior, a hero, a man of valour', and it has a long history of use in alliterative poetry down to the early 16th century (*OED*: BERNE). *Beorn*, of course, is the name of the 'great strong black-haired man' with whom Bilbo and the dwarves find shelter in chapter vii of *The Hobbit*. The etymological ambivalence of Beorn's name is translated by Tolkien into narrative, for at night Beorn the mighty man changes his shape from human to that of a huge black bear. Another allusion to the legendary background lies in the beehives which surround Beorn's hall and the honey which he mostly lives on. Furthermore, the hall itself is imagined as looking much like the halls described in *Beowulf* and other ancient Germanic poetry, a wooden building with a steep roof supported by two lines of pillars and a central fireplace. (As W. G. Hammond & C. Scull point out in *J. R. R. Tolkien: Artist and Illustrator* (1995), the picture drawn by Tolkien for *The Hobbit* may be compared with the plan and drawing of a Norse hall included in the *Introduction to Old Norse* (1927) by his friend and colleague at Leeds University, E. V. Gordon.) The tension in Beorn's character, between courteous, generous host and dangerous, savage fighter, itself reflects the contrasts in the character of Beowulf, portrayed by the poet as a polite, modest, self-controlled visitor to the Danish hall, and yet capable of superhuman feats such as tearing off Grendel's arm, fighting off sea-monsters underwater, and swimming home with thirty sets of battle-gear.

The linguistic duality of Beorn's name reflects what he is: a **skin-changer**. This term is defined by the *OED* as 'one supposedly able to metamorphose himself or herself', and is illustrated by a quotation from *The Hobbit* (chapter vi), where Gandalf explains that Beorn 'is a skin-changer: sometimes he is a huge black bear, sometimes he is a great strong black-haired man'. The *OED* records one earlier quotation for this compound, which (significantly) comes from Gordon's *Introduction to Old Norse* (mentioned above). In the extract, Gordon explains the origin of the Old Norse word *berserkr* (from which English *berserk* is derived): 'Berserks were probably named "bear-shirts" from a superstition that they were "skin-changers"'. Gordon also says that a *berserkr* was 'a wild warrior on whom a fighting-rage descended like madness' and that it was probably believed that 'they got superhuman strength from their animal nature'. This accords very well with Beorn's spectacular wrath at the Battle of Five Armies (*Hobbit*, ch. xviii). (See also **hame**.)

Both Tolkien and Gordon probably knew the word *skin-changer* from William Morris's romance *The Roots of the Mountains* (1889), chapter vii:

'Yet thou hast seen me', she said; 'yet not altogether as I am now;' and therewith she smiled on him friendly. 'How is this?' said he; 'art thou a skin-changer?'

✣ blunderbuss ✣

Farmer Giles of Ham is notoriously full of philological wordplays of the kind in which Tolkien rejoiced, and the introduction of the blunderbuss, the ancient gun which Giles kept hanging in his kitchen, provides an excuse for the author to make a thinly-veiled reference to the *OED* itself. The 'Four Wise Clerks of Oxenford', to whom (we are told) the question was put as to what a blunderbuss was, are undoubtedly the four Editors of the *OED* (James Murray, Henry Bradley, William Craigie, and Charles Onions); and the definition they are said to have given is indeed that of the *OED* itself, in the characteristically formal and slightly patronizing style of a 19th-century dictionary:

> A blunderbuss is a short gun with a large bore firing many balls or slugs, and capable of doing execution within a limited range without exact aim. (Now superseded in civilized countries by other firearms.)

Tolkien gently mocks the preciseness of the definition by pointing out that Giles's blunderbuss fired not balls or slugs but whatever he could stuff into it, and notes that, since the blunderbuss had not yet been superseded, Ham cannot have been 'civilized'.

Paul Kocher, in *Master of Middle-earth* (1972), comments: 'One would like to know exactly who composed that definition of *blunderbuss* for the *Oxford Dictionary*' (p. 181), wondering if it could perhaps have been Tolkien himself or one of his close colleagues. However, the section *Batter–Boz*, in which it appeared, was published in 1887. James Murray was the Dictionary's sole Editor at that time, although he had several assistants; it was Murray himself who put the finishing touches to the definition, including the addition of the comment about the blunderbuss being 'superseded in civilized countries'. The identity of the person who drafted the main body of the definition—probably one of Murray's in-house assistants—is unknown.

⟶ carrock ⟵

The Carrock is the 'great rock, almost a hill of stone' which stands 'right in the path of the stream which looped itself about it', on which Beorn made the steps and where he spends time at night (*Hobbit*, ch. vii). 'And why is it called the Carrock?' Bilbo asks. 'He called it the Carrock, because carrock is his word for it. He calls things like that carrocks,' answers Gandalf unhelpfully. In other words, *carrock* is intended to be taken as a common noun meaning a large isolated rocky outcrop. This is borne out by the fact that, in his manuscript notes for *The Lord of the Rings*, Tolkien referred to the island which was later called Tol Brandir as 'Tolondren the Great Carrock' (*HME* VII. 269).

Because Beorn is conceived in 'Anglo-Saxon' terms (see **bee-hunter**), it would seem natural to look to Old English for the etymology. The *OED* gives us CARR *n.*[1], found only in Old Northumbrian (*Se þe getimbres hus his ofer carr* 'he who builds his house on the rock' in the *Lindisfarne Gospels*) and in some place names. (This is probably one of the few Old English words borrowed from Celtic.) One possible explanation of *carrock* is that Tolkien formed it from *carr* by adding the suffix *-ock*, which is not now productive but was formerly used with a diminutive sense (as in *hillock*, a small hill).

However, a more likely origin lies in some similar-sounding place names. Tolkien spent two memorable holidays in Cornwall, in 1914 and 1932, and was fond of its rocky coastline. There are some rocks called The Carracks off the north coast of the Penwith peninsula (map ref. SW4640), the name being spelt *Carrocks* in 1742, and Carrick Roads (*Caryck Rood* c. 1540), an anchorage off Falmouth, takes its name from some prominent rocks close by. Both names are derived from Cornish *karrek* 'rock', related to Welsh *carreg* 'stone': both of these words are in turn derived from the ancient British (that is, Brythonic Celtic) root of the *OED*'s CARR *n*.[1] There is also a Carrock Fell in Cumberland, which may have a similar Celtic source.

Gandalf's unhelpful answer highlights the underlying character-istic of many of Tolkien's place names: like some of the personal names, they are in effect common names made specific. Among the most obvious examples of this are The Hill and The Water in Hobbiton: such names capture the essence of the hobbits' paro-chialism, which supposes that the hill standing above their town needs no other distinguishing title.

✦ confusticate and bebother ✦

Confusticate and bebother those dwarves! (*Hobbit*, ch. i)

Confusticate means 'confound', and the *OED* quotes this sentence from *The Hobbit* as its most recent example. The word is, in effect, an elaboration of 'confuse' with a Latinate suffix, as though a less than well-educated rustic or schoolboy were trying to sound im-pressive. The *OED*'s earliest source (Farmer's *Slang Dictionary* of

1891) seems mistaken in calling it 'American', since the *OED* files now have an example from a song in W. S. Gilbert's comedy *Ruy Blas* (1866), and the *English Dialect Dictionary* (1898) lists the similar word *confuscate* from south Lincolnshire (with the same meaning, but not nearly so good to say).

Bebother is found in the *OED* entry for the prefix BE- 2, in the form of the adjective *bebothered*. This use of the prefix *be-* adds the meaning 'thoroughly' to the word to which it is prefixed, so this means 'thoroughly bother'. Tolkien was to use the word again in his letters:

> I am hopelessly behind with the 'Appendices' to Vol. III; but I have been be-bothered with many things.
>
> (*Lett.* 157, 27 November 1954)

As well as 'positively flummoxed' (*OED*: FLUMMOX *v.*, 19th century), Bilbo is also described as 'altogether bewildered and bewuthered' by his unexpected guests. The *OED* does not list *bewuther*, but it is perhaps related to *wuther* (*OED*: WHITHER *v.*, variant spelling), a dialect word variously meaning 'to make a rushing sound, to whizz' and 'to tremble, shake, quiver'.

Another word in the same category, but which Tolkien eventually discarded, is *flabbergastation*. In an early draft of 'A Long-expected Party' (*LR* I. i), this describes the reaction to Bilbo's announcement of his plan to get married (*HME* VI. 15). The word is recorded by the *OED* with a single quotation from an 1856 issue of the humorous magazine *Punch*.

✦ corrigan ✦

A term used of the witch in Tolkien's poem 'The Lay of Aotrou and Itroun', which is based on Breton folk tales. It is an alternative spelling of *korrigan*, a word borrowed directly from Breton, and translated in Breton dictionaries by the French word *lutin*, i.e. goblin, brownie, or elf. It is the feminine of *korrig* 'goblin or dwarf', which is in turn a diminutive of *korr* 'dwarf'. The *OED* says that the korrigan is a fairy or witch noted especially for stealing children. (The first English writer to use the word was the novelist Charlotte Yonge, in her 1855 retelling of the tale of Tom Thumb. Within a few years of writing the story she became involved with the Dictionary herself, having agreed to subedit part of the letter N for Frederick Furnivall.)

⁕ daymeal and nuncheon ⁕

> There is the nuncheon, at noon or after as duties allow; and men gather for the daymeal, and such mirth as there still may be, about the hour of sunset. (*LR* v. i)

So Beregond informs Pippin of the daily schedule which he and his comrades in the Guard of the Citadel follow. The word **daymeal** is not recorded in the *OED*, nor does it seem to occur in Old or Middle English, although a similar Old English compound *dægmete* 'daymeat' does occur occasionally.

As with several of Tolkien's words, the explanation is perhaps to be found in Old Norse. Cleasby and Vigfusson's *Icelandic–English Dictionary* glosses the Old Norse word *dag-mál* as

> prop[erly] '*day-meal*', one of the divisions of the day, usually about 8 or 9 o'clock a.m.... The word is synonymous with dagverðarmál, *breakfast-time*, and denotes the time when the ancient Icel[anders] used to take their chief meal, opposed to náttmál, *night-meal* or *supper-time*.

Tolkien was not the first to use the compound in modern English: it also occurs in E. R. Eddison's fantasy *The Worm Ouroboros* (1922) (chapter xxvi: 'we halted for daymeal hard by Blackwood in Amadardale'). Here, though, the meal seems to be taken in the early morning (during a journey which began at dawn), closer to the 'breakfast-time' mentioned in the Icelandic dictionary than to the sunset hour of Beregond's daymeal.

The other meal mentioned by Beregond, **nuncheon**, is defined in *OED Online* as 'a light refreshment between meals; a snack'; Tolkien's wording carefully emphasizes the word's original link to the word *noon*. *(or: Hobbit snacks)*

✦ **dingle** and **dern** ✦

There [in the depths of a lake] he beheld strange shapes of flame bending and branching and wavering like great weeds in a sea-dingle.
(*Smith of Wootton Major*)

The *OED* defines *sea-dingle* as 'an abyss or deep in the sea'. The word **dingle** itself means 'a deep dell or hollow'. Curiously, though, it is not recorded until the 17th century, except in this compound, *sea-dingle*, which occurs four centuries earlier in the Middle English religious work *Sawles Warde* ('the Soul's Guardian'). Speaking of the blessed souls in heaven, it says *ha witen alle Godes reades, his runes, ant his domes þe derne beoð, ant deopre þen eni sea-dingle* (they know all God's designs, his private counsels, and his judgements, which are secret, and deeper than any sea-dingle). The Latin text from which this is translated says only that the counsels and judgements of God are innumerable abysses, but the English writer has expanded the sentence to fit the rhythmic, alliterative pattern in which much of the work is cast, and in doing so has produced this striking image. The passage was echoed by Tolkien's pupil and friend W. H. Auden in a poem published in 1932 and also quoted in the *OED*: 'Doom is dark and deeper than any sea-dingle.'

Sawles Warde is found in a number of early 13th-century manu-scripts: it is one of a group of texts from around 1200 that originated in the West Midlands and are written in a very distinctive dialect, the direct descendant of the Mercian dialect of Old English. Tolkien was greatly interested in and attached to the dialect and the texts written in it: he edited one version of the most important of these texts, the *Ancrene Riwle* (Rule for Anchoresses—an anchoress is a female religious recluse), and published a study of the dialect. His fondness for the dialect may explain his delight in reviving its words. As well as giving him the word *sea-dingle*, the phrase *derne beoð, ant deopre þen eni sea-dingle* may also have suggested the name of the place where the Entmoot takes place: '*Derndingle* men call it' (*LR* iii. iv; in an earlier draft it was *Dernslade*: *HME* VII. 420).

Tolkien writes in his 'Guide to the Names in *LR*': '*Dingle* is still known, meaning "deep (tree-shadowed) dell", but *dern* "secret, hidden" is long obsolete, as are the related words in other Germanic languages—except *Tarn-* in German *Tarnkappe* (in Middle High German)'.

The word **dern** (*OED*: DERN *a.*) also means 'serving to conceal', which underlies the German *Tarnkappe* (a cap of invisibility; *OED*: TARN-CAP, 19th century). Better known, but with much the same meaning, is *Tarnhelm*, the name of the magic helmet conveying invisibility in Wagner's *Ring of the Nibelungen*. The English equiva-lent of *Tarnhelm* is *Dernhelm*, the name that Éowyn adopts in her disguise as a male warrior (*LR* v. iii).

✦ dumbledore ✦

Many of those familiar with J. K. Rowling's Harry Potter books, or the films based on them, have been surprised to discover that the name of the headmaster of Hogwarts School also occurs in Tolkien's writings. (They might be even more surprised to find it in Thomas Hardy's *The Mayor of Casterbridge*.) The word is recorded by the *OED* as a dialect name for the bumblebee (and certain other insects), with quotations dating back to 1787. Tolkien used it in some versions of his poem 'Errantry', in which the 'merry passenger', we are told, 'battled with the Dumbledores' (*HME* VII. 86, 88).

✦ dwarf ✦

> Mr Baggins began as a comic tale among conventional and inconsistent Grimm's fairy-tale dwarves.
>
> (*Lett.* 19, to Stanley Unwin, 16 December 1937)

Dwarf is a well-established word for 'one of a supposed race of diminutive beings, who figure in Teutonic and especially Scandinavian mythology and folk-lore; often identified with the elves, and supposed to be endowed with special skill in working metals, etc.' (*OED*: DWARF *n.*, sense 1b). Perhaps it is surprising that this meaning is not instanced in the *OED* before the 18th century, when Scandinavian mythology began to be known in Britain. There is a great deal about *dvergar*, dwarves, in Old Norse literature, and one might have expected to find a mention of the same mythological beings in Old English literature. In fact there are only very slight traces, mainly reflecting the idea that the dwarves (like the elves) cause illnesses. There exists, for example, a charm which directs: *Wið dweorh man sceal niman VII lytle oflætan, swylce man mid ofrað, and writan þas naman on ælcre oflætan* (against a 'dwarf'—presumably meaning an illness inflicted by a dwarf—one must take seven small wafers, such as those offered at the Mass, and write the name on each wafer). One old name of the medicinal herb pennyroyal is *dweorge-dwostle*, of which the first element is 'dwarf' (and the second element is otherwise unknown).

Before Tolkien, the standard plural of *dwarf* in modern English had strictly been *dwarfs*. From the first, Tolkien consistently used *dwarves* for the plural. It is found, for example, in his 'Gnomish Lexicon' of 1917: '*Nauglafring*...the Necklace of the Dwarves' (*HME* II. 346). (A few exceptional uses of *dwarfs* occur in the manuscripts of the 'Quenta Silmarillion': *HME* V. 272–3.) He says, referring to its use (unnoticed by critics) in *The Hobbit*, that this began as a pure mistake:

> I am afraid it is just a piece of private bad grammar, rather shocking in a philologist; but I shall have to go on with it.
>
> (*Lett.* 17, to Stanley Unwin, 15 October 1937)

But he made a virtue of this error by using it as a 'technical' name for his mythical non-human race, in contrast to the ordinary sense referring to humans with unusually short stature (see *LR*, Appendix F). This decision had already been formulated in the same letter:

> Perhaps my *dwarf*—since he and the *Gnome* are only translations into approximate equivalents of creatures with different names and rather different functions in their own world—may be allowed a peculiar plural.

This is in line with several other instances where Tolkien deliberately used a variant form of a familiar word in order to distinguish his use of such terms, in the context of his stories, from the commonplace use. (Proofreaders would often correct *dwarves* to *dwarfs*, much to Tolkien's annoyance; he was particularly irritated by the 1961 Puffin edition of *The Hobbit*, which contained many such corrections: see *Lett.* 236.)

Tolkien's 'piece of private bad grammar' was not in fact private, and he was by no means the first to use the form *dwarves*. The *OED* records W. Taylor writing in 1818 of 'Laurin, king of the dwarves', and the spelling represents a spoken form that has presumably been in use for the best part of two centuries. The form *dwarves* is part of a trend that has been going on for a long time, by which English speakers have gradually replaced the regular form of the plural of nouns ending in *f* with an irregular form in *-ves*. Following the pattern of those words where this is original, such as *calf* – *calves*, *loaf* – *loaves*, and of course *elf* – *elves*, there have arisen over the last three centuries such plurals as *scarves* (early 18th century) and, most recently, *rooves* (early 20th century: Tolkien himself used it in 1923 in 'The Cat and the Fiddle') in place of the earlier and more regular forms *scarfs* and *roofs*. This kind of linguistic change is known as hypercorrection. It shows that even a philologist who might 'know better' is not immune to the drift of usage.

The *-v-* form is also reflected in the adjective *dwarvish*. This too is much older than Tolkien's use of it: the *OED*'s entry for DWARFISH quotes it from Edward Topsell's *Four-footed Beasts* of 1607, though it is there printed as *dwaruish*. (Interestingly, the word *dwarven*—not yet recorded in the *OED*—is now much commoner in this form than in the spelling *dwarfen*. Tolkien experimented with both forms in his early writings: e.g. 'a sword of dwarven steel' in the 'Tale of the Nauglafring' (*HME* II. 227), but 'the forged knife of dwarfen steel' in 'The Lay of the Children of Húrin' (*HME* III. 44).)

It is characteristic of Tolkien that he immediately resorted to philology to put the 'correct' plural *dwarfs* into a historical perspective:

> The real 'historical' plural of *dwarf* (like *teeth of tooth*) is *dwarrows*, anyway: rather a nice word, but a bit too archaic. Still I rather wish I had used the word *dwarrow*. (*Lett.* 17)

This observation echoes the *OED*'s etymological note on DWARF. After giving the original Old English form of the word, *dweorg* or *dweorh* (the last consonant of which was similar to the *ch* sound in *loch*), it says (slightly simplified here):

> In English the word shows interesting phonetic processes:... *dweorg* became regularly *dwarf* (*-eor-* became *-ar-* as in *bark*; final *-g* became *-f* as in *enough*). But the plural *dweorgas* became *dwerwhes, dwerwes, dwerows, dwarrows*. From these, by 'levelling', arose corresponding forms of the nominative singular.

In other words, the singular and plural passed independently through a series of changes, resulting in the quite dissimilar forms *dwarf* and *dwarrows*, so that even the 'correct' form *dwarfs* is actually a later hypercorrection, and the singular *dwarrow* is a subsequent 'logical' development from the historic plural, like the much more recent form *dwarves*.

In the event, Tolkien did not entirely forgo the 'nice' form *dwarrow*, but used it in *The Lord of the Rings* in the place name *Dwarrowdelf*. This is the English equivalent of the archaic Westron name *Phurunargian* (i.e. Khazad-dûm or Moria); its second element is *OED*'s DELF *n.*[1] (sense 1b) 'an excavation in or under the earth' (related to the verb *delve*).

The variant *dwarves* is now well established as a minority spelling, though *dwarfs* remains standard (for example) in astronomy, and the evidence indicates that, even in the mythological or fantasy context, Disney's *Snow White and the Seven Dwarfs* keeps the dominant spelling in the public eye.

→ **dwimmerlaik** ←

At a dramatic moment (*LR* v. vi), Éowyn of Rohan confronts the Lord of the Nazgûl with the words 'Begone, foul dwimmerlaik, lord of carrion!' *Dwimmerlaik* is an obsolete word which Tolkien has restored to a more robust condition by the application of a little etymological paintwork.

The *OED* entry is headed with the spelling DEMERLAYK, and the word is defined as 'magic, practice of occult art, jugglery'. Such '*w*-less' spellings of the word were common by about 1400, e.g. in the poem *Cleanness* (*Deuinores of demorlaykes þat dremes cowþe rede* 'diviners of occult arts who could interpret dreams') and in the *Wars of Alexander* (*And all þis demerlayke he did bot be þe deuyllis craftis* 'and all this sorcery he did only by the devil's crafts'). Earlier, in Laȝamon's *Brut*, the form was *dweomerlak* (*hem þe cuþen dweomerlakes song* 'those who knew magic songs'). The closest match to Tolkien's form, *dwimerlaik*, is attributed by the *OED* to the *Wars of Alexander* but in fact is not found in the original text: nevertheless, the *OED* entry may have influenced Tolkien's spelling of the word, even though this particular example appears to be a phantom. His own earlier spellings (*HME* VIII. 365, 368, and notes 2 and 6) were *dwimor-lake* and *dwimmer-lake*.

The word is derived from an Old English stem *dwimer-* which is found in *gedwimor* 'apparition, phantom; delusion; delusive practice, witchcraft'. The suffix *-layk*, a northern spelling of the Old

English suffix *-lac*, survives in modern English only in the word *wedlock*. (The *-lock* in *warlock* is from a different Old English root, *-loga*, meaning 'liar'.) In Middle English the word was, it appears, mainly abstract, but Tolkien has made it a concrete noun, presumably meaning 'sorcerer'.

The root *dwimer-* is seen also in the adjective *dwimmer-crafty*, a derivative of Old English *dwimercræft* (*OED*: DWEOMERCRÆFT) used by Éomer to describe Saruman (*LR* III. ii). It also appears in two place names, *Dwimorberg* (the Haunted Mountain at the rear of Dunharrow in Rohan), and *Dwimordene* (literally 'Vale of Illusion', the name used in Rohan for the Elvish land of Lothlórien). It may seem remarkable that the same word is used to refer both to evil magic and to the benign power of the Elves. However, it is clear from the words of Wormtongue ('webs of deceit were ever woven in Dwimordene': *LR* III. vi) that in the minds of the Rohirrim there was little distinction: both were extremely dangerous. The identification of the (essentially good) Elves with the power of evil magic is one of Tolkien's themes (see **elf**).

Relatively few of the many Old English words beginning with *dw-* survive in modern English (*dwarf* of course being one). It is notable that several obsolete ones had similar meanings, such as the *OED*'s DWALE *n.*[1] (error, delusion; deceit, fraud), DWALE *n.*[2] (stupefying drink, deadly nightshade), DWALM *v.* (to swoon), and DWELE *v.* (to go astray, to swoon).

The word *dweomer* is used in *Dungeons and Dragons* and similar fantasy games to mean a magical 'aura' imparted to an enchanted object. Why did the coiner (or reviver) of this word opt for a different spelling from that used by Tolkien in his Rohirric compounds? It is possible that they may have been reading Laȝamon's *Brut*, the one Middle English text in which the *dweo-* forms occur—

but it seems no less likely that mention of this spelling in the *OED* entries for DEMERLAYK and DWEOMERCRÆFT may have suggested it (and it does have the attraction of being a rather more exotic-looking word).

✤ Easterling ✤

In *The Lord of the Rings*, the peoples of the far east of Middle-earth, allied with Sauron, in the War of the Ring, are called Easterlings by the people of Gondor. In *The Silmarillion* (and the manuscripts which underlie it), the Easterlings (some of whom fight on both sides in the conflict with Morgoth) are the people who enter Beleriand from the East later than the three Houses of the Edain.

The word is found in the *OED* in two senses. The first refers to a native of eastern Germany or the Baltic coasts (it was chiefly applied to the merchants of the Hanseatic League of north German cities); the second applies more generally to an inhabitant of an eastern country or district. A quotation of 1609 is suggestive of Tolkien's use: 'A regiment of Easterlings got the upper hand'—the reference here is actually to Saracens. The word was also used by William Morris in his poem *The Earthly Paradise* (1870).

The *OED* explains that the word is formed from *easter* (an adjective derived from *east*) plus the suffix *-ling* (see **halfling**). In the first sense, according to the *Middle English Dictionary*, it dates back to about 1422. It is likely to have been modelled on the Dutch word *oosterling*.

(See also **Southron** and **Swertings**.)

✦ Elder Days ✦

And over Middle-earth he passed
and heard at last the weeping sore
of women and of elven-maids
in Elder Days, in years of yore.

(Bilbo's song of Eärendil at Rivendell, *LR* II. i).

Of this expression Tolkien wrote: 'This is naturally taken by English readers to mean "older" (that is "former"), but with an archaic flavour, since this original form of the comparative is now only applied to persons, or used as a noun in *Elders* (seniors). In inventing the expression I intended this, as well as association with the poetic word *eld* "old age, antiquity". I have since (recently) come across the expression in early English *be eldern dawes* "in the days of our forefathers, long ago"' ('Guide to the Names in *LR*').

Tolkien had come up with the expression long before he introduced it into the text of this song (whose gradual evolution is described in *HME* VII. 81–109), though if he thought he had 'invented' it, he certainly was not the first to do so (it was used by, among others, Longfellow, Swinburne, and Thomas Love Peacock). Its very first occurrence, according to Christopher Tolkien, is in a revision of 'The Fall of Númenor': 'Sea covered much that in the Elder Days had been dry' (*HME* V. 32). A little later in the 'Quenta Silmarillion' we find: 'These [mountains] Melko built in the elder days as a fence to his citadel, Utumno' (*HME* V. 259). In the first draft of the Prologue to *The Lord of the Rings*, Tolkien wrote 'Earliest Days' (*HME* VI. 311) but changed it to *Elder Days*, as it now stands. (The expressions *Elder Years* and *eldest days* are also found in *HME* V.)

The Middle English phrase *be eldern dawes* (in which *dawes* is the old plural of *day*) is very rare, being found only once each in two texts of a work named *Mum and the Sothsegger* from around 1400. One instance is quoted in the *OED* (at DAY *n.*, section A): *As it is said by elderne dawis*. It is striking that Tolkien introduced to his writing an expression that he thought sounded authentic, and long afterwards discovered that it was indeed genuine Middle English.

✦ eleventy-one and gross ✦

In the first chapter of *The Lord of the Rings*, Bilbo is about to reach the age of **eleventy-one**, 111, 'a rather curious number', and at his birthday party, his announcement 'I am eleventy-one today' is met with cheers from the assembled guests. In English there are other invented terms for numbers representing tens, most famously *umpty*, which is now almost forgotten, but on which was based the very common word *umpteen*. It would be easy to see this as a piece of whimsical fancy based on Lewis Carroll logic: if we can count to ninety, why not eleventy?

But as always with Tolkien, the roots go deeper, and are planted in the reality of the culture of the ancient world. In Old English, the next two tens after *hund* 'hundred' were *hundendlufontig* and *hundtwelftig*: the *hund-* was a prefix, which also occurred in *hundeahtatig* 'eighty' and *hundnigontig* 'ninety'; if we remove the prefix, we get *-endlufontig* 'eleventy' from *endlufon* or *endleofon* 'eleven' and *-twelftig* 'twelfty'. Why did the Anglo-Saxons count up to 'twelfty'? The answer lies in an ancient system of counting in twelves; much later, at the end of the Middle English period, certain commodities, such as fish, were counted in 'hundreds' that actually contained six score or 120, and this was known as the 'great hundred' or 'long hundred' (*OED*: HUNDRED *n.* and *a.*, sense 3). That this probably goes back to ancient times is shown by the fact that in Old Norse 100 was *tíu tigir* 'ten tens', 110 was *ellifu tigir* 'eleven tens' (exactly parallel to *eleventy*), and 120 was *hundrað* 'hundred'. There are even said to be ordinal numerals *títugandi* and *ellifu-tugandi* 'tentieth' and 'eleventieth'.

Similarly, the *OED* shows that, from around 1400, many commodities were reckoned by the **gross** (*OED*: GROSS *n.*³), which signified 12 dozen (144). We know that the hobbits used this reckoning from another place in the same chapter, where we are told that the invitations to the special family dinner party were limited to twelve dozen, 'a number also called by the hobbits one Gross, though the word was not considered proper to use of people'—Bilbo offends his guests later in the speech already referred to, by doing just that. The party is even punningly described as 'an engrossing entertainment', although the sentence containing this phrase no longer contains the mention of '144' present in the early draft (*HME* VI. 23), so many readers miss the pun.

Tolkien is imagining, as with many other matters, that the hobbits continued a practice used by our forefathers. But he presumably also knew that the *OED* has an entry for the similarly formed word *eleventeen* meaning 'twenty-one', which was used by a 17th-century writer named George Wither (and also revived in a Victorian farce by Charles Selby in 1858). It is also quite probable that he had come across this gloss for the Icelandic word *ellefu-tíu* in Cleasby and Vigfusson's *Icelandic–English Dictionary* (1874): '"eleventy" (i.e. one hundred and ten),…frequent in reckoning by duodecimal hundreds'.

✦ elf ✦

Tolkien transformed the meaning of this word: it would scarcely be an exaggeration to say that most of his Middle-earth writings are themselves a commentary on it. But his creative achievement is a matter for others to address; here we confine ourselves to a look at some of its linguistic aspects.

The entry for ELF *n.*[1] in the *OED* makes a number of relevant observations. According to early Germanic beliefs about elves, they were 'supposed to possess formidable magical powers, exercised variously for the benefit or injury of mankind'. However, the appearances of elves in surviving medieval literature are rather meagre, giving us only glimpses of what was believed about them.

In Old English literature there are a few mentions of elves. The *OED* quotes from *Beowulf*, where the Christian poet observes that from the evil brood of Cain (the slayer of his brother Abel in *Genesis*) arose *eotenas ond ylfe ond orcneas, swylce gigantas* (ettins and elves and orcs, likewise the giants). Elves thus appear in a distinctly negative light. The *OED* also quotes an Old English charm which prescribes: *Wið ælfe and wið uncuþum fidsan gnið myrran on win* (for an elf and for an unknown [word obscure] pulverize myrrh in wine). Another Old English source mentions *ylfa gescot* 'elf-shot' as a possible cause of a sudden pain, along with *hægtessan gescot* 'witch's shot' and *esa gescot*, the 'shot' or 'shooting' of the pagan gods (*esa* is the genitive plural of the noun *os*, which refers to the Germanic gods known in Norse literature as the *Æsir*). References to folk-beliefs attributing the ills of humans or their livestock to 'elf-shot' persisted in some rural areas of the British Isles into the 19th century (*OED*: ELF-SHOT *n.*, ELF-SHOOT *v.*).

The linking of the old gods with the elves in the everyday context of folk-medicine hints that, in ancient times, these beings must have been much more familiar concepts than the surviving tales reveal. Their names occur as the first element (*Os-* and *Ælf-*) of many fore-names: Osberht, Oslaf, Osred, Osric, Osthryth, Oswald, Oswig, and Ælfgar, Ælfgifu, Ælfheah, Ælfric, Ælfweard, Ælfred, and especially Oswine and Ælfwine (Tom Shippey, *The Road to Middle-earth*, p. 336, analyses Tolkien's use of this pairing in detail: see also **elf-friend**). The elves must have had a higher status in mythology than as mere causers of illness. The mismatch between the glimpses of a rather arbitrary, cruel nature that we get in surviving literature, and the exaltedness that we sense in the background is exploited by Tolkien throughout his writings. The ordinary people in his stories misconceive the elves as weavers of deceit and illusion, and the elves by their enigmatic behaviour seem to bear out their poor reputation. But those who seek them out discover their true nobility.

After the Norman Conquest, in Laȝamon's *Brut*, elves are still conceived of as human-sized and powerful—most notably when the wounded King Arthur is borne away to Avalon, *to Argante þere quene, aluen swiðe sceone* (to Argante the queen, the Elf most fair). But by the 16th century, the concept attached to the word *elf*, while still that of a being of a different order, having certain powers over human beings and dwelling beyond our reach, had become that of a diminutive, airy creature whose exploits are described with whimsy and sentimentality rather than dread and awe. By this time, too, the French-derived word *fairy* has appeared, used at first to denote the elf-realm or elf-magic (see **fairy**). Tolkien had a strong antipathy to this established tradition. In making his momentous break with it he obviously considered abandoning the word; he refers in a letter to the 'creatures which in English I call misleadingly Elves' (*Lett.* 131), and says 'I now deeply regret having used Elves, though this is a word in ancestry and original meaning suitable enough' (*Lett.* 151, September 1954). But though he abandoned *gnome*, he never found a replacement for *elf*. Its deep roots in Germanic legend probably induced him to stick to it.

In *The Hobbit* (chapter viii) we are told that the land of 'Faerie in the West' was where 'the Light-elves and the Deep-elves and the Sea-elves went and lived for ages': these terms all go back to early versions of the mythology. *Light-elves* would seem to be a translation of Old Norse *ljósálfar*, who in the Edda (one of the main repositories of the old mythology) are contrasted with the *døkkálfar or Dark Elves*; the latter term is used in *The Silmarillion* mainly to refer to elves that did not cross the Great Sea, though it also has other applications (see the Index to *The Silmarillion*).

❖ elf-friend ❖

The *OED* quotes *The Hobbit* for this word: 'The master of the house was an elf-friend' (chapter iii, referring to Elrond; in chapter xviii, Bilbo is named as elf-friend by the Elvenking). The concept of the Elf-friend, the human being who loves the Elves and possesses their learning and wisdom, was deep in Tolkien's mythos. The character originally called Eriol in *The Book of Lost Tales* is partly replaced by one bearing the Old English name *Ælfwine* (*HME* II. 278ff.), meaning literally 'elf-friend'. Its equivalent in Lombardic (the language of a Germanic people who invaded Lombardy in the 6th century) is *Alboin*, the name of a central character in the unfinished story 'The Lost Road' (*HME* V. 36ff.), which is based on the idea of 'the Elf-friends of old'. The name of the character *Alwin* Lowdham in 'The

Notion Club Papers' (*HME* IX. 159ff.) is a modern English equivalent of the same name (and the name of the philologist *Elwin* Ransom in C. S. Lewis's cosmic trilogy is also an echo of it). Beyond the name, there is nothing more in Old English literature to support or develop the concept, which seems to be essentially Tolkien's own. It persisted into *The Lord of the Rings*—for example, in Gildor's greeting of Frodo (*LR* I. iii), 'Hail, Elf-friend'—and is encapsulated in the name of *Elendil* (the Elvish equivalent of *Ælfwine*), a character who first emerges in 'The Lost Road'.

❧ elven ❧

Tolkien revived *elven* as an adjective meaning 'of or relating to the Elves' (used attributively, that is, standing in front of a noun to modify it). He described it himself as 'an archaic adjectival or composition form' ('Guide to the Names in *LR*'). The *OED* entry for ELVEN shows that the word originally existed in Old English as a noun meaning 'a female elf' (here the *-en* is an obsolete feminine suffix, found in modern English only in *vixen*). In Middle English the word was used for both sexes. (Because of a certain variability of weak endings, it is sometimes difficult to tell what singular form is represented by a plural form such as *elvene*: it could be *elven, elve, elf*, or *elfe*, all of which occur as the singular.)

Elven was occasionally used in the 14th and 15th centuries as a modifier before another noun: for example (from the romance *Guy of Warwick*) *A brond that was y-made in Eluene lond* (a sword that was made in Elfland). Tolkien exploited the possibilites of constructions like this to create his own compounds such as *Elvenking, Elven-tongue, Elven-kin,* and even *Elven-wise*. In modern English the *-en* ending suggests the adjectival suffix found in, for example, *flaxen*, *golden*, and *oaken*, and also has the archaic, poetic ring of *olden* in 'olden days'.

The conventional adjective from *elf* is *elfin*, which Tolkien did use in his early writings ('and such ships as fare that way must needs espy them or ever they reach the last waters that wash the elfin shores': *HME* I. 211); but he abandoned it, probably because it has quite the wrong sound, and would foster a conception of the Elves as gauzy, insubstantial creatures. *Elven* seems to occur first in the 'Lay of Leithian' (dating from the later 1920s: *HME* III): 'half elven-fair and half divine' (line 493), with 'Elvenland' replacing earlier 'Fairyland' (line 2193). Similarly, *elfin* is changed to *elven* in the 'Quenta' (1930: *HME* IV). With the emergence of the adjective *elven*, Tolkien was able to replace terms such as *Fairyland* and *Faërie* with **Elvenhome**, e.g. in the 1927 version of 'Over Old Hills and Far Away' (*HME* I. 108–110), and in the 'Quenta' and 'Ambarkanta' (*HME* IV).

❖ Elvenhome ❖

To haven white he came at last,
to Elvenhome the green and fair. (*LR* II. i)

Elvenhome is Tolkien's English equivalent of *Eldamar*, the part of Valinor where the Elves live. It also refers to a region in Beleriand inhabited by Elves, as in the 'Tale of Tinúviel' chanted by Aragorn (*LR* I. xi): 'Through woven woods in Elvenhome | She lightly fled on dancing feet'. The English word has a real-world counterpart in Old Norse *Álfheimar* (literally 'Elf-homes'), the region in the Norse mythological world inhabited by the elves.

❋ **ent** and **etten** ❋

> As usually with me they grew rather out of their name than the
> other way about. I always felt that something ought to be done about
> the peculiar A[nglo-] Saxon word *ent* for a 'giant' or mighty person of
> long ago—to whom all old works were ascribed.
> (*Lett.* 157)

The emergence of the ents from a single Anglo-Saxon word is one
of the key examples of Tolkien's linguistic imagination (see also
p. 58). His mythology (unlike the Norse and Classical) does not
contain giants, in the strict sense of huge humanoid creatures
(apart from casual and unintegrated appearances, such as that in
chapter iv of *The Hobbit*); but their mythological niche is partly
filled by these large, benevolent forest-dwelling creatures, who look
after trees and to some extent resemble them. One can imagine how
such a tiny word appealed to Tolkien's sense of humour as a term for
beings which he conceived of as not only large but also extremely
long-winded and unable to express anything in few syllables. It also
appealed to him that the entirely unrelated Latin form *ent-* is the
present participle stem of the verb 'to be' (as in the word *entity*),
suggesting the idea of essential being.

In Old English there were (at least) two inherited terms meaning
'giant': *eoten* and *ent*. An *eoten* (*OED*: ETEN, ETTIN) was a being
hostile to humans; the name is cognate with the Norse *jötunn*, which
denotes the inhabitants of Jötunheimr (see **Middle-earth**), the
giants against whom the gods fight. In *Sir Gawain*, the Green
Knight, on his first appearance, is described as 'half etayn' (a variant
spelling of the same word). The word comes down to early modern
English with all the unfavourable connotations of folk-tale flesh-
eating giants. Tolkien uses it in the place name *Ettenmoors*, an area

frequented by Trolls (which implies that inhabitants of Middle-earth used *etten* as a synonym for 'troll').

In the drafts of the first two books of *The Lord of the Rings* this region is called the *Entish Dales* or *Entish Lands*. At this stage of Tolkien's conception, *ent* and *etten* (or *ettin*) are interchangeable, both with a bad sense. Then, as the concept of Treebeard and his people gradually emerges from earlier hints about 'tree-men' or 'tree-giants', the two words part company. This can be seen in the plot plans: Treebeard is at first a dangerous giant (*HME* VII. 71), but then is planned to turn out 'a decent giant' (*HME* VII. 210). A pencilled note by Tolkien (*HME* VII. 411) expresses the 'difference between *trolls*—stone inhabited by goblin-spirit, *stone-giants*, and the "tree-folk"'; to which is added in ink: 'Ents'.

For the reader of ancient English literature, *ent* is a word with a mysterious feel. In several Anglo-Saxon poems the ruins of ancient buildings (often identified with ruined Roman cities) are described as *enta geweorc* (the work of giants). In one place we find the phrase *orþanc enta geweorc* (the cunning work of giants). In this single phrase we can see the likely genesis of two concepts that eventually came to stand in opposition: the name of Saruman's stronghold *Orthanc*, 'the tower of the cunning mind' (the Anglo-Saxon letter *þ* represented by modern English *th*), and the name of the ents, who lay waste Isengard and defeat the power of Orthanc, 'The Ents,' says Tolkien (*Lett.* 247), '...had mastery *over stone.*' Another echo of the Old English expression occurs in a description of the Hornburg: 'Men said that in the far-off days... the sea-kings had built here this fastness with the hands of giants' (*LR* III. vii).

The word *ent* hardly appears in English after the Old English period, and the *OED* (listing it under the Middle English spelling

EONT) includes just one example, from the *Lambeth Homilies* (c. 1225), here expanded: *Efter noes flode...eontas wolden areran ane buruh and anne stepel swa hehne þet his rof asti3e up to heofena* (After Noah's Flood the giants intended to erect a city and a tower so high that its roof would ascend to the heavens). This refers to the Christian legend that giants were responsible for building the Tower of Babel (perhaps another echo of Orthanc). The form of the word, beginning with *eo-*, perhaps indicates that *ent* had been influenced by *eoten.*

The adjective derived from *ent* is *entish* (also used for their language, *LR* III. iv: the term *Old Entish* is possibly a scholarly pun on the name of the Anglo-Saxon dialect Old Kentish). It reflects Old English *entisc*, which appears in *Beowulf* (together with the equivalent adjective derived from *eoten*):

> *eald sweord eotonisc, entiscne helm*
> the ancient ettenish sword, the giant-made helmet.

The children of the Ents are called *Entings*. This is a well-formed derivative using the Old English suffix *-ing*, which can indicate 'child of (someone)', 'member of the tribe of (someone)', or 'person characterized by (something)'. (Many English place names in *-ing* originate with people or tribal groups bearing such names.) In Tolkien's writings we find the *Swertings*, the *Bardings* (the people of Dale, ruled by Bard), the *Beornings* (Beorn's people), and the *Dunlendings* (the people of Dunland, with a change of *a* to *e* as mentioned at **Mannish**). In more archaic, Old English form we also find the *Eorlingas* (Eorl's people) and the *Helmingas* (Helm's people) of Rohan.

❧ éored ❧

An éored is a troop of cavalry of the Rohirrim. At the time of the War of the Ring it consisted of 120 men (more details can be found in note 36 to 'Cirion and Eorl', *Unfinished Tales* 315). This number probably reflects the ancient system of duodecimal counting (see **eleventy-one**).

Its Old English derivation is from *eoh* 'horse' and a worn-down form of *rad* 'riding', the antecedent of modern English words *road* and *raid* (it is regular in Old English for the *h* to disappear in the middle of the word, and for the vowel *eo* to be lengthened).

The element *éo-* representing 'horse' is found in other words and names of the Rohirrim, reflecting that people's concern with horses. Examples include the names *Éomer* (which was in real history the name of an ancestor of the Mercian royal house), *Éowyn*, and *Éomund*, and also the word *Éothéod*, which is what the Rohirrim call themselves, a compound created by Tolkien meaning 'horse-people'. (The name of *Eorl* and his people the *Eorlingas*, with a short *e*, do not contain the element *éo-*: *eorl* is an Old English word meaning 'nobleman' or 'warrior'; *OED*: EARL *n.*, sense 1, 1b.)

Éored is one of a number of words which Tolkien borrowed from Old English but which (unlike **Arkenstone**, **mathom**, and **smial**) he deliberately did not modernize, because they were intended to represent the archaic-sounding language of the Rohirrim, in contrast to the Common Speech or Westron. Other 'Rohirric' words which Tolkien took directly from Old English are *Mearas*, the special breed of horses to which Shadowfax belongs (literally just 'horses'; *OED*: MARE *n.*[1], etymology), the two parts of the flower name *simbelmynë* 'evermind', *Edoras*, the name of the dwelling of the king (the plural of an Old English word meaning 'enclosure' or 'court'), and *Meduseld*, the great hall (from *medu* 'mead' and *seld* 'hall').

❧ eucatastrophe ❧

All of a sudden I realized what it was: the very thing I have been trying to write about and explain…. For it I coined the word 'eucatastrophe': the sudden happy turn in a story which pierces you with a joy that brings tears.

(*Lett.* 89, to his son Christopher, 7–8 November 1944)

In his essay 'On Fairy-Stories', Tolkien identifies the consolatory happy ending as one of the principal defining features of the fairy story, and coins for this the word *eucatastrophe* (which he also gives a theological dimension by applying it to the Resurrection, the 'happy ending' of the Gospels). Although this word has not yet entered the *OED*, it has been taken up as a technical term by some writers on fantasy literature. As Tolkien explains, it is based on the Greek word *katastrophē* 'overturning, sudden turn, conclusion'.

The word *catastrophe* did historically have a neutral sense in English—'the change or revolution which produces the conclusion or final event of a dramatic piece' (Samuel Johnson's *Dictionary*, quoted in the *OED*, which gives as a modern equivalent the French loanword *dénouement*). However, its use is now dominated by the negative sense—'a conclusion generally unhappy' (Johnson); 'a disastrous end, finish-up, conclusion, upshot; overthrow, ruin, calamitous fate' (*OED*: CATASTROPHE *n.*, sense 2). The notion of a 'happy catastrophe' (as quoted by *OED* from a 17th-century writer) is so distant from the present understanding of the word that Tolkien felt obliged to invent a new term using the Greek-derived prefix *eu-*, meaning 'good, well'. He could then use the opposite term *dyscatastrophe* to refer specifically to a tragic ending.

❧ even ❧

Even meaning 'evening' is now a rare poetic word, familiar only in the compounds *evensong* and *eventide*. It bears the same relationship to *eve* 'the day before' and *evening* as *morn* does to *morrow* and *morning* (see **morrow**). Parallel to *morrowdim*, Tolkien formed *evendim*, which is also the name of a lake in the west of Middle-earth (i.e. the region towards sunset), and in Bilbo's song at Rivendell, Eärendil sets sail in the twilight 'from *Evereven*'s lofty hills' (*LR* ii. i).

Tolkien also revived the word *evenstar*, quoted in the *OED* (EVEN-STAR) from King Alfred's 9th-century translation of Boethius and not recorded since the 16th century (though the ever-inventive James Joyce did also use it in a short poem in 1907). It is best known as the surname of Arwen, the last, bright child of her kindred, but it also appears in its literal use in *Smith of Wootton Major*: 'It was evening and the Even-star was shining in a luminous sky close to the Moon'; and it is clearly identified with Eärendil in 'The Mirror of Galadriel' (*LR* ii. vii).

(See also **morrow**.)

❧ Faërie ❧

In the earliest versions of his mythology, Tolkien used *Faërie* (or *Faëry*) to mean 'the realm of the Elves (in the far West or in

Beleriand)'. This is more or less parallel to his use of *fairy* for an inhabitant of this realm. By using these two words in this distinct way, he marked the difference between older and newer meanings of the word *fairy* (see the article on this word below). After the period of the 'Lays of Beleriand' (*HME* III) this usage was abandoned, and *Faërie* was replaced by *Elvenhome* or by the Elvish names of the various realms, but a remnant of the older usage is preserved in *The Hobbit* (chapter viii):

> They [the Wood-elves] differed from the High Elves of the West, and were more dangerous and less wise. For most of them… were descended from the ancient tribes that never went to Faerie in the West.

The *OED* entry (FAERY, FAERIE) explains that these spellings, though they may perhaps have existed in Middle English, were introduced anew to early modern English by Edmund Spenser in his *The Faerie Queene* (1590), along with various other archaic words which he adopted or even invented (as later authors have done) to give a deliberate sense of antique mystery to his tale. (The dots or diaeresis over the ë, used by many later writers, indicate a separate syllable.) Spenser's spellings have given later writers a way of using *fairy* in its older sense, 'the realm of the fairies', while avoiding the undesirable connotations of *fairyland*. Tolkien himself uses it in this way in the essay 'On Fairy-Stories':

> *Faërie* contains many things besides elves and fays, and besides dwarfs, witches, trolls, giants, or dragons: it holds the seas, the sun, the moon, the sky; and the earth, and all things that are in it: tree and bird, water and stone, wine and bread, and ourselves, mortal men, when we are enchanted.

In the draft text of *Smith of Wootton Major* he experimented with using *Fairy* in the old sense, but preferred to change it to *Faery* for publication.

✤ fairy ✦

Fairy, as a noun more or less equivalent to *elf*, is a relatively modern word, hardly used until the Tudor period. The first quotation in the *Oxford Dictionary* (the only one before AD 1450) is significant. It is taken from the poet Gower: *as he were a faierie*. But this Gower did not say. He wrote *as he were of faierie*, 'as if he were come from Faërie'. ('On Fairy-Stories')

Here Tolkien encapsulates the history of the word *fairy*: in origin it literally meant 'the land of the fays' (*'fay-ery'*: see also **fay**). The three earliest senses of the word in the *OED* can be summarized as 'fairy-land', 'the inhabitants of fairyland', and 'enchantment'. It is only in the late 14th century that the word is transferred from this collective meaning to that of an individual member of the fairy people, which soon became its normal use. (For further discussion of the 'fairy-land' sense, see **Faërie**.)

Like the elves, the inhabitants of the fairy realm were originally imagined as powerful and terrifying (the word comes ultimately from the Latin *fata*, the Fates who control human destiny). In the 14th-century poem *Sir Orfeo*, the *fairi* steal away Orfeo's wife despite all the guards set round her. Later (like Smith in *Smith of Wootton Major*), Orfeo sees them frequently in the wilderness: sometimes their king is out hunting; sometimes an army of ten thousand fierce *fairi* knights is marching; and sometimes knights and ladies of *fairi* are elegantly dancing, and then disappear into thin air rather like the Wood-elves in chapter viii of *The Hobbit*.

In 'On Fairy-Stories' Tolkien claims to take issue with 'the lexi-cographer's definition of *fairies*':

> supernatural beings of diminutive size, in popular belief supposed to possess magical powers and to have great influence for good or evil over the affairs of man. (*OED*: FAIRY *n.*, sense 4a)

In reality, he is taking issue with the modern conception of fairies which the definition presents. He guesses that the notion of fair-ies as essentially diminutive (as reflected also in the 18th-century term 'little people') is largely a product of literary fancy, which had certainly taken hold by the time of Shakespeare's *A Mid-summer Night's Dream* (1600) and which similarly affected the use of *elf*.

In the earliest versions of his mythology, Tolkien used the word *fairy* with the same meaning as his later *Elf* and *Elvish*:

> Now on a time the fairies dwelt in the Lonely Isle after the great wars with Melko and the ruin of Gondolin.
> (Introduction to 'Kortirion among the Trees' (1915): *HME* I. 25)

> The Lonely Island, Tol Eressëa in the fairy speech, but which the Gnomes call Dor Faidwen.
> ('The Cottage of Lost Play' (c. 1917): *HME* I. 13)

He even provided an explanation, in terms of his own mythology, of their fading to small size, in a notebook of around 1917 ('The History of Eriol': *HME* II. 283). After this period, though, he increasingly laid the word aside, as too much associated with everything he rejected in the post-medieval conception of the elves: diminutive size, wings, and sickly sentimentality.

❖ fairy-story ❖

Tolkien begins his well-known essay 'On Fairy-Stories' by, as it were, providing necessary revisions to the *OED*. The first is this:

> What is a fairy-story? In this case you will turn to the *Oxford English Dictionary* in vain. It contains no reference to the combination *fairy-story*, and is unhelpful on the subject of *fairies* generally.

(In the original version of the essay, published in 1947, he mischievously comments that 'Volume F was not edited by a Scotsman', implying that fairies were not taken so seriously by the Englishman Henry Bradley as they might have been by a 'Celt' such as James Murray!) An entry for FAIRY STORY was eventually published in the *Supplement to the OED* (1972), which traces its history back to Dickens's *David Copperfield* (1850)—although more recent research has unearthed examples as early as 1687.

Tolkien goes on to acknowledge that *fairy-tale* (represented in the original *OED* only by an example from Tennyson dated 1864) does have a complete entry in the *OED Supplement* of 1933, but he considers its definition to be in need of further attention, since it focuses too much on 'fairies' rather than 'Faërie' at large:

> In the Supplement, *fairy-tale* is recorded since the year 1750, and its leading sense is said to be (*a*) a tale about fairies, or generally a fairy legend... The first sense is too narrow... For fairy-stories are not in normal English usage stories *about* fairies or elves, but stories about Fairy, that is *Faërie*, the realm or state in which fairies have their being. *Faërie* contains many things besides elves and fays, and besides dwarfs, witches, trolls, giants, or dragons.

The *OED*'s editors will no doubt bear his comments in mind when working on a future revised entry, which would helpfully document each of the different strands of meaning separately.

✤ farthing ✤

Each of the four parts into which the Shire is divided is called a *farthing*: a convincingly 'Old English'-sounding term. The word is, of course, in the *OED*, but the meaning which Tolkien gives to it is his own. The basic sense is 'one of four parts into which something is divided'. In Old English the word was *feorþing* (formed from *feorþa* 'fourth' plus the suffix *-ing*). The best known use is as the name of an old British coin worth a quarter of a penny. (This was not abolished until 1961, so when Tolkien was writing, the name would have neatly associated the small people of the Shire with the smallest British coin in circulation.)

Tolkien's adaptation of *farthing* (as he says explicitly in the 'Guide to the Names in *LR*') is based on the word *riding*—although Tom Shippey has suggested that his thoughts may have been set in motion by an encounter with the Northamptonshire place-name *Farthinghoe*, which is mentioned (though spelt *Farthingho*) in the foreword to *Farmer Giles of Ham*. *Riding* is the term for one of the three parts (East, West, and North) into which the historic county of Yorkshire was traditionally divided. It comes from Old Norse *þriðjung* 'a third part' (from the Norse equivalents of *third* and the suffix *-ing*), the initial *th* consonant having eroded away over the centuries from its nearness to the consonant of the preceding word (North-thriding = North Riding), and the connection with *third* having been forgotten. So, just as the Shire of York can be divided into three 'thirdings' or *ridings*, the Shire of the hobbits can be divided into four 'fourthings' or *farthings*.

Although the word *farthing* has old senses recorded by the *OED* referring to land, it never seems to have referred to each of four parts of a region. However, in Old Norse there was an equivalent word *fjórðung,* meaning in general 'quarter', and in particular 'one of four areas into which a region is divided'. Iceland was and still is divided into four *fjórðungar* which are named, like the Farthings of the Shire, after the four points of the compass.

✦ Fastitocalon ✦

Þam is noma cenned, fyrnstreama geflotan, Fastitocalon
to the sailor of the ocean is given the name of Fastitocalon
(from the Old English poem *The Whale*)

This is the first occurrence in English literature of this extraordinary name, and the poem turns on the mistaking of the whale for an island. Tolkien's verse 'Fastitocalon'—first published in *The Stapeldon Magazine* (1927: see also **oliphaunt**) and revised for *The Adventures of Tom Bombadil*—is based on this Old English poem, which is in turn based on the medieval Latin bestiary entitled *Physiologus* (or 'The Natural Philosopher'). The word there appears as *aspidocalon.* Scholars believe that *Fastitocalon* is the result of a series of textual corruptions which occurred as one scribe after another, copying the *Physiologus,* encountered this unfamiliar word and tried to make something of it. In a letter of 5 March 1964 (*Lett.* 255), Tolkien opined that the initial *F* was probably added by the Anglo-Saxon poet simply to make the word fit his alliterative metre.[1] The Latin text is based on a Greek one, so behind

---

[1] An older theory suggests that it arises from transmission of the word, at some point, through Old Irish. The 'mutation' of consonants in Celtic languages causes words with initial *f* to shift, in certain contexts, to initial *fh*, which is silent. A scribe may therefore suppose an unfamiliar foreign word beginning with a vowel sound to have an initial silent *fh*, and so 'reinstate' a spurious initial *f*. Since Old Irish lacked the sound *p* in native words, the change of *-asp-* to *-ast-* also supports this theory.

the Latin *aspidocalon* almost certainly lurks the Greek word *aspidochelōne* ('shield-turtle'), and the tale of the false island may originally have been inspired not by a whale but by a giant turtle of the Indian Ocean.

➤ **fay** ◆

While in the process of abandoning the word *fairy* in his mythological writings, Tolkien experimented with *fay* as an alternative: 'brownies, fays, pixies, leprawns, and what else are they not called' (early draft of 'The Coming of the Valar': *HME* I. 66), and 'half a fay of the woods and dells' (description of Tinfang Warble: *HME* I. 94). This word—a borrowing of French *fée* in use since the 14th century—might have seemed preferable to *fairy*, which did not originally apply to individual creatures (see **fairy**). Gradually, however, he seems to have found this word unsatisfactory too, at least as a description of any of the inhabitants of Middle-earth, and it occurs less and less often in his later Middle-earth writings. A late echo is to be found in 'Of Tuor and his Coming to Gondolin'—written in 1951 (though drawing on earlier texts)—where Tuor believes the cry of a gulls to be 'a fay-voice' (*Unfinished Tales* 24). Another example occurs in his unfinished alliterative poem 'The Fall of Arthur' (quoted in Carpenter's *Biography*), where Guinever is described as 'fair as fay-woman and fell-minded'.

Fay once appears as an adjective, in *Smith of Wootton Major*: ' "It is *fay*," said Prentice. "It comes from Faery." ' This use is covered only implicitly by the *OED*, which cites an example from Gower (the same poet who gives us our earliest use of *faërie*): 'My wif[e] Constance is faie'. The *Middle English Dictionary* (at FAIE) treats the word in more detail, noting several medieval uses of *faie* or *faye* to mean 'possessed of magical powers or properties; enchanted' (and also the name of the Arthurian character *Morgan le Fay*); and Tolkien's use makes plain the historic link between *fay* and *faërie*.

It should be noted that this is not, historically, the same word as *fey* 'fated to die, doomed to death' (Old English *fǣge*), though since the early 19th century this word has often shifted to mean 'disordered in mind like one about to die' or more generally 'displaying magical, fairylike, or unearthly qualities', and so has converged in sense with the much rarer word *fay*. Tolkien used this word too:

> Alas that such a fey mood should fall on a man so greathearted in this hour of need. (*LR* v. ii)
> Théoden could not be overtaken. Fey he seemed. (*LR* v. v)

❧ flammifer ❧

In Bilbo's 'Song of Eärendil', the poetic name 'the Flammifer of Westernesse' is given to the mythologized Morning Star (though it is not wholly clear whether it refers to Eärendil the mariner himself or to the bright ship in which he sails the heavens). *Flammifer* is unusual in being a Tolkien coinage with Latin rather than Germanic roots, though this is appropriate in the context of the rather post-Renaissance vocabulary of the poem. The Latin word *flammifer* literally means 'flame-bearer'; it sits easily with a small group of English words of this type, such as *aquifer* ('water-bearer'), *conifer* ('cone-bearer'), *crucifer* ('cross-bearer'), *signifer* ('standard-bearer'), *thurifer* ('incense-bearer'), and the name *Lucifer* (literally 'light-bearer', and long used as a name for the Morning Star, although now avoided because of its Satanic associations); however,

Tolkien's use of it as an English word has no precedent, and the *OED* lists only the corresponding adjective *flammiferous* (itself very rare, and first found in a dictionary of the mid 17th century).

⁕ flet ⁕

> Near the top the main stem divided into a crown of many boughs, and among these they found that there had been built a wooden platform, or *flet* as such things were called in those days: the Elves called it a *talan*. (*LR* ii. vi)

Flet is an adaptation by Tolkien of an old word for a flat surface, derived from the adjective *flat*, with the change of vowel also seen in pairs of related words like *man–men* and *fall–fell*. The first sense given by the *OED* is 'the floor or ground under one's feet'; the examples show that it usually means the floor of a room or building, e.g. (from *Beowulf*) *heo on flet gecrong* (she collapsed to the floor)—this is in the monster Grendel's underwater hall—or (from *Sir Gawain and the Green Knight*) *a tule tapit tyȝt ouer þe flet* (a carpet of rich material spread on the floor). By extension, the word could be used to mean 'a hall or dwelling', a use also found in *Beowulf*. These meanings did not survive beyond Middle English. In Scots the word came to mean the inner part of a house. The *OED* shows that in early modern English there arose a quasi-legal formula, *fire and flet* 'fire and house-room'. This expression often occurred in wills, where it was essentially a guarantee that the deceased's heir, especially a dead man's wife, would have the right to these amenities while living in a house owned by someone else. The expression is sometimes spelt *fire and fleet*, as in the line 'fire and fleet and candle-light' in the opening verse of the 17th-century ballad *A Lyke-Wake Dirge*.

Before Tolkien the word *flet* never, as far as we know, meant a platform built amid the boughs of a tree, whether by Elves or human beings. The word was introduced into the draft of the Lothlórien chapter as it was written (*HME* VII. 227). Tolkien weaves the spell of antiquity by taking up the little-known word *flet* and adding the aside 'as such things were called in those days', as usual calling up a fictional continuity between the past of his story and the present in which he writes. He also neatly binds together two of its distinct meanings, 'dwelling' and 'flat surface', into a single image.

✦ gangrel ✦

> He is only a wretched gangrel creature, but I have him under my care
> for a while.
>
> (Frodo, speaking of Gollum to Faramir: *LR* IV. iv)

The choice of this unusual word is doubly appropriate. The first sense in the *OED* is 'a vagabond' and, when used as an adjective, 'vagrant':

> Was it a light thing that gangrel thieves should burn and waste in
> Mid-mark and depart unhurt, that ye stand here with clean blades
> and cold bodies? (William Morris *The House of the Wolfings*, chapter xxii)

The second sense is 'a lanky loose-jointed person', which may seem equally apt for the agile Gollum. The word is a Middle English formation which adds a disparaging suffix (also seen in *mongrel* and *wastrel*) to a stem apparently meaning 'go or walk'. Tolkien also used the word (but only in the first sense) in Fëanor's dismissal of Melkor: 'Get thee from my gate, thou gangrel' ('Annals of Aman': *HME* X. 97).

❖ gladden ❖

They took a boat and went down to the Gladden Fields, where there were great beds of iris and flowering reeds. (*LR* I. ii)

Gladden is Tolkien's updating of the Old English word *glædene* 'iris'. This is recorded in an Old English document from the 9th (or possibly the 8th) century. In the names *Gladden River* and *Gladden Fields* in *The Lord of the Rings*, Tolkien intended the word to refer to the 'yellow flag' (*Iris pseudacorus*), which grows by streams and in marshes (*Lett.* 297). The Old English word in fact continued in later use in the slightly different form *gladdon*, though, as Tolkien went on to explain, the name is now usually applied to a different species, the purple-flowered *Iris foetidissima* (or 'stinking iris'). The word is now rarely found outside regional dialects.

The *OED* entry (GLADDON) quotes a line from the Middle English romance *The Wars of Alexander*, evoking an image reminiscent of the Gladden Fields: *a dryi meere was full of gladen & of gale & of grete redis* (a dry lake was full of gladdon and bog-myrtle and great reeds).

❖ glede ❖

It was hot when I first took it, hot as a glede.
(Isildur describing the Great Ring: *LR* II. ii)
Full on the town he fell. His last throes splintered
it to sparks and gledes. (*Hobbit*, ch. xiv)

Tolkien perhaps deliberately favoured an archaic-looking spelling of this word (*OED*: GLEED), which in Isildur's account of the Ring fits well with other old word-forms such as *seemeth* and *loseth*. The word means 'a live coal' or 'an ember', and goes back to Old English: ultimately it is related to the verb *glow*. It was once much used in similes such as *red, hot,* or *fierce as a gleed*: the phrase 'hot as any gleed' occurs in the *Troy Book,* by the poet John Lydgate, and the romance *Guy of Warwick,* both from the 15th century.

✦ Gnome ✦

In his earliest Elvish tales, Tolkien used the word *Gnome* for the second of the great Elf-kindreds, corresponding to the Elvish word *Noldo* (or its predecessor). He persisted with this use for a long time, believing (as Tom Shippey observes in *The Road to Middle-earth,* p. 333) that his readers would understand this in the light of the Greek word *gnōmē,* which is connected with *gnōsis* 'knowledge'. However, this erudite use of the word was always in danger of being undermined by association with nursery tales, or with the absurd bearded and red-capped garden gnomes (probably introduced in around the 1860s and widespread in Britain by the 1940s). It is just as well that he decided to replace it with the Elvish word. Even so, the language generally known as Sindarin was called *Gnomish* even in some writings later than *The Lord of the Rings.*

The *OED* lists two separate English words of this spelling. The first of these (*OED:* GNOME *n.*[1]) means 'a pithy saying' and is indeed derived from the Greek word *gnōmē* (plural *gnōmai).* This word is mainly in technical use, especially to describe what is called 'gnomic' literature, which makes general statements about things in the world and forms part of both Old English and Old Norse traditions.

The second English word (*OED:* GNOME *n.*[2]) was introduced in the Latin form *gnomus* by the 16th-century natural philosopher Paracelsus. The *OED* suggests that he may not have conjured the word up from nowhere: it could be an adaptation—deliberate or mistaken—of a Greek compound *gē-nomos* 'earth-dweller'. Paracelsus suggested that each of the four classical elements was inhabited by its own being: sylphs in the air, salamanders in fire, undines in water, and gnomes in the earth. This conceit was adopted by Alexander Pope in *The Rape of the Lock* (1712); from there the gnome was quickly drawn into whimsical fairy lore, and developed into the diminutive dwarf-like creature fashioned in pottery for the adornment of suburban gardens (the *OED*'s files contain an American example of *garden gnome* from 1933).

It is likely that Tolkien deliberately combined elements of the meanings of both of these words. While GNOME[1] implied wisdom but did not refer to a being, GNOME[2] referred to a being, but merely an earth-dwelling one, without the connection with wisdom. As his concept became clarified, the Gnomes shed most vestiges of earthiness (though retaining their ancient link to Aulë, the god of the earth, and a tendency to a somewhat Dwarvish love of jewels) and their greater dignity demanded a better name. There appears to be a kind of linguistic wordplay in the names *Nóm* 'Wisdom' and *Nómin* 'the Wise' given by Men to Finrod and his people (the Noldor) in their own language (*Silmarillion*, ch. xvii).

⟡ goblin ⟡

> Now goblins are cruel, wicked, and bad-hearted. They make no beautiful things, but they make many clever ones. (*Hobbit*, ch. iv)

In writing *The Hobbit*, Tolkien was content to use *goblin* for the ugly, malevolent enemies of Elves, Dwarves, and Men, encountered by Bilbo and his companions. His reasons for ceasing to use it as a general term in his later tales may be guessed: the word has deep roots in the 19th-century romantic world of Christina Rossetti's *Goblin Market* (1862), and even the serious intent of a story such as George MacDonald's *The Princess and the Goblin* (1872) could not rid it of its associations with more whimsical nursery tales. Even the goblins of *The Hobbit* are a more serious prospect than their earlier manifestation, as the malevolent but rather unthreatening vermin which, according to Tolkien's letters to his children in the guise of Father Christmas, infest tunnels and caves near the North Pole (*The Father Christmas Letters*, letters for 1932 and 1933). Also, *goblin* is not an inherited Old English word like *elf* or *dwarf*, but was borrowed in the 14th century from French or Latin, though it may ultimately be Germanic if, as etymologists think, it is related to German *Kobold* (a spirit haunting mines and caves).

However, the word was not entirely dispensed with, and appears in *The Lord of the Rings* denoting various individuals or types of *orc*: 'four goblin-soldiers of greater stature, swart, slant-eyed, with thick legs and large hands' (*LR* III. i); 'he looks more than half like a goblin' (*LR* I. xi; the adjective *goblinish* appears in an earlier draft: *HME* VI. 165); 'dozens of other goblins had sprung out of the trees' (*LR* III. iii). And there are 'goblin-barkers' among Gandalf's fire-works.

There is some evidence that, in the earliest tales, Tolkien experimented with using the name *goblins* for the beings later known as the *gnomes* (*HME* I, Appendix, under *Noldoli*); this accords with the nomenclature of George MacDonald, who in *The Princess and the Goblin* suggested that *gnome, kobold,* and *goblin* were all names for the same race of beings.

❧ halfling ❧

Tolkien wrote of this word that 'it is not actually an English word, but might be (that is, it is suitably formed with appropriate suffix)' ('Guide to the Names in *LR*'). In fact, *halfling* did exist, though with a very slightly different meaning, quite a long time before Tolkien used it in this specific way. The *OED* says that it is a northern and Scots word, and gives examples as far back as the late 17th century. It means 'one not fully grown; a stripling'—which is, of course, how a hobbit superficially appears to a human being. The Gondorian boy Bergil says to Peregrin Took: 'I am ten years already, and shall soon be five feet. I am taller than you.' This is a little younger than the age ascribed to the adjectival use of *halfling* by the *OED*: 'not fully grown; about the age of 15'.

The form of the word is transparent, if slightly archaic to modern ears: *-ling* is a familiar suffix forming nouns for persons whose nature or status is indicated by the first part of the word, such as *firstling*, *nurseling*, and *weakling*. It is also found in *Easterling*, in *beardling*, a derisive term for a dwarf used by the orcs of Moria (*LR*, Appendix A), and earlier by George Dasent in his version of *Njal's Saga* (see pp. 67–8); and in *hagling*, an insulting term used to Lobelia Sackville-Baggins by Saruman's ruffians (*LR* vi. viii).

In the early drafts of *The Lord of the Rings*, the term *half-high* is used. This is a modernized form, but its Old English equivalent *Halfheah* actually appears in an early version of 'The Riders of Rohan' (*HME* VII. 405, note 20). (Tolkien had noted the appearance of Old English *Healf-heah* as a nickname in a charter—presumably for a short person—in his lectures in the 1930s, published as *Finn and Hengest*.) He continued to use this term as far as the point in 'The Window on the West' where Faramir says 'If then you are the Halfling that was named', at which point *Halfling* first appears as an emendation (*HME* VIII. 166). No similar use of the adjective compound *half-high* as a noun is recorded in the *OED*, and most readers would probably agree that the coinage or adoption of *halfling* was a great improvement on the original 'Common Speech' name for a hobbit.

Fantasy role-playing games take their terminology from a wide range of mythological and fictional sources, including Tolkien's works. It is notable that *halfling* rather than *hobbit* is generally adopted as a generic term for the short humanoid race appearing in these games, presumably because it sounds like an English word of general application, rather than being specific to the Tolkienian world.

✦ hame ✦

Gandalf Greyhame is known in the Mark. (*LR* III. ii)

Tolkien explains the name Greyhame as the modernized form of Old English *greghama* (representing the usage of Rohan), meaning 'greycoat' ('Guide to the Names in *LR*'). A slightly different form, *græghama*, occurs in the fragmentary Old English text *The Fight at Finnesburg*; Tolkien (in *Finn and Hengest*) explains this as 'the greycoated one', i.e. 'wolf'. The second part of this compound is the *OED*'s HAME *n.*[1] (in Old English *hama* or *homa*), defined as 'a covering, especially a natural covering, integument; skin, membrane'; this word became obsolete in the 16th century.

In illustrating the use of *hame*, the *OED* mentions a character in the Middle English romance *King Alisaunder* putting on and taking off a dragon's hame. This brings to mind chapter xix of *The Silmarillion*, where Beren disguises himself in 'the ghastly wolf-hame of Draugluin' (in the earlier 'Lay of Leithian', lines 3398–3401 'a wolfhame huge…the werewolf cloak of Draugluin': *HME* III. 278). Though the situation here is exceptional, it echoes the widespread folk-tale image of a person (human or divine) changing his or her shape into that of a wolf (*wolf-hame* is an exact equivalent of Old Norse *úlfa-hamir* 'wolf-coats'). The Old Norse word *hamr* (the equivalent of Old English *hama*) was often used in the legendary sagas to express the idea of another creature's skin or likeness: eagle, falcon, horse, or troll. The Norse phrase *skipta hömum* 'to change one's shape' (*skipta* corresponds to the English *shift*) reflects this, as do compounds such as *hamhleypa* 'a skin-changing witch' (literally 'one who jumps skin') and *hamfarir* 'magical travel in the shape of an animal'. (See also **bee-hunter** and **skin-changer**.)

Parallels to Old English *greghama* or *græghama* include two words for the human body: *flæsc-hama* (literally 'flesh-coat') and *lic-hama* (literally 'body-coat'), a word used so much that it usually had the worn-down form *licuma* (*OED*: LICHAM). There is also the picturesque term *feðer-hama* (*OED*: FEATHER-HAM) meaning 'plumage' or 'wings'.

⤖ hemlock ⤙

Of the evocative images at the emotional centre of Tolkien's writings, one of the earliest and most personal is that of Beren watching Lúthien as she dances among the hemlocks in the woods of Doriath. To those who have heard of hemlock mainly as a poisonous weed whose noxious effect caused the death of Socrates, this may seem rather a curious plant to be found in such a romantic context. However, Tolkien was using the name not for the particular plant that usually bears this name (*Conium maculatum*; *OED*: HEM-LOCK, sense 1a), but in a more general sense with roots in regional English. As *OED* records (sense 1b), the name is 'also applied in rural use to the large Umbelliferae generally', that is, to any of the various plants whose flowers and seeds are borne on delicate, many-branched umbels. These are familiar plants of British woodlands and hedgerows, but their modern common names are less apt to Tolkien's purpose: the mention of 'Queen Anne's lace' would have been jarring in a tale of the Elves, and for Lúthien to dance amid the 'cow-parsley' would perhaps have conjured up thoughts of a rustic milkmaid rather than an elven princess. According to his son Christopher, Tolkien did not sympathize with the botanist's habit of applying distinct English names to closely similar plants which popular usage made little or no attempt to distinguish (J. Garth *Tolkien and the Great War*, p. 238, footnote). This appreciation of old and rural plant names is seen also in his use of the names *gladden* and *nasturtian*.

Incidentally, *OED*'s sense 2 records the use of the name *hemlock* in North America for a quite different kind of plant, a large evergreen tree also called *hemlock-spruce*. This American use of the word has apparently betrayed at least one artist into representing the dancing Lúthien not glimpsed through a filigree of lacy umbels but dwarfed by the trunks of enormous trees.

✦ hobbit ✦

I. A DEFINITION OF *HOBBIT* FOR THE *OED*

The *OED* entry for HOBBIT was published in 1976, in Volume II (H–N) of the *Supplement to the OED*. In December 1969, when this entry was in preparation, the Editor, R. W. Burchfield, sent a draft of the entry to Tolkien (who had been his teacher), asking for his comments. Tolkien did not reply until the following August: 1970 had turned out to be a year of 'great pressures for me and domestic distresses', as he explained in an apologetic letter to Burchfield. Fortunately there was still time to make use of his comments, which he included in a further letter (cf. *Lett.* 316) dated 11 September 1970:

> Unfortunately, as all lexicographers know, 'don't look into things, unless you are looking for trouble: they nearly always turn out to [be] less simple than you thought'. You will shortly be receiving a long letter on *hobbit* and related matters, of which, even if it is in time, only a small part may be useful or interesting to you.

> For the moment this is held up, because I am having the matter of the etymology: 'invented by J. R. R. Tolkien': investigated by experts. I knew that the claim was not clear, but I had not troubled to look into it, until faced by the inclusion of *hobbit* in the Supplement.

> In the meanwhile I submit for your consideration the following definition:

>> One of an imaginary people, a small variety of the human race, that gave themselves this name (meaning 'hole-dweller') but were called by others *halflings*, since they were half the height of normal Men.

> This assumes that the etymology can stand. If not it may be necessary to modify it: e.g. by substituting after 'race'

>> ; in the tales of J. R. R. Tolkien said to have given themselves this name, though others called them.....

> If it stands, as I think it will even if an alleged older story called 'The Hobbit' can be traced, then the '(meaning 'hole-dweller')' could be transferred to the etymology.

> This definition, since it is more than twice as long as the one that you
> submitted and differs from it widely, will need some justification. I
> will supply it.

The 'long letter on *hobbit* and related matters', in which presumably
the 'justification' was going to be supplied, was never received, and
no more was heard of the 'investigation by experts'.

The entry which was actually published and now appears (with
the addition of Tolkien's death date) in the *OED* (Second Edition)
reads:

> In the tales of J. R. R. Tolkien (1892–1973): one of an imaginary
> people, a small variety of the human race, that gave themselves this
> name (meaning 'hole-dweller') but were called by others *halflings*,
> since they were half the height of normal men.

II. THE ORIGIN OF *HOBBIT*: INVENTED

Are not these the Halflings, that some among us call the Holbytlan?
(*LR* iii. viii)

Having as far as he knew invented the word, Tolkien provided an
imaginary etymology for *hobbit*, in order to fit the word into the
linguistic landscape of Middle-earth. This was a remarkable feat of
reverse engineering, not quite like any of his other etymological
exploits amongst the tongues of Middle-earth.

On encountering the Rohirrim, the hobbits notice that their speech
contains many words that sound like Shire words but have a more
archaic form. The prime example is their word for the hobbits themselves: *holbytla*. This is a well-formed Old English compound (because Tolkien represents the language of the Rohirrim as Old
English). It is made up of *hol* 'hole' and *bytla* 'builder'; it just happens,
as far as we know, never to have existed in Old English, and if *hobbit*

turned out to be a genuine word from folklore it is most unlikely that this would be its actual etymology.

Tolkien is playfully suggesting that if there had been an Old English word *holbytla* (its accentuation would have been similar to that of *hole-builder*) it might well have come down into modern English as *hobbit* (though actually a more likely form would be *hobittle*, with a first syllable like that of *hobo*). But just to complicate things further, in a note at the end of the Appendices to *The Lord of the Rings*, Tolkien is at pains to explain that 'really' the human languages of Middle-earth were quite different from the English and Old English which he has 'translated' them into. *Hobbit* was 'really' *kuduk* and *holbytla* was 'really' *kûd-dûkan*; but he claims to have devised the English equivalents in order the better to convey the flavour of the world he is writing about.

III. THE ORIGIN OF *HOBBIT*: ACTUAL

The first quotation in the *OED* entry is the famous first line of *The Hobbit*: 'In a hole in the ground there lived a hobbit.' It is well known that Tolkien scribbled this sentence on an examination paper he was marking in a moment of boredom (*Lett.* 163). The word is Tolkien's most famous coinage—if it is indeed a coinage. His letter of September 1970 to the Dictionary department (quoted above) makes it clear that Tolkien was not entirely certain that he had invented the word, but neither he nor anyone else had at this time uncovered any earlier instance. A correspondent to *The Observer* on 16 January 1938 had claimed to recall the word from an earlier story, but this could not be traced; Tolkien's response (*Lett.* 25) shows that he at least acknowledged the possibility, though he commented: 'I suspect that the two hobbits are accidental homophones.' In another letter written in 1971 on the same subject (*Lett.* 319), he wrote of his 'unsupported assertion that I remember the occasion of its invention... However, one cannot exclude the possibility that buried childhood memories might suddenly rise to the surface long after.'

Then, after Tolkien's death, an example of the word did turn up, in a long list of 'supernatural beings' appearing in the so-called *Denham Tracts*, compiled by the Yorkshire merchant M. A. Denham (1800 or 1801–1859). Denham was an amateur folklorist who published many books and pamphlets, including twenty *Minor Tracts on Folklore* (1849–c.1854). The majority of these Tracts were collected in an edition prepared for the Folklore Society in the 1890s, and the word *hobbit* appears in the second volume (1895) of this edition.

The discovery of the word in the *Denham Tracts* was reported in *The Times* on 31 May 1977. The article records that Tolkien, when asked whence he had got the name, 'replied that he could not remember: perhaps he invented it; or "I may have picked it up from a nineteenth century source".' (Perhaps Tolkien still recalled that exchange of letters in 1938.) The *Times* writer rather boldly asserted that this 'nineteenth century source' had now been identified as Tolkien's inspiration. But could Tolkien have read the relevant *Denham Tract*? It certainly seems an unlikely origin for 'buried childhood memories'.

The *Denham Tracts* are a bibliographically untidy collection of texts. It seems that Denham would write a short piece and have it printed in a relatively small number of copies which were then distributed, probably mostly to his own circle. There is no single complete collection in existence, and in any case this would be hard to achieve since it also seems that Denham used to publish rewritten versions of his Tracts.

We know of four versions of the Tract in question. The original version (to which the others refer back) is in fact an article entitled 'Seasonable Information' published in the *Literary Gazette* of 23 December 1848 (p. 849, column 2). It is really no more than a light-hearted joke for the Christmas season, along the following lines: the glossarist and folklorist Francis Grose observes (says Denham) that those born on Christmas Day cannot see spirits; what a happiness this must have been seventy or eighty years ago for those who had the luck to be born on this day, when the whole earth was overrun with them—and there then follows a list of 131 'supernatural beings' of various kinds, beginning with 'ghosts, boggles, bloody-bones, spirits, demons', and ending with 'silkies, cauld-lads, death-hearses, and goblins and apparitions of every shape and make, kind and description'. The list contains beings drawn from both classical tradition and British folklore. Some are very familiar, some are evidently drawn from Denham's own research, and some appear to be unique to the list. His sources for the lesser-known words are uncertain, but he does share material with such sources as Reginald Scot's *Discoverie of Witchcraft* (1584). It is not a scholarly piece but just an opportunity to exhibit the vastness of the vocabulary of supernatural beings.

The second version (1851) is a separate Tract with a title page inscribed: 'To all and singular the Ghosts, Hobgoblins, and Phantasms, of the United Kingdom of Great Britain and Ireland, These brief Pages are Fearlessly Inscribed, In utter defiance of their Power and Influence, By their verie hvmble Seruaunte, To Com'aund, M:A:D.' The list is essentially the same but now contains 165 items. The new names have been added en bloc at the end of the list, with a few rearrangements and changes in spelling, and seven quasi-scholarly footnotes. The third version (1853) is similar, with almost the same title page. It contains 198 items and 31 footnotes. The additional new names have been inserted almost, but not quite, at the end of the list, i.e. within the section that was inserted in 1851. The word *hobbits* is the first word of the new section, which continues with 'hobgoblins [a repetition: the word is already in the original list], brown-men, cowies, dunnies, wirrikows...'. Unfortunately 'hobbits' is not footnoted. The fourth version is the reprint in the *Publications of the Folk-lore Society* mentioned above, where the word *hobbits* was first detected. This is in all important respects identical to the 1853 version. A very small number of changes appear to have been made, perhaps by the editor responsible for the republication.

The 1895 version would have been readily available in university libraries accessible to Tolkien (there is a copy in Oxford), and he was interested in folklore. Alternatively, he could have seen a list copied out by one of his friends or colleagues—someone like C. S. Lewis who read all kinds of abstruse writings. If there were any other unusual items in the list which also occurred in Tolkien's writings, we might suspect that the Tract was the source for all of them; but even though such curious words might have been quite handy for some of his more light-hearted poems, there is no trace of them. There seems to be nothing that tips the scales in favour of the theory that he had somehow come across the word from the Tract.

Even if Tolkien had in fact picked the word up from the Tract, this would only replace one mystery with another, for we do not know where Denham found the word, or what its meaning and etymology are. The other words newly added to Denham's list do not seem to be traceable to particular sources that might contain *hobbit*, unnoticed. It is possible that the first syllable *hob-* is the same as that of the next word in the list, *hobgoblin.* This element *hob* (*OED*: HOB *n.*[1], sense 2a) has the same meaning as the full word *hobgoblin* (but is about a century or so older). It originated as a familiar form of *Rob*, short for

Robert (of which *Robin*, used in the sprite name *Robin Goodfellow*, is a diminutive). It could be hypothesized that *hobbit* is a derivative of this word *hob*; the ending *-it* could be explained as the diminutive suffix more usually spelt *-et*, found in *midget, moppet*, and *snippet*, and the word would mean 'a small goblin or sprite'.

Another idea is that it might be a shortening of *hobbity-hoy*, a variant (quoted by the *OED* from a glossary of Yorkshire dialect) of HOBBLEDEHOY, meaning 'a clumsy or awkward youth': of course this is not a supernatural being, but not all Denham's words actually are. Either of these suggestions requires the assumption that it was a genuine word used by country people and recorded by Denham or an informant of his, but by no one else.

Alternatively, could the word have been suggested to Tolkien by something other than the Tract? There is the distinct possibility that a similar word (not necessarily with the meaning he gave to it) listed in the *OED* might have lodged, submerged, in his memory. One candidate is the word *hobbity-hoy* already mentioned. Another is the entry HOWITZ, HAUBITZ, meaning 'howitzer', which has the variant spellings (unchanged in the plural) *hobbits* or *hobits*, illustrated by the following quotations:

> *Hobits* are a sort of small Mortars from 6 to 8 Inches Diameter. Their Carriages are like those of Guns, only much shorter.
> (J. Harris *Lexicon Technicum* II (1710))

> Little Hobbits charged with the various kinds of Fire-Balls.
> (G. Shelvocke *Artillery* (1729) V. 377)

When one recalls that *Bilbo* meant a kind of sword and was often used in the 17th and 18th centuries as the name of a sword personified, the idea seems quite attractive. However, this is just one more unproven speculation; the real origin of Tolkien's word remains obscure.

IV. ON TRANSLATING *HOBBIT*

It is surely no surprise that, having taken such care over his use of
English in *The Hobbit* and *The Lord of the Rings*, Tolkien should take
a considerable interest in how these works were translated into
other languages. The word *hobbit* itself posed particular problems.
It seems that Tolkien was not consulted over the very first translation of *The Hobbit*, namely the Swedish version by Tore Zetterholm
which appeared in 1947 under the title *Hompen*. By 1956 he was
certainly ready to remonstrate with his publishers over a proposed
Dutch translation of *The Lord of the Rings*. In a letter concerned
mainly with proposals to translate some of the place names of
Middle-earth into Dutch (to which he objected 'as strongly as is
possible', describing himself as 'actually very angry indeed'), he also
says regarding *hobbit* that he 'will not have any more *Hompen* [...],
nor any *Hobbel* or what not. Elves, Dwarfs/ves, Trolls, yes: they are
mere modern equivalents of the correct terms. But *hobbit* (and *orc*)
are of that world, and they must stay, whether they sound Dutch or
not' (*Lett.* 190). Tolkien thereafter left his publishers in no doubt
that he would prefer *hobbit* not to be translated—a comment to this
effect appears in his 'Guide to the Names in *LR*'—and most of the
subsequent translations of the book reflect this: German (*Kleine
Hobbit und der grosse Zauberer*, 1957), Polish (*Hobbit*, 1960), Spanish
(*El hobito*, 1964), Danish (*Hobbitten*, 1969), French (*Bilbo le hobbit*,
1969), Norwegian (*Hobbiten*, 1972), Italian (*Lo hobbit*, 1973), Catalan
(*El hòbbit*, 1983), Russian (*Khobbit*, 1977), Czech (*Hobit*, 1979), and
so on. Even so, there have been occasional exceptions, including the
versions in Hungarian (*A babó*, c. 1975) and Estonian (*Kääbik*, 1977).

Icelandic has a special place in this story. In 1973 Tolkien commented to Ungfrú Aðalsteinsdottir, who was preparing a translation

of *The Hobbit,* that it was 'a language which I think would fit it better than any other I have any adequate knowledge of' (*Lett.* 352). He did not live to see the publication of the first Icelandic translation, which only appeared in 1978, and which followed the majority of other translations in using the word *hobbit* in unchanged form. In fact Tolkien had been consulted about an Icelandic version of *The Hobbit* over twenty years earlier, when a former Icelandic pupil of his, Benedikt Benedikz, began work on his own translation. Dr Benedikz has kindly allowed us to reproduce his recollection of the occasion in 1952 when he approached Tolkien, after a lecture, about how he might translate the word *hobbit* in the famous opening sentence: 'He was charm itself, and [...] discussed with me what should be the Icelandic equivalent. He was quite firm on this. "The definition of the word is in that sentence, and the philologically accurate word is *holbúi* 'hole-dweller' and no one should ever use any back-formation or re-formation from *hobbit.*"' This makes a striking contrast with the view he expressed only a few years later in relation to the Dutch translation.

V. THE AFTERLIFE OF *HOBBIT*

Hobbit has several derivatives and compounds listed in the *OED*: *hobbitish, hobbitomane,* and *hobbitry.* The first example of this last was used in an abstract sense by C. S. Lewis, writing about *The Hobbit* in 1947: 'As the humour and homeliness of the early chapters, the sheer "Hobbitry", dies away we pass insensibly into the world of epic.' Tolkien himself then used it, in a collective sense, in the Prologue to *The Lord of the Rings*: 'The Thain was the...captain of the Hobbitry-in-arms'. Others that have been used include *hobbit-lore* (*LR* i. ii), *hobbitic* (used by commentators including Tom Shippey and Paul Kocher, but not in the *OED*), and *hobbitized* (used by Kocher, but not in the *OED*).

In the 1960s a Tolkien craze swept American campuses, and it seems that the first people to identify themselves with the hobbits were the hippies, as an example in the *OED* tells us:

> The consistently good people in the Tolkien books are Hobbits and they have the lowliest status of all the groups of characters in the books. The hippies thought of themselves as being or becoming Hobbits; from time to time as the winter wore on, a sign would appear in the window of one of their gathering places to this effect: Do not add to the street confusion this weekend... Be good little Hobbits and stay home. (H. Perry *Human Be-In* (1970) i. 20)

In 2004 archaeologists in Indonesia found the fossil bones of a group of human beings who were one metre tall and lived on the island of Flores until about 12,000 years ago. These were repeatedly referred to as 'hobbits', and not without reason: they were closely related to *Homo sapiens*, like Tolkien's hobbits, and may even have been enshrined in the legends of the present inhabitants of Flores, which mention little people called *Ebu Gogo*. (The species has now been named *Homo floresiensis*.) Tolkien might well have been amused that his fiction of a hidden halfling race related to human beings could turn out to have some basis in reality.

✦ kingsfoil ✦

In an amusing exchange (*LR* v. viii), Aragorn asks Ioreth, one of the women in the Houses of Healing, for leaves of the plant *athelas* (in Quenya, 'the Valinorean tongue', called *asëa aranion*) and when she professes ignorance, he tells her, 'It is also called kingsfoil.' This leads her to reminisce: "'Kingsfoil", I said, "'tis a strange name, and I wonder why 'tis called so; for if I were a king, I would have plants more bright in my garden."'

It sounds like an authentic plant name, because Tolkien has based the formation on existing English types: *bifoil* or *dufoil* is twayblade, *caprifoil* is honeysuckle, *cinquefoil* is potentilla, *milfoil* is yarrow, *rockfoil* is saxifrage, and *trefoil* is a kind of small clover, as well as a name for many kinds of three-leaved plant. The *-foil* element simply means 'leaf' (from Latin *folium*). 'Only the leaf of *asëa* was valued,' Tolkien notes ('Guide to the Names in *LR*'). There are not many traditional English plant names involving kings, but some kinds of clover or melilot were known to medieval writers as *king's clover* or *king's crown*, and the name *kyngeswort* is identified (perhaps inaccurately) by a 14th-century glossary as belonging to the herb sweet marjoram. The herb basil also has a kingly connection, taking its name from the Greek *basilikon*, meaning 'royal'.

❧ legendarium ❧

This legendarium [i.e. the 'Silmarillion'] ends with a vision of the end of the world, its breaking and remaking, and the recovery of the Silmarilli and the 'light before the Sun'.
(*Lett.* 131, to Milton Waldman, 1951)

The adjective *legendary* is familiar to most people, but there is also a noun with the same spelling, the oldest sense of which is defined in the *OED* as 'a…collection of legends, esp. of lives of saints', with quotations dating from 1513 onwards. This derives from a medieval Latin word *legendarium* with the same meaning. Such collections of saints' lives circulated widely throughout Christendom during the

Middle Ages, both in Latin and in various European vernaculars; some of them are important Middle English texts, such as the *South English Legendary* (which is quoted in the article on **Mannish and Man**). Tolkien was no doubt reminded of these collections when he was trying to find a suitably all-embracing word to describe the totality of his imaginative writings relating to Middle-earth. But *legendary* itself would not quite do, as it usually denoted a physical object; nor would *mythology*, as many of his writings were too 'historical' to be described as myths. In the end he settled on *legendarium*, a word which, although not yet recorded in the *OED*, was current in various other European languages, and has been occasionally used by some English writers since the early 20th century in preference to *legendary*. Tolkien's use of the word has so far only found application in discussion of his own writing—an indication of the uniqueness of his imaginative achievement.

⟡ lockholes ⟡

The hobbit version of 'lock-up (house)'. ('Guide to the Names in *LR*')

The lockholes are the Shire equivalent of prison. In early drafts of 'The Scouring of the Shire' (*LR* vi. viii) it sounds as if the Lockholes had existed before Saruman's ruffians took over the Shire ('they've made the old Lock-holes into a regular fort'); but in the final text Farmer Cotton says 'there's the Lockholes, as they call them: the old storage-tunnels at Michel Delving that they've made into prisons'.

In the late 16th century, both *lock-hole* and *key-hole* were introduced as terms for the hole into which a key is inserted, but it was 'keyhole' that became standard, and *lockhole* was available for Tolkien to adapt. The new meaning is his own creation, but it makes perfect sense. The word is respectably old, it is reminiscent of *lock-up* (a word that would be too modern to use, being recorded only from the early 19th century), and it is well-grounded historically, given that *hole* can mean 'dungeon or prison-cell' (*OED*: HOLE *n.*[1], sense 2b, first recorded in 1535)—and, of course, among hobbits a *hole* is the equivalent of a building among the 'Big Folk'.

✤ maid-child ✤

'Half the maidchildren of the Shire are called by such names,' says Frodo (*LR* VI. ix), and his comment is quoted as the most recent example of the word in *OED Online*. It is a shortening (dating from the 13th century) of *maiden-child* (dating from Old English), as *maid* is a shortening of *maiden*, and it means, of course, a female child. Its original male equivalent was *knave-child*, later replaced by *man-child*, which subsequently gave rise to the parallel modern term *woman-child*. More common in contemporary English is *girl-child*, recorded in the *OED* from 1886.

✤ malefit ✤

English is full of 'unmatched pairs': the form of many common words implies the existence of an opposite which is far less common, if indeed it occurs at all. These implied antonyms can be used for comic effect: the word *gruntled*, for example, was coined by P. G. Wodehouse in opposition to *disgruntled*. In some cases the idea of coining a particular 'missing' antonym may occur independently to several writers; this seems to have happened with *malefit*, which Tolkien uses in 'The Notion Club Papers' ('Made for the Malefit of Men': *HME* IX. 217), almost certainly unaware of the fact that the word had appeared in an actress's memoirs of 1755 (*A Narrative of the Life of Mrs Charlotte Charke*). Tolkien could not have found the word in the *OED*, as an entry has only recently (2000) been published. Nor does it seem likely that Philip Howard—the next person recorded in the *OED* entry as having used the word—would have encountered either of these earlier uses. The word is relatively unusual among Tolkien's coinages in being derived from Romance rather than Germanic elements—the starting point being the word *benefit*, with *ben-* (deriving ultimately from Latin *bene* 'well') being replaced by *mal-* 'badly'; but the Notion Club Papers contain a fair smattering of such unusual Latinate words, including *bibliopoly* for bookselling (the 'School of Bibliopoly': *HME* IX. 156) and *longeval* for 'long-lived' (p. 198); these are not coinages of Tolkien's, but are certainly unusual enough to impart something slightly 'other-worldly' to the milieu of Arry Lowdham and his companions.

The analogous but slightly less rare word *maleficial*, which Tolkien uses in the same passage, was used in the 17th century but then fell out of use. Jeremy Bentham re-coined it in his *Essay on Language*, but it has not caught on, though interestingly it was used by E. R. Eddison in *The Worm Ouroboros* (1922).

✦ Mannish and Man ✦

But the native speech of the Númenóreans remained for the most part their ancestral Mannish tongue, the Adûnaic. (*LR*, Appendix F)

Tolkien's use of the word here is not the usual modern sense 're-sembling a male human being', but the archaic sense 'of, relating to, or characteristic of the human species; human' (*OED Online*: MAN-NISH *a.*, sense 1). Originally in Old English this adjective had the form *mennisc* (with the same change of vowel from *man* that is seen in *English* from *Angle* and *French* from *Frank*); but in early Middle English, under the influence of the parent word *man*, it changed to *mannish*. For example, around 1300 a collection of saints' lives, the *South English Legendary*, says of St Mary of Egypt: *Heo ne et no mannische mete bot weodes and wilde more* (she ate no human food but weeds and wild roots); and John Gower, in the 14th century, describes a statue as *Most lich to mannyssh creature; Bot as of beaute hevenlich* (most like to a human creature, but heavenly in beauty).

When referring to human beings as a race in contrast to hobbits, elves, dwarves, or other beings, Tolkien generally uses *Men* with a capital initial. For example, in 'Concerning Hobbits' (*LR*, Prologue) he writes: 'This art [i.e. that of disappearing swiftly and silently] they have developed until to Men it may seem magical.' He even uses *Man* in the singular when the contrast is important: 'He [Frodo] stepped quickly away, and eyed with alarm the tall Man, nearly twice his height' (*LR* II. x).

Mannish is used by Tolkien as the adjective corresponding to this use of *Man* in *LR*, Appendix F: e.g. 'the *Westron* was a Man-nish speech'. In the draft *Appendix on Languages* which preceded this Appendix, Tolkien wrote: 'We have in these histories to deal with both Elvish and Mannish tongues': *Mannish* here replaces the previously written word 'human'. Commenting on this, Christopher Tolkien writes: 'So far as I have been able to discover, my father never used the adjective "Mannish", whether of language or tradition, before its occurrence in this work. The change of "Human" to "Mannish"…therefore marks the entry of this term' (*HME* XII. 61).

Mannish is the appropriate ethnic adjective corresponding to *Man* in this contrastive sense. 'Human' would not have been so suitable, in view of its connotations and its habitual contrast with 'animal'; besides, it has Latin roots, whereas *Mannish* is Germanic, and so fits with the early English atmosphere that Tolkien strove to create. *Mannish* fits neatly into a sequence of other 'ethnic' adjectives in Tolkien's work, *dwarvish, elvish, entish, and orkish*. The suffix *-ish* now usually has the sense 'somewhat, tending towards (whatever the first element means)', but in Old English it more commonly bore the specific sense it has in these words, 'belonging to the people denoted by (the first element)', as in *Scottish* and *Danish*.

✦ march and Mark ✦

The principal sense of the Old English word *mearc* (*OED Online*: MARK *n.*[1]) was 'a boundary, a frontier, a limit' (this became obsolete in the 16th century, though it was revived in the 19th century); it could also mean 'district'. Old High German *marca* had similar uses, and modern German *Mark* means 'border country', especially in the names of particular territories, such as the *Mark of Brandenburg* in eastern Germany. The corresponding Old Norse *mörk* meant 'a forest, especially one forming a boundary', but could also mean 'land' as the second part of a compound, as in *Danmörk* 'Denmark'. In William Morris's *The House of the Wolfings* (1889), a romantic tale of the war between the Goths and the Romans, the parts of

Mirkwood inhabited by the Goths are known by them as the Mark and they call themselves the Mark-men.

All these uses in related Germanic languages underlie Tolkien's adoption of the word as the name of the country of the Rohirrim, the **Mark**, which is situated on the northern border of Gondor and defends it. Its fuller name *Riddermark* is a modernization of Old English *riddena-mearc* ('land of the knights', as the Index to *The Lord of the Rings* puts it, *riddena* being the genitive plural of *ridda* 'a rider'). Tolkien's use is cited among other archaic or historical examples in *OED Online* (MARK *n.*¹, sense 2).

The word **march** (*OED Online*: MARCH *n.*³) is borrowed from Anglo-Norman and Old French *marche* 'border, border territory', which is itself a borrowing into French of the same Germanic word from which *mark* is derived. It is especially used in the plural to refer to the part of England bordering on Wales. It is otherwise rarely encountered, except when used to mean a territory as an equivalent to *mark* in place names (e.g. in the *March of Brandenburg*). When used in the *March of Wales*, the *OED* says, it represents the post-classical Latin name *Mercia*, which comes from the Old English name of the inhabitants of the area, *Merce*, which in turn comes from the word *mearc* (*mark*). Tolkien always counted himself a native of this region and had a special love for its language, especially as used in certain Middle English texts (see **dingle and dern**). Writing of this dialect in his Preface to M. B. Salu's translation of *Ancrene Riwle* (1955), he says that 'the soil in which it grew was that of the West Midlands and the Marches of Wales'. Tolkien's affection for the western borderlands is surely displayed in the name *Westmarch*, given by the hobbits to the region between the Far Downs and the Tower Hills, added to the Shire in SR 1452, and so borne by the Red Book of Westmarch, in which the whole tale of the end of the Third Age is supposed to have been preserved.

OED Online lists the compound *march-ward* 'a person appointed to guard or administer the marches', suggesting that it is modelled on Old English *mearc-weard*, though oddly this is only recorded as a poetic metaphor (kenning) for 'wolf'. The example given is from Tolkien: 'Thingol...sent Mablung after her, with many hardy march-wards, to find her and guard her' (*Silmarillion*, ch. xxi). The only earlier occurrence mentioned is an entry in *Webster's American Dictionary* of 1864, but on what evidence that entry was based is not known. Tolkien also refers to 'the ancient halls of the Mark-wardens mist-enshrouded' in the alliterative account of the eastward ride of the Rohirrim (*LR* v. iii).

✦ Marish ✦

The Marish is a low-lying marshy area in the east of the Shire, beside the Brandywine River. *Marish* is not strictly a proper name, but just a common noun familiarly applied to a district, and Tolkien's use is quoted as an example in *OED Online*:

> The folk of the Marish and their offshoot across the Brandywine were
> in many ways peculiar, as has been told. (*LR*, Appendix F)

The word goes back to about 1327 in English, and is based on an Anglo-Norman and Old French form which is ultimately derived from the same Germanic root as *marsh*. It is frequently used in English literature as a synonym of *marsh*, having the convenience for verse of having two syllables, which also gave it (in our ancestors' opinion) greater dignity. The Authorized Version of the Bible (1611) uses it in Ezekiel 47:11: 'the myrie [i.e. miry] places therof, and the marishes therof, shall not be healed'. The *OED* quotes a report from *The Times* as late as 1880 that 'In the carrs and marishes [of York-shire] both corn and turnips are under water'. (The plural form *Marishes* survives today as a place name in North Yorkshire.) It has a more specialized, toponymic ring than plain 'marsh', which is per-haps why Tolkien borrowed it to use as a Shire name.

✦ mathom ✦

Anything that hobbits had no immediate use for, but were unwilling to throw away, they called a *mathom*. (*LR*, Prologue)   *hoarding?*

Tolkien deliberately revived this word, which was common in Old English in the forms *maþm, maþum, maþþum,* or *madm,* and meant 'something valuable, an item of treasure'. It descends from a com-mon Germanic word probably meaning 'something exchanged' or 'gift', as does the related word *maiþms* in the earliest recorded Germanic language, that of the 4th-century Goths. The 1st-century Roman writer Tacitus, describing the Germanic nations, tells how war-chiefs constantly made gifts of horses or spears to secure their retainers' loyalty, and how gifts were exchanged between neighbour-ing communities: 'choice horses, splendid arms, metal discs, and collars'. The giving of gifts was the social cement of the period.

Old English poets celebrated an aristocratic society which still retained this and other customs of their continental Germanic ancestors. The *OED*'s quotations illustrate this tradition: the author of *Beowulf,* describing the funeral of an ancient king, says *him on bearme læg madma mænigo* (in his bosom lay a multitude of treas-ures). The *Old English Chronicle* for 1110 says that the king of England sent his daughter to marry the Emperor of Germany

mid mænigfealdan madman (with manifold treasures). The word
was also used in Christian contexts: each of the Three Kings,
according to the *Ormulum* (c. 1200), opens *hiss hord off hise
madmess* (his hoard of treasures). The word is last attested in
works of the 13th century that look back to the Anglo-Saxon world.

'The word was playfully revived in a slightly different sense by
J. R. R. Tolkien,' observes *OED Online*. Tolkien brought it down in
the world, for among the hobbits it denotes a piece of bric-a-brac,
something that is only subjectively a treasure because you don't
want to part with it, although at the same time it is clear that
the giving of presents, many of which were probably mathoms,
was a highly important part of hobbit life. He also modernized
the Old English word *maþmhus* 'a treasury' as the *mathom-
house*, a museum where some of the Shire's antiquities are displayed.
This fits the cultural framework of Tolkien's story very well. The
warriors of Rohan, whose society bears many resemblances to that
of the Anglo-Saxons, share a number of words with the hobbits,
mathom included (we are told in the Prologue); but the latter are
peace-loving rather than heroic, middle-class rather than aristocratic. The adaptation of the word into a worn-down modern English form with a domestic sense mirrors the cultural status of the
Shire with gentle humour.

✣ Middle-earth ✣

> Hobbits had, in fact, lived quietly in Middle-earth for many long
> years before other folk became even aware of them. (*LR*, Prologue)

Middle-earth means 'the world regarded as a middle region between
heaven and hell, or as occupying the centre of the universe' (*OED*

Online: MIDDLE EARTH *n.*, sense 1). It is not an invention of Tolkien's, and he did not intend it to convey the idea of an imaginary or other world. On this he insisted more than once:

> Middle-earth is not an imaginary world. The name is the modern form (appearing in the 13th century and still in use) of…an ancient name for the *oikoumenē*, the abiding place of Men, the objectively real world, in use specifically opposed to imaginary worlds (as Fairyland) or unseen worlds (as Heaven or Hell). The theatre of my tale is this earth…but the historical period is imaginary. (*Lett.* 183)

> Middle because thought of vaguely as set amidst the encircling Seas and (in the northern-imagination) between ice of the North and the fire of the South. (*Lett.* 211)

The compound has a long history and prehistory. It is a Germanic formation, found in the oldest Germanic language, Gothic (recorded in the 4th century) in the form *midjun-gards*, the first element being related to English *mid*, and the second element ultimately the same word as *yard* (i.e. an enclosed space in which beings dwell), the whole therefore meaning 'the middle enclosed region'. An equivalent word appears in Old Norse cosmography in the form *Miðgarðr* (*OED*: MIDGARD *n.*). This refers to the world of human beings, surrounded by the sea, one of a number of distinct regions of the universe, including *Ásgarðr* the dwelling of the gods (*Ás* means a god) and *Jötunheimr* the home of the giants.

This Germanic word appears in Old English (recorded c. 8th–12th century) in the form *middangeard*, which was the ordinary word for 'the earth on which we live'. It occurs, for instance, in one of the oldest English poems, *Cædmon's Hymn*, with reference to God's creation of the world. By the 12th century its form had changed, with the loss of the *g* (pronounced as *y*), to *middenerd* (*OED*:

MIDDENERD *n.*). The first part of the compound having now become unfamiliar, it was remodelled as *middle-erd*, the second element of which was understood as the word *erd*, meaning 'region' (*OED*: MIDDLE-ERD *n.*). But the word *erd* became unfamiliar in its turn and was replaced, around 1300, by the familiar word *earth*, giving the compound *middle-earth*.

The word was formerly common, as the quotations in the *OED* show. Shakespeare has 'I smell a man of middle earth' in *The Merry Wives of Windsor*; Sir Walter Scott (by whose day it was probably an archaic or poetical word) has 'That maid is born of middle earth, And may of man be won' (from *The Bridal of Triermain*, 1813); and interestingly, E. R. Eddison, in his fantasy novel *The Worm Ouroboros* (1922), has 'At length when winter was gone in middle earth, and the spring far spent, back came that last little martlet.'

In Tolkien's early writings, the lands east of the Great Sea are called the *Great Lands*, the *Hither Lands*, or the *Outer Lands* (though the latter in some writings, confusingly, can mean the lands beyond the Western Sea). Tolkien's earliest poem about Eärendel, written in 1914, does refer to 'the mid-world's rim' (*HME* II. 268), but the term *Middle-earth* is never used in *The Book of Lost Tales* (*HME* I and II) and does not appear in *The Hobbit*; it seems to have been adopted in the writings of the later 1930s published in *HME* V (the Old English *middangeard* is found already in Tolkien's Old English version of the 'Earliest Annals of Valinor'). It then became established as the normal term in *The Lord of the Rings*. In the earlier version of 'The Shadow of the Past' (*LR* I. ii) 'the middle-world' appears several times, but is once changed to 'the middle-earth'. Perhaps by an oversight, 'the Great Lands' survives from the earlier draft in Faramir's exposition of the history of Gondor (*LR* IV. v) in one place, but in another is replaced by *Middle-earth*.

✦ Mirkwood ✦

West lies Mirkwood the Great. There are Spiders.
(Thror's Map, endpaper to *The Hobbit*)

Mirkwood is the name of the vast forest to the east of the Misty Mountains, introduced in *The Hobbit*. As a proper name, it is not found in the *OED*, but its constituent elements are *wood* (of course) and the less familiar word *mirk*, which is a way of spelling *murk* (*OED*: MURK *n.*[1] and *a.*[1]) 'dark', 'darkness'. The compound therefore literally means 'dark or murky wood'. The name is also applied to the even more terrible forest Taur-na-Fuin in the 'Quenta Silmarillion' (*HME* V. 282), which dates from the same period as *The Hobbit*. And Tolkien invented an Old English equivalent *Myrcwudu*, which occurs in the poem *King Sheave*.

The word is not pure invention. It is a calque—an expression formed by translating the elements of a foreign expression into elements of one's own language that are as close as possible to them. It is modelled on Old Norse *Myrkviðr*, the name of the eastern European forest in Norse legend in which some of the epic battles take place and 'which divides the land of the Huns from the land of the Goths', according to one Old Norse poem (the Goths and Huns being the antagonists in these epics). In Old Norse, *myrk* is the equivalent (and cognate) of *mirk* and *viðr* of *wood*.

It was not Tolkien himself who first adapted *Mirkwood* from the Old Norse word. William Morris's *The House of the Wolfings* (1889) is set in *Mirkwood*, where the settlements of the Goths stand in forest clearings, rather like those of the Woodmen of Mirkwood in *The Lord of the Rings* or the earlier Woodmen of Brethil in *The Silmarillion*.

welsh poet Dylan Thomas [handwritten annotation]

✦ mithril ✦

> Here alone in the world was found Moria-silver, or true-silver as
> some have called it: *mithril* is the Elvish name... The beauty of *mithril*
> did not tarnish or grow dim. (*LR* II. iv)

Mithril is the first Elvish word to have entered the *Oxford English
Dictionary*: an entry appeared in Volume II (H–N) of the *Supplement to the OED* (1976) with the succinct definition 'Name given by
J. R. R. Tolkien to a mythical precious metal' and two examples from
The Lord of the Rings. The *OED Online* entry (version released June
2002) adds an earlier instance of the word, from a letter of 29
November 1944, and notes that although Bilbo's corslet of mithril
appears in *The Hobbit* (chapter xiii), the word was coined only during the composition of *The Lord of the Rings*, and then added to the
revised third edition of *The Hobbit* (1966); earlier editions called it
'silvered steel'. Its Elvish etymology is from *mith* 'grey' + *ril* 'bril-
liance'.

The name *true-silver* means 'silver properly so called, real silver'
(*OED*: TRUE *a.*, sense 5). The form of this word recalls *quicksilver* (in
which *quick* means 'alive'), and also recalls an earlier candidate for
the Elvish name (*HME* VI. 465), *Erceleb*, in which the element *-celeb*
means 'silver'.

Very few words from invented languages ever achieve sufficient
use outside their original context to be recorded in the *OED*, but one
rather striking parallel to *mithril* exists in the word *vril*. In Edward
Bulwer-Lytton's early science fiction novel *The Coming Race* (1871)
the strange beings living beneath the surface of the earth are said to
have discovered a mysterious power source which they call *vril*.
Lytton's novel was popular enough for *vril* to be mentioned from
time to time in other contexts (the *OED* gives an example from the

Pall Mall Gazette of 1888), but it has now rather faded from view—except as the inspiration for the trade name *Bovril*. The similarity of *Thilevril*, another candidate briefly considered by Tolkien as a name for mithril (*HME* VII. 184), is surely no more than coincidence.

✴ moot ✴

> 'Hoo, eh? Entmoot?' said Treebeard… 'It is not a place, it is a gathering of Ents—which does not often happen nowadays.'
> (*LR* III. iv)

The word *moot* principally means 'a meeting, an assembly of people, especially for legislative or judicial purposes' (*OED Online*: MOOT *n.*[1], sense 1): it is related to the verb *meet*. As *OED Online* notes, although this word has undergone a partial revival since the 19th century—including a specific sense in law (sense 4: 'the discussion of a hypothetical case by law students for practice')—it had become an archaism after the medieval period. In fact it was often used just as a learned term in legal history, written *mote*, reflecting the Old English form *mot* and the Middle English form *mote*. In such cases it was often the second part of a compound, the first part showing the kind of 'moot' it was: e.g. *borough-moot*, *hallmote*, *hundred-mote*, *portmote*, *wardmote*. The *folkmoot* (or *folkmote*), in particular, was an assembly of the community going back to ancient times, at which both legislative and judicial proceedings took place. The holding of a folkmoot is vividly imagined in Tolkien's story 'The Wanderings of Húrin' (*HME* XI. 281): 'The next day it was proclaimed that the Folkmoot for Judgement should be held on the following morning, for already five hundred of the headmen had come in, and that was by custom deemed the least number which might count as a full meeting of the Folk.' A similar scene is described in chapter vii of William Morris's *The House of the Wolfings*, entitled 'The folk-mote of the Mark-men'.

This kind of compound is imitated in Tolkien's word *entmoot*, the great gathering of ents at which the decision is (very gradually) taken to destroy Isengard. Many members of the Tolkien Society are also familiar with the considerably livelier event known as 'Oxonmoot'—the Society's annual gathering in Oxford.

✥ morrow ✥

Through halls of iron and darkling door,
And woods of nightshade morrowless. (*LR* I. ix)

Morrow is familiar to most people as meaning 'the day after this one', but its earlier sense was 'morning', in use from Old English to the 16th century and revived as an archaism in the 19th century. The Old English form was *morgen*, which split into two forms: one kept the -*n* but was contracted into *morn*, from which *morning* was formed, and one developed into the Middle English form *morwen*, then lost the -*n*, and finally became *morrow*. From the latter Tolkien formed *morrowdim* (*LR* Appendices)—a noteworthy compound because *dim* is not usually a noun—and *morrowless*, which had previously been used to mean 'having no tomorrows', but is also listed in the *OED* as meaning 'morningless', quoting Tolkien's verse.

There is also a passing reference in the 'Grey Annals' (*HME* XI. 84) to *morrowgift*—evidently Tolkien's preferred alternative, at least in this archaic context, to *morning gift* 'a gift traditionally given to a bride by her husband on the morning (or day) after their marriage' (*OED Online*: MORNING GIFT *n.*). The latter is one of three different variations on an original Old English word *morgengifu* which are covered in the *OED*, the others being *moryeve* (which seems to have fallen out of use in the 15th century) and *morwyngift* (recorded only in 16th-century Scots). Etymologically related words with the same meaning are found in other Germanic languages (e.g. German *Morgengabe*), indicating how widespread the custom was.

(See also **even**.)

❖ nasturtian ❖

The plant name *nasturtium* has a history stretching back to the classical world, and arrived in England with the writings of the early medieval herbalists; it is Latin in origin, and at first it referred to various plants with pungent-tasting leaves, particularly cress and watercress. In the late 16th century a plant with a similar taste was introduced into Europe from Peru, and was given the Latin name *Nasturtium Indicum*; a century later another Peruvian plant made the transatlantic journey. Both of these plants belong to the genus *Tropaeolum*, and it is these plants, with their showy orange flowers and peppery-tasting leaves, which are familiar to today's gardeners as nasturtiums.

There is a long tradition of referring to the plant by the Latin form of its name. However, Tolkien preferred to use the form *nasturtian*, regarding the change in spelling as 'a natural anglicization that started soon after [the plant] was naturalized (from Peru, I think) in the 18th century' (*Lett.* 148). He may well have taken this information from the *OED*, as the entry for *nasturtian* in the First Edition includes quotations from around 1740 onwards. In fact, *OED Online* now traces English spellings ending in *-n* as early as the

Grete Herball of 1526. In this important volume of plant lore, the writer used the name form *narsturcion* (in the older sense, for cress and watercress), seemingly combining the French spelling *nasturtion* (used in the text he was translating) with the medieval Latin spelling *narsturcium*.

'Nasturtians' were among the flowers to be found in Bilbo's garden in a passage drafted in the late 1930s (*HME* VI. 235) which eventually found its way into 'A Long-expected Party' (the passage is cited in the revised *OED Online* entry). Tolkien knew that his preferred spelling was 'a minority usage'; however, he was not pleased when this, and some of his other less common spellings in *The Fellowship of the Ring*, were changed without reference to him by a proofreader. Tolkien 'dug [his] toes in about *nasturtians*', and his spelling was restored. (Tolkien recounts this episode in 1954, in the letter already quoted, where he also criticizes *nasturtium* as 'bogusly botanical, and falsely learned'. He also recalls a conversation with the college gardener whom he consulted on the subject, who considered that *nasturtian* was the name for the garden flower, whereas *nasturtium* was still an alternative name for watercress.)

✦ ninnyhammer ✦

> You're nowt but a ninnyhammer, Sam Gamgee.
> (*LR* IV. i, as quoted in *OED Online*)

The word has a long history of use, beginning in the printed record with Thomas Nashe, a master of invective, in *Strange Newes* (1592). Lawrence Sterne, in *Tristram Shandy* (1767), classes ninnyhammers with 'numskuls, doddypoles, dunderheads…and other unsavory appellations'. It was probably a current colloquialism down to the late 19th century, the last example in the *OED* before Tolkien's being from 1879. More recently it has been taken up by Georgette Heyer as one of a range of slang terms used to impart 'period colour' to her historical novels, e.g. *The Toll-Gate* (1954). No one knows the full derivation: the first part is presumably *ninny* (although this word, on its own, is known only from a year later, 1593); the *hammer* may have something to do with the earlier opprobrious epithet *hammer-headed* 'stupid', which Nashe also used.

In an earlier draft, Sam refers to himself as 'numbpate and ninnyhammer' (*HME* VIII. 89); but *numbpate*—perhaps a variation on *numbskull*—is not in the *OED*.

Another insulting word for a foolish or stupid person is the 19th-century term *Tomnoddy*, which appears in Bilbo's taunting song to the spiders of Mirkwood in *The Hobbit*. Probably originating in regional dialect, it is simply made up of *Tom*, the personal name (as in *tomfool*), and *noddy*, also meaning a foolish person. /drunk

❖ north-away and south-away ❖

Tolkien is quoted by the *OED* for **north-away**: 'Going swiftly to lesser posts and strongholds north-away' (*LR* VI. ii). It is a spatial adverb which probably has its roots in regional dialect, though in fact many of the examples given in the *OED* (NORTH-AWAY *adv.*) are from literary sources: as meaning 'towards the north' (sense 1) it is cited from Defoe, Coleridge, and Browning, and as meaning 'in the north' (sense 2, the sense Tolkien uses here) from Walter Scott and William Morris. It is probably connected with a use of 'away' (*OED*: AWAY *adv.*, sense 10, used after 'where', 'here', and 'there') which goes back to the 16th century, but which by the

1880s was limited to Scottish dialect ('he lives here-away'). The phrase *up away*, not recorded in the *OED*, is found in 'Homeward Bound' (*LR* vi. vii): Barliman Butterbur lists 'Willie Banks from up-away' as one of the hobbits who have been 'killed, killed dead' in the recent troubles.

Tolkien is the only author recorded in the *OED* as using **south-away**: he seems to have liked the word and uses it several times:

> The folk of the Marish…came…up from south-away. (*LR*, Prologue)

> A lot of Men…came with great waggons, some to carry off the goods south-away, and others to stay. (*LR* vi. viii)

> South away! and South away!
> Seek the sunlight and the day.
> (*Hobbit*, ch. ix, as the Wood-elves are dispatching barrels into the river)

It did make an occasional appearance in the 19th century, mainly in the works of 'Celtic Revival' authors such as the Irish poet William Allingham (1824–89), and the *Scottish National Dictionary* records the Scots form *sooth awa* from Aberdeen in 1952.

There is also *east-away* ('east-away towards Doriath', in the 'Narn I Hîn Húrin': *Unfinished Tales* 117), not recorded in the *OED*, though it was used by E. R. Eddison in *The Worm Ouroboros* (1922).

✦ oliphaunt ✦

> I've heard tales of the big folk down away in the Sunlands. Swertings we call 'em in our tales; and they ride on oliphaunts, 'tis said, when they fight. They put houses and towers on the oliphauntses backs and all. (*LR* iv. iii, quoted in *OED Online*: OLIPHANT *n.*, sense 1a)

Thus says Sam Gamgee, who has recited 'the old fireside rhyme of *Oliphaunt*' to Frodo and Gollum; and who in the following chapter has his wish and sees a stampeding oliphaunt at close hand. The powerfully visualized scene echoes some of the medieval texts quoted in the *OED*; for example, from *Arthour and Merlin* (early 14th century): *Felled was king Rion standard And þe four olyfaunce yslawe, Baners and castels adoun yþrawe* (King Rion's standard was felled and the four elephants slain, banners and castles thrown down).

Of the spelling *oliphaunt*, Tolkien comments: 'It is an archaic form of "elephant" used as a "rusticism", on the supposition that rumour of the Southern beast would have reached the Shire long ago in the form of legend' ('Guide to the Names in *LR*'). A common medieval spelling, by the end of the 16th century it had been largely displaced by the modern form of the word. The initial *o-* has not been fully explained, but all the major European languages had similar forms during the Middle Ages (and in modern Dutch the word is still spelt *olifant*). As well as giving the 'rustic' feel that Tolkien mentions, it also imparts a suitably unfamiliar and legendary flavour to the modern reader, for whom the familiar word *elephant* may conjure up more comfortable images than that of the fierce and exotic *mûmak* (plural *mûmakil*), the war-elephant of the Haradrim.

Tolkien had used the word long before in one of his 'Adventures in Unnatural History and Medieval Metres, being the Freaks of Fisiologus' (published in *The Stapeldon Magazine* in June 1927). The first of these is ***Fastitocalon***, and the second is 'Iumbo, or ye Kinde of ye Oliphaunt': and here is another of Tolkien's playful anachronisms, setting into the context of a supposed medieval bestiary the name Jumbo, which originated with a London Zoo elephant of the 1880s!

❧ orc ❧

The Ring slipped from his finger as he swam, and then the Orcs saw him and killed him with arrows.

('The Shadow of the Past', *LR* I. ii)

He became visible to his enemies, and the goblins slew him.
(early draft of the same chapter: *HME* VI. 78)

The word *orc* appears only once in the first edition of *The Hobbit*, in the rather facetious, unheroic style so often used there: 'the slopes of the Grey Mountains…are simply stiff with goblins, hobgoblins, and orcs of the worst description' (ch. vii); the usual word there is **goblin**. However, in the published text of *The Lord of the Rings*, with its higher tone, the word *orc* is ubiquitous, as it is in all Tolkien's preceding legends, from *The Book of Lost Tales* onwards, as the term for a very specific, sharply visualized creature, the degraded and thoroughly nasty antagonist of humans, elves, and dwarves. Some early passages seem to imply that '"Orcs" are to be regarded as a more formidable kind of "Goblin"' (*HME* VI. 437).

The Old English word *orc* appears in *Beowulf* in the compound *orcneas*, which refers to evil spirits or walking corpses: *eotenas ond ylfe ond orcneas* (giants and elves and demons). It probably comes from the classical Latin *Orcus*, the name of the god of the underworld, but is so rarely attested in Old English literature that we can deduce little about how it got into English, to become the companion of such native Germanic words as *eotenas* and *ylfe*. (It is not the same word as *orc* meaning 'a cetacean or sea-monster', from Latin *orca*, which *OED Online* separates out as ORC *n.*[1]) Tolkien states clearly that 'the word is as far as I am concerned actually derived from Old English *orc* "demon", but only because of its phonetic suitability' (*Lett.* 144, 25 April 1954). The sense of the Old English word does not suit the orcs that Tolkien had in mind: 'In days of old they were strong and fell as demons. Yet they were not of demon kind' (*HME* X. 109).

As *OED Online* points out (ORC *n.*²), because there is no evidence for the word in Middle English or in the 16th century, it is unlikely that the Old English word *orc* survived. It is notable, then, that exactly the same word-form reappears with a similar meaning in 17th-century English, surfacing first in Sylvester's 1605 translation of Du Bartas's *Divine Weeks and Works.* Here it is probably a borrowing of Italian *orco* meaning 'man-eating giant, demon, monster', which also comes from Latin *Orcus.* In the earliest examples the *Orque* or *Orke* is a grotesque monster, able (in Sylvester) to devour numbers of creatures, or (in Samuel Holland's *Don Zara* of 1656) having several heads. Since Tolkien's orcs are ugly and violent, with hints that they eat human flesh, but not supernatural, his use of the word seems closer to that of Sylvester and Holland than to the Old English word which was his stimulus. By the 19th century, orcs were appearing in company with monsters of Germanic folklore, and in *Hereward the Wake* (1865) Charles Kingsley lists dragons, giants, and orcs as if all were equally familiar creatures of fable. By this date it seems likely that, with the rise of Anglo-Saxon studies, writers had become aware of the Old English word.

In *The Lord of the Rings* the corresponding adjective is *Orkish*, in accordance with English spelling rules, and in fact Tolkien later said that the word *orc* itself ought really to have been written *ork* (*HME* X. 422). (A rare published instance of the latter spelling occurs in the poem 'Bombadil Goes Boating' (*The Adventures of Tom Bombadil*): 'I'll call the orks on you: that'll send you running!') However, the adjective is fairly common in subsequent fantasy games and stories, but usually spelt *Orcish*, so this is the form at the head of the entry in *OED Online*.

❧ pipe-weed ❧

It was Tobold Hornblower, of Longbottom in the Southfarthing, who first grew the true pipe-weed in his gardens, about the year 1070 according to our reckoning. (*LR* III. viii)

Pipe-weed is the hobbits' name for tobacco. It is not a particularly old term, and the *OED* (Second Edition) illustrates it only from Tolkien, though subsequent research for *OED Online* has located examples as far back as an American magazine of 1792. *Weed* on its own has been used to mean 'tobacco' since 1606 (*OED*: WEED *n*.[1] 3a). In the earliest draft of the passage quoted above, Merry spoke of *weed* (as Gimli still does in the published text), but this was replaced by *pipe-weed* in a subsequent stage of rewriting (*HME* VI. 36–7). It is a natural-sounding compound of English words (resembling other old plant names ending in -*weed*), and is clearly more suited to hobbit-speech than the exotic Caribbean loanword *tobacco* (though this does appear in the more anachronistic text of *The Hobbit*). The similarly alien word *potato* sometimes appears in the English colloquial form *taters*, which helps to disguise the covert anachronism of a New World plant in a supposedly Old World setting (see also Shippey's *The Road to Middle-earth*, pp. 78–9).

❧ Precious ❧

Precious is a word with a long history in English before Tolkien made it his own (or Gollum's). It is most widely used as an adjective: the

OED's entry for the word traces it back to Middle English. But it is as a noun that it has become most strongly associated with Tolkien, and with the Ring: Gollum's use of the word immediately precedes the first appearance of the Ring in *The Hobbit*, and 'his last wail *Precious*' marks its destruction in the Cracks of Doom. (Gollum also uses 'precious' to refer to himself, but the Ring is distinguished as 'the Precious', with a capital letter.)

In fact its use as a noun, in the sense that Gollum uses it, also goes back a long way. As a term of endearment, similar to *dear* or *darling*, it is first recorded in the Elizabethan tragedy *Antonio and Mellida* by John Marston (c. 1575–1634): 'Nay, pretious, If youle be peeuish, by this light, Ile sweare Thou rail'dst vpon thy love.' Not that Tolkien would have known this from the *OED* entry as he saw it: the First Edition of the Dictionary gave as its first example a quotation from Susanna Centlivre's comedy *The Basset-Table* of 1706 ('With all my Heart, my Jewel, my Precious'). The example from Marston, only recently added to the *OED* database, extends the known history of this sense by over a century.

Tolkien also uses the adjective in its familiar sense 'valuable', and occasionally in an ironical sense, also recorded in the *OED*, when referring in a belittling or depreciative manner to things considered of little or no value—for example, when one of Saruman's ruffians asks Merry where 'those precious Shirriffs' have got to (*LR* VI. viii).

❧ Púkel-men ❧

There were great standing stones that had been carved in the likeness of men, huge and clumsy-limbed, squatting cross-legged with their

> stumpy arms folded on fat bellies,... The Púkel-men they [the Riders]
> called them. (*LR* v. iii)

> A Rohan name for the effigies of men of a vanished race. It represents
> Old English *púcel* (still surviving as *puckle*), one of the forms of the
> *puk-* stem (widespread in England, Wales, Ireland, Norway and
> Iceland) referring to a devil, or to a minor sprite such as Puck, and
> often applied to ugly misshapen persons. ('Guide to the Names in *LR*')

Tolkien respelt the word *Púkel* (*Pookel* in an earlier draft) in order to
avoid mistaken pronunciation of the Old English spelling *púcel*. The
modern English descendant of the Old English word, as Tolkien
says, is *puckle* (*OED*: PUCKLE *n.*[1]), listed with the fire-drake, hobgoblin, and other 'bugs' by Reginald Scott in his *Discoverie of Witchcraft* (1584). It is a derivative of *puck* (*OED*: PUCK *n.*[1]), which was
originally the name of a spirit so formidable that it was identified
with the devil, and only later became the 'tricksy sprite' of literature.

In an earlier draft, Tolkien experimented with the form *Hoker-
men* or *Hocker-men* (*HME* VIII. 245–6), the first part of which
probably represents a modernized form of the Old English word
hocor 'derision' (*OED*: HOKER *n.*).

✳ Quickbeam ✳

> I am Bregalad, that is Quickbeam in your language...They have
> called me that ever since I said *yes* to an elder Ent before he had
> finished his question. (*LR* III. iv)

The name *Quickbeam* is typical of Tolkien's linguistic puns. It
depends on two uses of *quick*, and possibly on two uses of *beam*.
On the surface, the name is a compound of *quick* in its familiar
sense 'distinguished by, or capable of, prompt or rapid action or

movement' (*OED*: QUICK *a*. III), appropriate to Quickbeam's hasty behaviour as a young Ent. This is also the purport of his Elvish name, in which *bre-* represents a root meaning 'sudden' or 'violent'. The second element of the Elvish name is *-galad*, which means 'light' (as in *Gil-galad*), implying that the second part of the English name is *beam* as in *sunbeam* ('a ray, or "bundle" of parallel rays, of light emitted from the sun or other luminous body' (*OED*: BEAM *n.*[1], sense 19a)).

However, on another level, the name is an adoption of an ancient English word for the mountain ash or rowan tree (*OED*: QUICKBEAM), the tree which Bregalad tells Merry and Pippin that he most loves. Here the second element is *beam* in the now archaic sense 'tree' (*OED*: BEAM *n.*[1] 1)—perhaps echoed in an Elvish half-pun on *galadh* 'tree'. The *OED* says that in the name of the tree 'the force of the adjective [*quick*] is not clear', but it probably involves the much older meaning 'characterized by the presence of life' (*OED*: QUICK *a*. I), as in 'the quick and the dead'.

✦ read and riddle ✦

Who will read this riddle for us? (Elrond, in *LR* II. ii)

This is not the ordinary sense of *read*—'to look over or scan (something written, printed, etc.) with understanding of what is meant by the letters and signs' (*OED*: READ *v.*, sense 5a)—but the more specific sense 'to make out or discover the meaning or significance of (a dream, riddle, etc.)' (*OED*: READ *v.*, sense 2a: e.g. 'Then by my word,...the riddle is already read', Sir Walter Scott, *Lady of the Lake*, 1810). The verb *read* probably meant 'to interpret, discover the meaning of' before it was narrowed down to the familiar meaning 'to interpret written characters'.

The expression *read a riddle* was originally the same kind of construction as *sing a song*, for *riddle* (*OED*: RIDDLE *n.*[1]) and *read* come from the same root. One can see this more clearly from their Old English ancestors *rædels* (*ræd-* + noun suffix *-els*) and *rædan* (*ræd-* + verb infinitive suffix *-an*). Another expression of this kind appears close by in the narrative: 'What shall we do with the Ring…? That is the doom that we must deem' (*LR* II. ii). Here the chime is between the related words *doom* (*OED*: DOOM *n.*, sense 2: 'judgement or decision, especially one formally pronounced') and *deem* (*OED*: DEEM *v.*, sense 4: 'to decide'). The *OED* quotes a similar medieval example from Laȝamon: *He hæhte alle cnihtes demen rihte domes* (he commanded all knights to make right determinations).

The only example which the *OED* gives for *riddle-game* (*OED*: RIDDLE *n.*[1]) is from the Prologue to *The Lord of the Rings*: 'Gollum challenged Bilbo to the Riddle-game'. This, of course, refers back to the riddle-game recounted in *The Hobbit*. The game is there presented as something 'sacred and of immense antiquity' which had 'ancient laws' attaching to it. The nine riddles exchanged are more formal and enigmatic than the modern humorous riddle: they are descriptions of something expressed in a way that makes it sound like something else, or nothing recognizable at all, the meaning of which must be worked out. Riddles of this kind are found in the Old English Exeter Book (late 10th century); their forerunners are Latin riddles, which were popular from the 5th century onwards in Europe (and of which several collections from 8th-century England have survived), and before that, a tradition of riddle-making which stretches back to the Sphinx of the ancient world and beyond. Riddles are a well-established feature of folk tales and fairy literature, as some other quotations in the *OED* testify. F. J. Child, in his collection *English and Scottish Popular Ballads* (1882), writes 'riddle-craft is practised by a variety of preternatural beings', and in discussing ballads from the same collection, M. J. C. Hodgart writes: 'The basic theme of these is that of a mortal outwitting a supernatural being by quickness of wit, and of the magic power of the Word expounded in riddles' (*Ballads*, 1950). Gollum is not strictly a 'preternatural being', yet the situation referred to is very close to that vividly realized in *The Hobbit*. (Unsurprisingly, Tolkien was not the first to use the compound *riddle-game*: the *OED*'s files include a recently discovered example from 1901.)

✤ ruel-bone ✤

When he was writing 'Of Tuor and his Coming to Gondolin', Tolkien jotted down (in some brief notes about how the story was to go on, *Unfinished Tales* 56) that Turgon bore a sword in a sheath of ruel-bone. The word is also used in the 'Lay of Leithian' (*HME* III. 236: 'teeth [of the hounds of Valinor] like ruel-bone'), and many years later his poem 'The Sea-Bell' (included in *The Adventures of Tom Bombadil*) mentioned 'cliffs of stone pale as ruel-bone'. The *OED* records *ruel-bone* as an obsolete word meaning 'ivory (possibly that of the narwhal)', with quotations entirely confined to the Middle English period; it also records the simple word *ruel* as a synonym. Tolkien could of course have picked up the word from any of the Middle English sources which use it; but it is surely significant that the *OED* entry for *ruel* is cited in the etymology of WALRUS—the drafting and redrafting of which had occupied Tolkien for so long (see p. 23). The etymological discussion notes that in Old French *rohal* (or *rochal*) meant 'walrus-ivory'. (In fact in the *Middle English Dictionary*'s entry for *rouel*, also spelt *ruel*, the word is defined as 'walrus-ivory', with no mention of the narwhal.) Tolkien's use of the word evidently arose directly out of his work on the *OED*—even though it does not begin with W. Whether his interest in this word was heightened by its coincidental similarity to his unusual given name 'Reuel' (from the Hebrew Bible) we can only speculate.

✦ rune ✦

> A king he was on carven throne
> In many-pillared halls of stone
> With golden roof and silver floor,
> And runes of power upon the door.
> (Gimli's song in Moria, *LR* ii. iv)

'A letter or character of the earliest Teutonic alphabet, which was most extensively used (in various forms) by the Scandinavians and Anglo-Saxons' (*OED*: RUNE *n.*², sense 1; linguists would now say 'Germanic' rather than 'Teutonic'). The Germanic runic alphabet originally had 24 letters: in England this was expanded to at least 28, whereas in Scandinavia the number was eventually reduced to sixteen. Use of runes began in about the 3rd century and continued in some places until the 12th century or so. They were sometimes arranged into sets of six letters; the first set contained the runes standing for F, U, TH (Þ), A or O, R, and K, and hence the alphabet is sometimes known as the Futhark or Futhorc (*OED*: FUTHORC).

In *The Hobbit*, Tolkien used the Germanic runic alphabet with the Anglo-Saxon or Old English values of the symbols. They occur principally on Thror's Map but are also used to decorate the title pages and covers. In the preliminary note Tolkien explains that the Dwarves' runes 'are in this book represented by English runes': in other words, the runes we see in *The Hobbit* are supposed to be transliterated from the runes actually used in Middle-earth. (And presumably also, the language on Thror's Map would not really have been English, but the Common Speech or Westron of Middle-earth.) 'The runes (Anglo-Saxon) and the dwarf-names (Icelandic), neither used with antiquarian accuracy, and both regretfully substituted to avoid abstruseness for the genuine alphabets and names of the mythology into which Mr Baggins intrudes' (*Lett.* 15, 31 August 1937).

'On the slab runes were deeply graven' (*LR* II. v). These are the runes inscribed on Balin's tomb in Moria, and it was at this point in the early draft of the book that Tolkien decided 'to abandon the Old English (or "Hobbit") runes and to use the real runes of Beleriand' (*HME* VI. 467, note 40). Memorably Tolkien provided an illustration showing the tomb inscription. These runes, consisting entirely of vertical and oblique strokes, are very similar to the Germanic runes, but they quite clearly have different values. The first word of the tomb inscription reads BALIN, but if the symbols were taken with their Germanic meanings it would read RUNIX. The full details of this alphabet, called in Elvish *Certar* or *Cirth*, are given in Appendix E of *The Lord of the Rings*. An important feature is that (as in the Elvish or Fëanorian letters) the shapes are related to each other phonetically: the sign for B reversed makes V, without its 'leg' makes P, the latter reversed makes F, and so on. By contrast, Germanic runes are arbitrary, like the Roman alphabet.

It is partly owing to Tolkien's application of the word to an alphabet similar to the Germanic Futhorc but with additional shapes and different values that the following was added to the original *OED* entry for RUNE in the Second Edition: 'Also, a similar character or mark having mysterious or magical powers attributed to it; applied to a letter or character of a non-Germanic alphabet (esp. in fictional writings) having a resemblance to the Germanic runes.' Supporting quotations, referring to Tolkien's invented runes, the *Cirth*, are given from *The Lord of the Rings* and *The Silmarillion*, as well as his use (in Appendix E of *LR*) of the technical term *rune-row*, originally applied in 1868 to the Germanic runes. Other alphabets adapted for carving on stone and wood, and therefore having similar shapes, have also been called runes, notably one found in inscriptions in Orkhon, Siberia and used for writing an ancient form of Turkic, but Tolkien's rather subtle extension of the term is the best known.

The fascination of runes lies partly in the magical powers attributed to them. In ancient Germanic times runic inscriptions seem to have been used in magical ceremonies and to confer power upon objects. They appeal because they seem like a secret code: and indeed, the etymological meaning of *rune* is 'secret'. In Old and early Middle English, *run* could mean 'a secret or mystery' or 'a secret consultation or counsel' (*OED*: ROUN; a Middle English example is quoted in the article on **dingle and dern**). The word died out in later Middle English, and *rune* was borrowed anew from Scandinavian languages in the 16th century.

Tolkien's influence was partly (perhaps largely) responsible for the appearance of runes in many other works of fantasy, such as the *Earthsea* trilogy by Ursula Le Guin (also quoted in the *OED* entry for the word); and this widespread fictional use may well have helped to fuel interest in runes as a popular medium of fortune-telling.

❧ Shirriff ❧

Shirriff, the hobbits' term for a member of their 'police', is listed in the *OED* as an obsolete spelling of the word SHERIFF. This is a compound of the two words *shire* and *reeve*. A reeve, in Anglo-Saxon times, was an official responsible for local government, so *sheriff* means 'shire (or county) official'—in many cases a relatively powerful office, and not, as among the hobbits, one of twelve humble folk concerned mainly with straying animals. The word has had literally dozens of slightly differing spellings through history, partly as a result of varying pronunciation. Tolkien used one in which the *-i-* of the parent word *shire* still remains, and said himself ('Guide to the Names in *LR*') that he did so primarily because it makes plain the link between the word and the name of the Shire. It also represents an earlier stage in the word's development, and therefore appears archaic. The second part of the word retains the familiar spelling, but the alteration of the first part prevents the reader from forming too many inappropriate associations, either of the gun-toting sheriffs of the cinema Western or of the quaint ceremonial of the English town hall.

Along similar lines, Tolkien briefly considered giving to the office of **Thain** the name of *Shirking* ('shire-king'). However, despite the tempting hobbitish puns which would have been possible, he thought better of it (*HME* XII. 5–6).

❧ sigaldry and glamoury ❧

Now was he Morgoth's mightiest lord
...and foul enchantments and dark sigaldry

did weave and wield. In glamoury
that necromancer held his hosts
of phantoms and of wandering ghosts.
('Lay of Leithian', lines 2069–75, describing Thû
(later called Sauron), *HME* III. 228)

Sigaldry, meaning 'enchantment, sorcery', is recorded only in Middle English texts until its revival by Tolkien. Although it looks as if it might be French in origin, it is in fact derived from the Old English word *sigalder*, meaning 'a charm or incantation'. The Old English roots of the word are *sige* 'victory in battle or conflict' (*OED*: SI3E) and *galdor* (*OED*: GALDER), also meaning 'a charm or incantation' (the treasure guarded by the dragon in *Beowulf* was secured by a *galdor*). The Middle English form *sigaldrie* occurs in one of the manuscripts of *Ancrene Riwle*, the medieval religious work edited by Tolkien.

As well as appearing in the 'Lay of Leithian' (quoted above and written in 1928), Tolkien's modernized form *sigaldry* is used in the poem 'Errantry' (written in the early 1930s). In a letter to Rayner Unwin in 1952 (*Lett.* 133), Tolkien discusses the curious history of 'Errantry': through the circulation of a typescript at an informal meeting in Oxford, the poem passed into 'oral tradition' and was transmitted by copying and from memory among people who had no idea of its origin. He comments that it bore out his theory that unusual 'hard words' tend to be preserved in oral tradition. In a later letter to Donald Swann (1966; quoted in *HME* VII. 107), he notes explicitly that the word *sigaldry* was one of the 'hard words' which had survived the process unchanged.

The word **glamoury** occurs in close proximity to *sigaldry* both in the 'Lay of Leithian' and in several texts transitional between 'Errantry' and Bilbo's song of Eärendil:

> Of glamoury he tidings heard
> And binding words of sigaldry. (*HME* VII. 92)

Glamoury ('occult knowledge, magic, necromancy') does have French roots. It is a relatively modern word (the first example in the *OED* files is from a Scots poem of 1811), adapted from *glamour* by the addition of the suffix *-y*, which the *OED* suggests may be due to the influence of a related word, *gramarye*. The connection between magic and grammar is perhaps not instantly obvious to the modern reader. The *OED* explains that, in the Middle Ages, the Latin word *grammatica* (and the corresponding Old French word *gramaire*) chiefly meant the knowledge or study of Latin. Since all academic learning was done in Latin, the word became synonymous with learning in general, and as this was popularly supposed to include magic and astrology, the Latin and English words became used specifically as a name for these 'occult sciences'. The word was memorably employed by E. R. Eddison to refer to the sorcerous powers of King Gorice XII:

> Being minded that he singleth you out, the twelfth, as potent in grammarie, all my care was that these Demons should be detained within reach of your spells. (Lord Gro, in *The Worm Ouroboros*, 1922)

❖ Silharrows ❖

The words which Tolkien rejected are sometimes just as interesting from a philological point of view as those which he finally settled on. *Silharrows* is one of several possible names for the Haradrim ('men of the South', or **Southrons**), which Tolkien jotted down as part of an early plot outline for the siege of Minas Tirith (*HME* VII. 435). As

Christopher Tolkien points out (p. 439), several of these names derive from Tolkien's investigation of the Old English word *Sigelhearwan* 'Ethiopians', which was published in the journal *Medium Ævum* (in two parts, December 1932 and June 1934). (One of Tolkien's suggestions was that in using the name *Sigelhearwan*, rather than something more similar to 'Ethiopians', the writer's intention must have been to bring to mind an established type of being from Northern mythology, namely a creature with a soot-black face and red-hot eyes that shed sparks—an idea which has been seen as the germ of what we now know as a Balrog.) Tolkien concluded that, while the first element of this name was evidently an Old English word *sigel* 'sun', the meaning of the second could not be deduced: it was 'a symbol...of that large part of ancient English language and lore which has now vanished beyond recall, *swa hit no wære*'. However, even though no precise meaning could be assigned to *-hearwan*, Tolkien was prepared to use it—in the 'evolved' form *-harrow*—as a component of an invented ethnonym (the name of a people). The element also appears in the related names *Harrowland* and *Sunharrowland* which he considered at the same time. In the end he abandoned these in favour of the place name *Sunlands* (Sam speaks in *LR* iv. iii of 'the big folk down away in the Sunlands')—which in the alliterative verse of Rohan becomes *Sunlending* ('Six thousand spears to Sunlending', *LR* v. iii).

The reader might suppose that this *-harrow* also appears in the name *Dunharrow* (which Tolkien substituted for the earlier candidate *Dunberg*: see *HME* VII. 447). However, in a toponym (place name) as distinct from an ethnonym, the *-harrow* of *Silharrows* is less suitable as a word-element. In fact the second element of *Dunharrow* is a different word (and one found in several English place names): Old English *hearg* 'heathen holy place'.

✦ sister-son ✦

The *OED* (sister *n.*, sense 9) gives two quotations from Tolkien for this compound: 'Fréalaf, Helm's sister-son' (*LR* vi. vi) and 'The King...looked with liking upon Maeglin his sister-son' (*Silmarillion*, ch. xvi). These are the first recorded examples for over two centuries: the *OED* entry includes a 1680 instance of the synonym *sister-bairn*, and we now know of other Scottish examples as late as 1729.

The formation is an unusual and very archaic one. We would normally compound relationship terms like *sister* or *brother* with other such terms such as *daughter* or *son* by using the genitive of the first term, e.g. *sister's son*, if we did not in fact use a special term, such as *nephew*. But originally in Old English the word *sister* did not add the *-s* ending to form its genitive; it remained in the same form. So in a quotation in the *OED* (referring to a campaign of 1054 in Scotland in which Earl Siward of Northumbria drove out Macbeth) we read of the deaths of *his sunu Osbarn and his sweostor sunu Sihward* (his son Osbarn and his sister-son Sihward). Words denoting other family relationships were similarly uninflected in the genitive: hence such compounds as *mother tongue* (meaning one's mother's language).

But why is this compound important, as its long history from Old English to the 17th century implies? The answer lies in Anglo-Saxon and ancient Germanic custom. As in many societies, the relationship between a man and his sister's son was held to be especially close and binding (possibly because the uncertainties of paternity made a man more confident of blood-relationship to his sister's son than to the offspring of his own marriage). It was the sister-son's duty to champion his uncle. The hero of the epic *Beowulf* is described as the son of the sister of King Hygelac, for whom he loyally fights and whom he eventually succeeds. To fail, betray, or harm one's mother's brother was particularly heinous, which is why Mordred's usurpation of King Arthur, his maternal uncle, is so grievous. In Laȝamon's chronicle *Brut*, a messenger says: 'If it happened—God forbid—that Mordred thy sister-son had taken thy queen and usurped thy kingdom...and had treacherously done all this...thou couldst yet avenge thyself'; and goes on to shock the court into silence with the announcement that this has indeed happened. The word also occurs in a passage in Tolkien's verse play *The Homecoming of Beorhtnoth*, which again illustrates his awareness of the importance of these relationships:

> ... His sister-son! The songs tell us,
> Ever near shall be at need nephew to uncle.

The same customs apply in Middle-earth. After the Battle of Five Armies we are told that the dwarves Fili and Kili fell defending the mortally wounded Thorin Oakenshield, 'for he was their mother's elder brother' (*Hobbit*, ch. xviii). On this Tolkien comments: 'The sentiment of affection for sister's children was strong among all peoples of the Third Age, but less so among Dwarves than Men or Elves among whom it was strongest' ('The Making of Appendix A' in *HME* XII. 285). Similarly the important position of Éomer in the kingdom of Rohan is due to his being the son of Théodwyn, sister of King Théoden.

❖ smial, Smeagol, and Smaug ❖

The hobbits' name for their underground dwellings, **smial**, is currently not in the *OED*. Tolkien fashioned it as an authentic modern

English form of Old English *smygels* 'a burrow', a word which did not survive the Norman conquest. This word contains the noun-making suffix *-els*, as in Old English *rædels* 'a riddle' (see **read and riddle**), and Tolkien has plausibly surmised that, as in the latter word, so in *smygels*, the final *-s* would have got lost over the years through confusion with the ordinary English plural *-s*. (Early drafts also had the form *Smiles*, but this was perhaps changed to avoid absurdity: *HME* IX. 107.) The first part of the word comes from the Germanic root of the verb *smugan* 'to creep or penetrate gradually'.

It seems that Tolkien especially liked this root. From it comes also another Old English verb *smeagan*, meaning 'to scrutinize, inves-tigate', and from that Tolkien created Gollum's true name **Smeagol**, which has the shape of an Old English adjective ending in *-ol*; an example of this kind of adjective survives in *fickle*, Old English *ficol*, from a root meaning 'deceive'. Another example of an adjective formed this way in Old English is *deagol* 'secret', which Tolkien borrowed for the name of Smeagol's best friend (a variant of this word is in *OED*: DIGHEL). It is highly appropriate that this unpleasant pair are named 'inquisitive' and 'secretive'.

Yet another derivative of this root is an Old English word *smeag* meaning 'sagacious', used in Old English to describe a 'worm' (i.e. a reptile: see **worm**). The equivalent of *smeag* in Old Norse, the lan-guage of the Northlands, would be *smaug*. This must be how Tolkien hit on the name of his dragon, **Smaug**, who can be said to be pene-trating in both the literal and the figurative sense. The name does not actually exist in Norse, but the word *smaug* is found as the past tense of another related verb *smjúga* 'to creep through an opening', as Tolkien himself explained (*Lett.* 25, 20 February 1938).

Smial is now firmly established in the Tolkien Society as a name for local branches of the Society.

✦ Southron ✦

Some of the Southrons have broken from the trap and are flying from the road. (*LR* iv. iv)

Southron is a Scots alteration of *southren*, which is a variant form of 'southern'; the ending has been altered through the influence of *Briton* and *Saxon* (*OED*: SOUTHRON *a.* and *n.*). The word was originally used by the Scots specifically of people living south of the Border, in England, and the *OED*'s examples imply that the original context was that of hostility and warfare between the two communities, though it was also used to denote the English, as opposed to Scottish, variety of English.

It is perhaps the antagonistic connotations that the word has collected which led Tolkien to adopt it as the (hostile) term for the people of the South who are allied with Sauron during the War of the Ring. The word was introduced in the drafts for the chapter 'Of Herbs and Stewed Rabbit', replacing *Barangils*, the Gondorian word also found on Tolkien's First Map alongside *Swertings* (*HME* VIII. 136):

(See also **Westron**.)

✦ springle-ring ✦

The springle-ring is mentioned in 'A Long-expected Party' (*LR* i. i) as 'a pretty dance, but rather vigorous', which is danced by young hobbits during a pause in Bilbo's farewell speech. In the previous draft of this passage (*HME* VI. 24) the dance was called *flip-flap*: the meaning here is perhaps the one given in the *OED* as 'a kind of somersault in which the performer throws himself over on his hands and feet alternately; also, a peculiar rollicking dance indulged in by costers' (*OED*: FLIP-FLAP *n.*, sense 3a, quoting a *Slang Dictionary* of 1864).

Tolkien wrote that *springle-ring* was 'an invention' and defined it as 'a vigorous ring-dance in which dancers often leaped up' ('Guide to the Names in *LR*'). Certainly the *OED* has no entry for *springle-ring*, and Tolkien perhaps intended *springle* simply to suggest the frequent *springing* or leaping. Yet the *OED* does mention an 18th- and 19th-century word *springle*, meaning 'a young man, youth, or stripling' (*OED*: SPRINGALD), which is used, for example, in Charles Kingsley's *Hereward the Wake*. This sense of *springle* would be quite appropriate even if Tolkien had used it only to imply that the dancers were normally young; but it could also be a learned joke, based on the fact that *springle* or *springald* has a meaning very similar to that of *halfling*.

❖ staggerment ❖

The *OED* (Second Edition) defines the word as 'great amazement; astonishment', and the earliest recorded example is from a letter of 16 March 1933, written by Tolkien himself to Kenneth Sisam at OUP, and reproduced here (from the OUP archives: see Fig. 15). The letter, in circular fashion, refers back to the *OED* (First Edition), on which Tolkien had worked thirteen years before, and which was just then being reissued in twelve volumes with a Supplement.

The *OED*'s second quotation is also from Tolkien, from *The Hobbit* (1937), chapter xii:

> To say that Bilbo's breath was taken away is no description at all.
> There are no words left to express his staggerment.

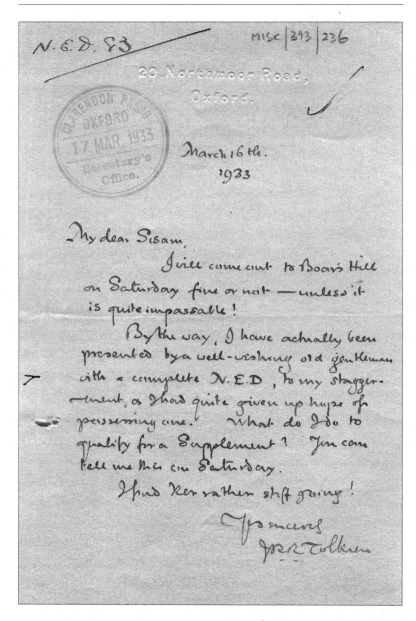

FIGURE 15. Tolkien's 1933 letter using the word *staggerment*.

Only the *OED*'s third example is from another writer, describing (in the *Church Times* in 1975) his or her feelings on being frisked in a cathedral.

Tolkien also used the word in a letter to Stanley Unwin (*Lett.* 17, 15 October 1937):

> At the moment I am suffering like Mr Baggins from a touch of 'staggerment'.

The word is derived from the common expression *to be staggered*, which seems to have been part of Tolkien's ordinary vocabulary:

> He [Frodo] felt staggered to think that he had been walking about with the price of the Shire under his jacket. (*LR* II. iv)

The form of the word is regular, the most obvious comparison being with words such as *bewilderment* and *wonderment*, and the 19th-century colloquial term *botherment*. Tolkien also used the relatively uncommon words *evolvement* (in a letter to W. H. Auden, *Lett.* 163) and *vanishment* (in some early drafts of 'A Long-expected Party': *HME* VI. 14, 23), recorded in the *OED* from 1852 and 1831 respectively. Other authors have used such one-off inventions as *shatterment* (1841) and *usherment* (1887).

✤ Stonebows ✤

The Bridge of Stonebows was the ancient name of the Brandywine Bridge (*LR*, Prologue; in an earlier draft it is just 'the great stone bridge': *HME* XII. 9). The word means simply 'an arch of stone' (*OED*: STONE-BOW, sense 1), but the *OED* notes that this sense is generally obsolete except as the name of one of the gates of Lincoln. The sole example of the general use of the word in the *OED* is from *Beowulf*: as the hero approached the mound which is the dragon's lair, *Geseah þa be wealle…Stondan stanbogan* (he caught sight of the stone arches standing in the wall). From these arches the hot breath of the dragon is issuing, and the next moment Beowulf challenges the dragon to fight.

That Tolkien chose to revive this almost unused compound noun seems to illustrate how thoroughly he had absorbed the language of *Beowulf*.

⁕ sub-creation ⁕

What really happens is that the story-maker proves a successful 'sub-creator'. He makes a Secondary World which your mind can enter. Inside it, what he relates is 'true': it accords with the laws of that world. ('On Fairy-Stories')

In Tolkien's essay 'On Fairy-Stories', he introduces the word *sub-creation* as a technical term for what the truly creative storyteller does. Rather than seeking to represent the real world of experience, or to interpret it symbolically by making analogies between one experience and another, the sub-creator uses and recombines the elements of experience to create a coherent fictional world. Although this world may be strange compared to the real world, its internal consistency enables the reader's mind to be captivated, passing beyond both 'disbelief' and mere conscious 'suspension of disbelief' into what Tolkien calls 'secondary belief'. This principle—that successful fantasy requires self-consistency (rather than mere whimsical oddity or illogicality)—is also expressed by Owen

Barfield, whose writing on language and meaning influenced Tolkien deeply:

> Almost any kind of strangeness may produce an aesthetic effect… On examination, the sole condition is found to be this, that the strangeness shall have an interior significance; it must be felt as arising from a different plane or mode of consciousness, and not merely as an eccentricity of expression.
>
> (Owen Barfield *Poetic Diction* (1928, second edition 1952), ch. 11)

The term *sub-creator* can be seen to have emerged in Tolkien's thought some years before he gave his lecture. It appears in a short piece of verse which he quotes in the essay, describing it as 'from a letter I once wrote to a man who described myth and fairy-story as "lies"':

> Man, Sub-creator, the refracted Light
> through whom is splintered from a single White
> to many hues, and endlessly combined
> in living shapes that move from mind to mind.
> We make still by the law in which we're made.

The recipient of the letter was C. S. Lewis, and the verse is an extract from *Mythopoeia*, a poem (not published in its entirety until 1988) which Tolkien wrote as a contribution to their friendly but passionate debate on the nature of mythology and its relationship with reality. The very form of the word *sub-creator* (*sub-* prefix implying lower position or lesser status; *creator*, maker, applied in Christian thought principally to God as maker of the world) implies the perspective which Tolkien is trying to present: the human myth-maker or storyteller may appropriately be likened to God as creator, while acknowledging that human imagination is a secondary expression of the divine creative power.

Tolkien's word has been found useful by literary commentators on fantasy, and sufficient evidence of its use was found for an entry in the *Supplement to the OED* for both *sub-creation* and, as a derivative, *sub-creator*—though admittedly, both words are used especially by writers on Tolkien's works, and the works the *OED* cites are Paul Kocher's *Master of Middle-earth* (1972) and Randel Helms's *Tolkien's World* (1974).

Tolkien is credited as the coiner of *sub-creation* in the *OED*'s entry for the word; and indeed in the sense in which he used it, he was. But a word composed of such readily available elements—in this case the productive prefix *sub-* and a term of standard English like *creation*—is always quite likely to have been formed and used independently of, and earlier than, its most well-known user. In the case of the related adjective *sub-creative* the *OED* notes that Oliver Wendell Holmes used the word as early as 1860, though it also records Tolkien's use. And, although not yet recorded in the *OED*, an example has recently come to light of *sub-creation* itself being used before Tolkien coined it. ('Coined' is still the appropriate term, in that there is no evidence that Tolkien was aware of, let alone influenced by, these earlier uses.) The political philosopher Ernest Barker's 1942 book *Reflections on Government* includes the following observation, in the course of a discussion of the setting up of committees by Parliament: 'The creator, when once it has exercised its power of creation, will refrain from playing with that power by such acts of sub-creation.'

✦ Swertings ✦

I've heard tales of the big folk down away in the Sunlands. Swertings we call 'em in our tales. (Sam, in *LR* iv. iii)

> The body of a mighty warrior, a giant among the Swertings. (*LR* IV. iv)

Swertings is the name in the Shire for the *Haradrim*, the people of the far South, known to hobbits only in folk tales. (Originally, perhaps, it was not going to be restricted to Shire-speech, since it was written on the first Map of Middle-earth, and Gollum used it in the first draft of 'The Black Gate is Closed'.)

The word is clearly derived from *swart* (Old English *sweart*), which means 'dark in colour', especially with reference to people's skin colour (*OED*: SWART *a.*, sense 1b). This word appears, for example, in *The Lord of the Rings*, describing some dead goblin-soldiers (*LR* III. i). *Swerting* has a precedent in *Beowulf*, where a person named *Swerting* is mentioned in passing, and in Old Norse literature, which mentions a man named *Sverting* and a family called the *Svertingar* (plural), though in these cases there is no suggestion that these people are foreigners.

The related term *Swartmen* is used in some of Tolkien's earlier writings as a name, though not for people of the far South, but for the *Easterlings* of the First Age (that is, the people who entered Beleriand after the people of the Three Houses of the Edain):

> The swart Men, whom Uldor the Accursed led, went over to the foe.
> ('Quenta' §11: *HME* IV. 118)

> *Ulfang, Uldor, Ulfast, Ulwarth*, names of Swartmen.
> (under ÚLUG- in 'The Etymologies': *HME* V. 396)

A similar switch in application occurs with the term *Swarthy Men*, used at first for Easterlings of the First Age:

> At this time the Swarthy Men came first into Beleriand... Now the Easterlings or Rómenildi, as the Elves named these newcomers, were short and broad...their skins were swart or sallow.
> ('Of the Swarthy Men': *HME* V. 286)

but later (once in *The Lord of the Rings*) for the Southrons:

> You may at the least disturb the Orcs and Swarthy Men from their feasting in the White Tower. (*LR* v. ii)

Tolkien says ('Guide to the Names in *LR*') that *Swarthy Men* is the Common Speech equivalent of the hobbits' word *Swertings*.

✦ Thain ✦

> They chose from their own chiefs a Thain to hold the authority of the king that was gone. (*LR*, Prologue)

The Thain is the hereditary ruler of the Shire, though at the time when the action of *The Lord of the Rings* begins the post has become largely honorific or ceremonial. The relevant definition in the *OED* reads: 'a person who in Anglo-Saxon times held lands of the king or other superior by military service' (*OED*: THANE *n.*[1], sense 3). In Old English the word was *thegn*, and historians sometimes use the word with this spelling as a technical term. The word died out in England at the end of the medieval period and survived only in Scotland, where the regular Scots form was and is *thane*, a word familiar to anyone who has read or seen Shakespeare's *Macbeth*. Had the word continued in use in England, it would have retained the Middle English form *thain*, just as Old English *regn* has the modern form *rain*. As with **Shirriff**, Tolkien's chosen spelling helps to convey the feeling that the speech of the Shire is a dialect in which an old word has been preserved in a special form and with a special meaning: the Thain of the Shire is not exactly a thane in the usual sense—there is no longer a king from whom he holds lands. The spelling also avoids associations with Macbeth, Macduff, and their peers, which the conventional spelling might conjure up.

When King Théoden formally accepts Merry's service (*LR* v. ii), he uses two words for the role or rank which he is bestowing. One is *esquire*, which has its roots in French and Latin and originally meant 'shield-bearer'. The other—with a Germanic flavour more appropriate to the context of Rohan—is *sword-thain*. Here *thain* has the slightly different Old English sense 'attendant, servant' (*OED*: THANE *n.*[1], sense 1). This still carries the notion of allegiance to a lord or master, and occurs in several Old English compounds, such as *bedd-þegn* and *burþegn* 'chamberlain', although *sweordþegn* is not itself attested in the records.

✦ Tolkienian and Tolkienesque ✦

Tolkienian was the first of these two words derived from Tolkien's name to enter the English language. An entry for it was published in the *Supplement to the OED*, Volume IV (1986), with the definition 'of or pertaining to the philologist and author of fantasy literature John Ronald Reuel Tolkien (1892–1973) or his writings'. The first example is from a review by C. S. Lewis in the literary magazine *Time and Tide* (14 August 1954). Lewis spells the word *Tolkinian*, a spelling also used by C. N. Manlove in his book *Modern Fantasy* (1975). This reflects a pseudo-scholarly assumption that the stem of the name *Tolkien* is to be taken as *Tolkin-*, but later authors have almost invariably adopted the more obvious form *Tolkienian*. In fact, the first known use of the word is even earlier, from a private letter by Tolkien's friend Christopher Wiseman written in around 1916 (John Garth *Tolkien and the Great War*, p. 133).

The same entry in the *Supplement to the OED* contains a subentry for the word **Tolkienesque**, defined as 'characteristic of or resembling Tolkien or his writings'. The earliest example is from the science magazine *Nature* (18 July 1970). This word is a little more distinctive, as the suffix *-esque* is typically used in adjectives which refer to a resemblance in style or characteristics, rather than in general adjectives. As well as being prominent in a group of words including *arabesque, burlesque, grotesque, picaresque,* and *picturesque*, it is used in a host of words derived from the names of visual artists and writers, from *Adamesque* (resembling the 18th-century architecture or furniture designed by the Adam brothers) to *Whitmanesque* (characteristic or suggestive of the 19th-century American poet Walt Whitman). Hence the word *Tolkienesque* is clearly a descriptive adjective of a more particular application than *Tolkienian*, reflecting a comparison or association with the visual or creative aspects of Tolkien's world (often rather imperfectly or superficially characterized). Words in *-esque* sometimes carry a slight air of deprecation, but it can be hard to tell—if the word is used in a faintly disapproving way—whether the writer is expressing disapproval of a poor imitation of Tolkien, or disapproval of its resembling Tolkien's work at all.

The evidence in the *OED* files shows that the word *Tolkienesque* continues to be in constant use in the media—in reviews of books, films, rock music, and video games, as well as in more general cultural contexts. It is used to conjure a range of associations, mainly relating to fantastic or mythological artwork or fiction. The most typical connotations are the natural beauty or grandeur of Tolkien's settings, the resonances of Germanic or Celtic art, or, more prosaically, the liberal use of invented names. (A publisher's reader working for George Allen & Unwin, given some of Tolkien's tales to review during the hunt for a 'sequel' to *The Hobbit*, referred to the names as 'eye-splitting'!) Sometimes it evokes the ecological or nature-loving theme within *The Lord of the Rings*, which became an important element in the public perception of Tolkien's work during its rise in popularity in the 1960s.

Other words such as *Tolkienish* can be found in use, but are not sufficiently common to have been listed in the *OED*, though *Tolkienist* has recently achieved a certain currency, particularly in connection with role-playing enthusiasts of eastern Europe.

✦ troll ✦

In Scandinavian mythology, one of a race of supernatural beings formerly conceived as giants, now, in Denmark and Sweden, as dwarfs or imps, supposed to inhabit caves or subterranean dwellings. (*OED*: TROLL *n.*², sense a)

This word is not (as far as we know from surviving evidence) an ancient term in English. It was borrowed from Scandinavia by mid-19th-century English writers, though it had been in use in the northern isles of Scotland, usually in the form *trow*, since the 17th century. Trolls soon made themselves at home in English fairy tales—and were no doubt further popularized by the success of Henrik Ibsen's *Peer Gynt* (1867)—but scarcely feature in Tolkien's early writings, being mentioned only in an outline of the incomplete 'History of Eriol or Ælfwine' (*HME* II. 283). They make their entrance in fairy-tale mode in *The Hobbit* as oafish, man-eating, giant-sized creatures that are turned to stone at sunrise, and then reappear in *The Lord of the Rings* in more malevolent and powerful guise in Moria and in the armies of Sauron. (Only as the story developed did trolls become clearly distinguished from ents: see **ent** and **etten**.)

❋ tweens ❋

The appearance of a strong and rather large and well-built hobbit just out of his 'tweens'. (second main draft of *LR*; *HME* VI. 251)

The tweens are 'the irresponsible twenties between [hobbit] childhood and coming of age at thirty-three' (*LR* I. i). This Tolkienian invention is obviously based on *teens*, which is a 20th-century word, derived, of course, from the numeral ending -*teen*. *Tweens* is a portmanteau word, a blending of *teens* with either of two possible words beginning with *tw-*. One of them is *'tween*, a shortened form of *between* (the tweens being *between* childhood and coming of age); the other is *twenties*. Ultimately, as Tolkien knew well, it doesn't matter which, since both *'tween* and *twenty* are derived from the same root, the base of the word *two*.

The word *tweens* is paralleled in more general modern use by inventions such as *tweenie* (1919), *tween-age* (1938), *tween* (1946), and *tweenager* (1949); but these of course lack the connection with *twenty* made possible by the longer lifespan of hobbits.

Incidentally, the *OED* (BETWEEN *prep.* and *adj.*) explains that the word *between* resulted from the combination of two words: the original construction was *bi...tweonum*, as in *bi sæm tweonum*, a poetic phrase meaning literally 'by seas twain'. This phrase is found four times in *Beowulf* as a way of saying 'in the whole land' or even 'in the whole world' (imagining the world as having a sea on either side). Tolkien introduces the modern form of the phrase in *Farmer*

Giles of Ham: 'such wonder and uproar as had seldom been seen between the two seas before'.

✦ unlight ✦

Tolkien is credited in the *OED* as the first person to use this word as a noun. The compilers of the *Supplement to the OED* noticed his use of the word to describe the cloak of darkness woven by Ungoliant in *The Silmarillion* (1977), and an entry was published in the fourth Supplement volume in 1986 (the word appears to have been introduced in Tolkien's rewriting of the 'Quenta Silmarillion' in the 1950s: *HME* X. 285). The word had in fact appeared in print ten years earlier, in *Smith of Wootton Major* ('the blue waves like snow-clad hills roll silently out of Unlight to the long strand').

Vivid as the word *unlight* may be, it is extremely simple in formation—consisting as it does of the prefix *un-* and the common noun *light*—and it could easily have been coined independently by other writers. Tolkien had particular reason to be aware of the ease with which words could be formed with *un-*: during his time as Henry Bradley's assistant on the *OED*, Bradley's fellow Editor, William Craigie, was having some of his most difficult struggles with the immense number of words beginning with *un-* for which evidence had accumulated in the Dictionary's files. Craigie wrestled with the difficulties of *un-* for several years, and Tolkien must have been aware of the arguments between the publishers at OUP and the lexicographers over how much time, paper, and money could be expended on what many regarded as words of very little importance or interest. He must also have seen the bundles of paper slips for some of the more marginal words, many of which were omitted.

The noun *unlight* does not seem to have been among these marginal words; on the other hand, Craigie did include entries for four distinct adjectives with the same spelling, as well as for a verb.

Indeed, the prefix *un-* combines so readily with just about any word in the language that it is all too easy for any writer to coin a previously unrecorded '*un*-word' without realizing it. The *OED* records Bilbo's description of Smaug as '*unassessably* wealthy' (*Hobbit*, ch. xii) as another first use for Tolkien; other words which Tolkien may have been the first to use, but which have not yet been listed by the *OED*, include *unfey* (in 'The Lay of the Children of Húrin': *HME* III. 117), *unbegrudged* (in *The Homecoming of Beorhtnoth*), and *unthrottled* (in 'The Passage of the Marshes' (*LR* IV. ii) Frodo and Sam find themselves 'alive and unthrottled'). It also provides a useful writer's device for combining unfamiliar appearance with a clear meaning. For example, Tolkien also used *undead* (*LR* v. vi), which is paralleled by Old Norse *údauðr* and had been revived by Bram Stoker in *Dracula* (1897) after 300 years' disuse. Among other authors, one might note the *Unman* in C. S. Lewis's *Perelandra* (1943); Ursula Le Guin uses both the rare coinage *unlife* and the established but archaic *untrusty* in *A Wizard of Earthsea* (1968). Of course, William Morris was doing this much earlier: for example, *unangry*, *undark*, and *unwrongful* all occur in his *Sigurd the Volsung* (1876)—and in each case the *OED* records his use as the only evidence for the word.

✢ warg ✢

In the tales of J. R. R. Tolkien, a wolf of a particularly evil kind.
(*Supplement to the OED*, Vol. IV)

In Old Norse, *vargr* means either 'outlaw' or 'wolf'. The corresponding Old English *wearg* (Middle English *wari*) means 'felon, outlaw, or villain' (*OED*: WARY *n.*). In Middle High German the related word *warc* could mean 'monster'. Tolkien's *warg* rolls all these meanings up into a vividly imagined monstrous wolf with supernatural (or at least preternatural) powers: the bodies of the wolves slain by the Fellowship in the night could not be found in the morning (*LR* II. iv). The spelling was intended to convey this generalized or combined meaning by representing the ancestral Germanic form of the word: 'The word *Warg* used in *The Hobbit* and the *L.R.* for an evil breed of (demonic) wolves is not supposed to be A[nglo]-S[axon] specifically, and is given prim[itive] Germanic form as representing the noun common to the Northmen of these creatures' (*Lett.* 297). In the same note, Tolkien also remarks that 'it seems to have "caught on"', mentioning the appearance of the word in a science fiction story.

Old English *wearg* also appears in the invented compound word *Bealuwearg* (not found in Old English literature), which appears as an 'equivalent' of Elvish *Balrog* in a list of names compiled in connection with Tolkien's Old English translation of part of the 'Quenta Noldorinwa' (*HME* IV. 208–13)—the first element of the compound is *bealu* 'evil, harm' (*OED*: BALE *n.*¹). This is not a 'translation' of *Balrog* (which means 'demon of might' in Elvish) so much as an evocative 'sound-alike'; the several similar 'equivalents' to other names in the list must have rather pleased Tolkien in the way that they provide the Elvish names with additional resonances. For example, *Engbend*, given as an 'equivalent' of *Angband* (Elvish 'iron prison'), contains the Old English words *enge* 'narrow, strait' and *bend* 'bond, fetter', while *Bansil* ('fair-gleam') is rendered as *Béansigel*, composed of Old English *béam* 'tree' and *sigel* 'sun' (see **Silharrows**).

❧ waybread ❧

> This waybread of the Elves had a potency that increased as
> travellers relied on it alone and did not mingle it with other foods.
> (*LR* vi. iii)

In ordinary English usage, this (*OED*: WAYBREAD) is a folk-name of
the plantain (*Plantago*), meaning literally 'broad-leaved plant growing beside the way'. The second part of the word is related to *broad*,
and has nothing to do with *bread*. However, Tolkien has punningly
adopted the word as if it were a literal compound of 'way' and
'bread' in order to have an English equivalent to the Elvish *lembas*
(explained as being from *len* 'way' and *bas* 'bread'), the cakes provided in Lothlórien which kept the Fellowship, especially Frodo and
Sam, nourished on their journeys. It does not occur in Tolkien's
earlier writings, but appears in 'Of Tuor and his Coming to
Gondolin' (1951) in *Unfinished Tales*.

Spiritually minded etymologists might also discern here a scholarly link with the word *viaticum*. In Roman Catholic practice, this is
the consecrated bread of the Eucharist administered to someone
who is dying or in danger of death. The Latin word *viaticum* originally meant simply 'provision for a journey'; it comes from Latin
via 'way', and from it developed the word *voyage* (borrowed from
French into English and originally meaning simply 'a journey').
Tolkien acknowledged the comparison between *lembas* and the Eucharist as miraculously sustaining forms of bread: the waybread
provides food for Frodo and Sam on a journey that, to the best
of their knowledge, leads to death. He comments that 'far greater
things may colour the mind in dealing with the lesser things of a
fairy-story' (*Lett.* 213, 25 October 1958).

✦ weapontake ✦

The weapontake was set for the morrow. When all is ordered we will
set out. (Théoden, in *LR* v. iii)

The word *wapentake* (*OED*: 'a subdivision of certain English shires,
corresponding to the "hundred" of other counties') is well known in
the context of English history, but not in the sense in which Tolkien
uses it. It derives from the Old Norse *vápnatak*, and clearly consists
of the two components *weapon* and *take*; the corresponding word in
Icelandic was used to mean (among other things) the taking up once
more of weapons which had been laid aside by those attending the
Althing (the Icelandic parliament). The route by which this word
came in English to mean an administrative region rather than an
event can only be guessed at; the *OED* entry offers some ideas.
Tolkien decided to take the word at face value, and thereby assign
to it (or rather to the respelt form *weapontake*) an obvious meaning
which he needed for his narrative.

✦ weregild ✦

In ancient Teutonic and Old English law, the price set upon a man
according to his rank, paid by way of compensation or fine in cases of
homicide and certain other crimes to free the offender from further
obligation or punishment. (*OED*: WERGELD, -GILD)

'This I will have, as weregild for my father, and my brother,' says
Isildur of the Ring, fatefully deciding the future of Middle-earth
throughout the Third Age (*LR* ii. ii). The word has not descended
into modern English direct from Old English *wergeld, wergild,* or
weregild: in this word the *g* sounded like *y*, and so its regular modern

English descendant, if it had survived, would have been something like *wer-yield*. Medieval and later lawyers used *wergeld* or *wergild* to represent the Old English word in legal documents. Tolkien chose the form *weregild*, which is shown by the *OED* to have also been used by 19th-century writers. He may have felt that it suggested a pronunciation of the first syllable rhyming with *pear* or *peer*, rather than *per*. *Weregild* is a compound, the first part (*OED*: WERE *n.*[1]) being a word for 'man' obsolete since the 13th century. The second is an old sense of the word *yield* (*OED*: YIELD *n.*, sense 1b) meaning 'payment, compensation'.

The *were-* appearing in *weregild* has often been compared to the first element of *werewolf*, though there is some evidence that they may not be the same word. Werewolves appear in *The Silmarillion*, devouring the companions of Beren and Felagund in Tol-in-Gaurhoth ('Isle of Werewolves'). There are none in *The Hobbit* and *The Lord of the Rings*, where wargs perhaps take their place, though Bilbo Baggins appears to have coined a similar (perhaps facetious) equivalent: 'If I have to walk from here to the East of East and fight the wild Were-worms in the Last Desert' (*Hobbit*, ch. i).

✦ Westernesse ✦

> Not all Men were estranged from [the Elves]. The Men of Westernesse came to their aid. (*LR* i. ii)

Westernesse is a translation of the Elvish name *Númenor* (from *númen* 'west, western'), the land given to the faithful Men who aided the Elves against Morgoth in the First Age, and drowned by the ocean at the end of the Second Age.

Tolkien had found the word *Westernesse* and adopted it for his mythology even before Númenor existed, using it at first for the Undying Lands of Valinor in the uttermost West: 'Westland or Westerness' (together with 'Eastland or Easterness') occurs on Map IV of 'Ambarkanta' (*HME* IV. 249); the form *Westerland* occurs even earlier, in fact in his very first poem about Earendel, written in 1914 (*HME* II. 267–9). Later, we read of the land of the Men of the West: 'It was called Númenor, that is Westernesse, and Andúnië or the Sunsetland' (*HME* V. 14). As Tolkien explained: 'It is meant to be *western* + *ess*, an ending used in partly francized names of "romantic" lands, as *Lyonesse*, or *Logres* (England in Arthurian Romance). The name actually occurs in the early romance of *King Horn*, of some kingdom reached by ship' ('Guide to the Names in *LR*'). Elsewhere, discussing the Middle English use of *Westernesse*, he writes: 'the meaning is vague, but may be taken to mean "Western lands" as distinct from the East inhabited by the Paynim [i.e. Pagans] and Saracens' (*Lett.* 276).

The *OED* has no entry for *Westernesse*, but it does record it in three quotations from the Middle English poem *King Horn*. One of these may even remind us of Númenor: *Þe se bigan to posse Riȝt in to Westernesse* (the sea began to thrust right into Westernesse). It is not clear exactly how this word was formed, whether simply by omission of an -*n*- from 'western-ness' or (as Tolkien suggests) by direct borrowing of the ending in the name *Lyonesse* (which in some Arthurian sources is said, rather significantly, to have been situated to the west of Cornwall, and to have been drowned by the sea). There is a Middle English parallel in the development of the obsolete word HEATHENESSE. Its first meaning is straightforward: 'the quality or condition of being heathen', that is 'heathen-ness'. A second meaning, though, refers to a region, 'heathendom, the heathen world; the lands outside Christendom', a vaguely conceived realm in which knights might go on crusade, and from which the Three Kings came to seek the birth of Christ. The *OED*'s etymology says: 'From an early date one of the two *n*'s was generally omitted, so that the word was sometimes treated as analogous to such words of French origin as *noblesse, Lyonesse.*' This use of *heathenesse* as the name of a region is early enough (early 13th century) to be a possible model for *Westernesse* in *King Horn* (from around 1300). Tolkien himself seems to have been so familiar with the name as perhaps to forget that it was not in standard modern use, since he uses it more than once as an 'explanation' of the name *Númenor*: in 'The Notion Club Papers Part Two' (*HME* IX. 240), Alwin Lowdham says: 'But take the name Nūmenōre…It means Westernesse.'

There is an intriguing possibility that Tolkien may have first encountered the name *Westerness* not in the Middle English *King Horn* but in a poem by his contemporary Laurence Binyon. Binyon's *Collected Poems* (1931) includes a long narrative poem called 'Ruan's Voyage'—strikingly reminiscent in places of Bilbo's song of Eärendil at Rivendell—which includes the lines 'Heavily Ruan thought on his home | In Westerness across the foam.'

The Elvish name *Eldamar* (see **Elvenhome**) is sometimes translated by the similar word *Elvenesse*, with the ending *-esse* again carrying connotations of a mythical land. In the earlier texts, where Tolkien is still using the adjective *elfin* rather than *elven*, the name is spelt *Elfinesse* (e.g. in 'The Hiding of Valinor': *HME* I. 211), but this is later changed (e.g. in the later version of the 'Lay of Leithian': *HME* III. 354, 360).

> …Felagund fought,
> And all the magic and might he brought
> Of Elvenesse into his words.
>
> (*Silmarillion*, ch. xix)

❧ **Westron** ❧

They [the hobbits] forgot whatever languages they had used before, and spoke ever after the Common Speech, the Westron as it was named, that was current through all the lands of the kings from Arnor to Gondor, and about all the coasts of the Sea from Belfalas to Lune. (*LR,* Prologue)

In Tolkien's Middle-earth writings, ordinary English is said to have been used to represent *Westron,* the human language used generally throughout the western part of Middle-earth. The slightly earlier term for this, used alongside it, is 'the Common Speech', found first in the drafts of *The Fellowship of the Ring* (*HME* VII. 223); other expressions also occur, such as 'the Common Tongue'. In the drafts of the Appendix on Languages we find at first *Westnish* (of uncertain formation; perhaps from the obsolete adverb *westen* 'from the west' + *-ish*), which was later changed to *Westron* (*HME* XII. 32, 55).

Christopher Tolkien notes that the word *Westron* was 'apparently devised by my father on the analogy of the old form *southron,* itself an alteration of *southern*'. Unlike **Southron,** it is not recorded in the *OED,* either as a word in its own right or as a variant of *western,* and it appears almost exclusively as meaning 'a language spoken in the West'. Only once does it appear in the more general sense 'a westerner': 'The Easterlings were dismayed, fearing that their Master would…give back the land to the Westrons' ('The Wanderings of Húrin': *HME* XI. 252).

The form *Eastron,* which has no record of use in English before Tolkien, also appears in 'The Wanderings of Húrin' (*HME* XI. 253): 'But Húrin coming to the gates looked on the Eastrons in scorn.' This word generally gave place to **Easterling.**

❖ wight ❖

A shadow came out of dark places far away, and the bones were stirred in the mounds. Barrow-wights walked in the hollow places with a clink of rings on cold fingers. (*LR* I. vii)

Until the 19th century the word *wight* was used in regional dialect with the meaning 'person'. Chaucer famously observes of the Knight on the Canterbury pilgrimage *He neuere yet no vileynye ne sayde In al his lyf vn to no maner wight* (he never in his life used offensive language to anyone of any kind). This sense has also survived in archaic literary contexts, as for example in the poetry of Thomas Hardy. The root meaning of the word is 'a living being, a creature' (as in Middle English *alle quike wihte* 'all living beings'), a sense obsolete after the 16th century. In later use it was often used 'implying some contempt or commiseration' (*OED*: WIGHT *n.*, sense 2). There is perhaps a hint of this in Tolkien's occasional use of the word: as Aragorn's company rides off to take the Paths of the Dead, some of the Rohirrim watching say: 'They are Elvish wights. Let them go where they belong, into the dark places, and never return' (*LR* v. ii).

Another early use of *wight*, which has survived till recent times, was to denote supernatural beings in general, or in particular a ghost or demon. In the 10th-century gloss to the *Lindisfarne Gospels* (quoted in the *OED*), the disciples think Christ, walking on the water, is (in Latin) a *phantasma*, in Old English *yfel wiht* (evil wight). The *OED* further tells us that in the 17th century the word was used for the four beasts in the Revelation of St John; and William Morris, in *The Wood Beyond the World* (1894), writes of 'our protection against uncouth wights'.

Tolkien, of course, uses the word in this sense for a baleful phantom creature haunting the grave-mounds on the Barrow-downs:

'Get out, you old Wight! Vanish in the sunlight!' sings Tom Bombadil (*LR* 1. viii). This concept is specifically expressed by the compound *barrow-wight*, which makes its first appearance in his writings in an early version of the poem 'The Adventures of Tom Bombadil', published in the *Oxford Magazine* of 15 February 1934. Then, when the writing of *The Lord of the Rings* had progressed only as far as the fourth version of 'A Long-expected Party', he wrote in some rough notes about the future development of the tale: 'They turn aside..., get lost and caught by Willowman and by Barrow-wights. T. Bombadil comes in' (*HME* VI. 42). The barrow-wights briefly had a role similar to the Black Riders, before attaining their final form, in which, of course, they play no further part in the story. However, they are mentioned in the later *Homecoming of Beorhtnoth*, when Tídwald says, 'And your eyes fancied barrow-wights and bogies.'

Tolkien notes that *barrow* 'is a recent adoption by archaeologists of the English dialect word *barrow* (earlier *berrow*, from [Old] English *beorg, berg* "hill, mound")' ('Guide to the Names in *LR*'). *Beorg* was also applied in Old English to a burial mound, but according to the *OED* the word is scarcely attested between that period and the 16th century, when it is identified as a West Country word for a sepulchre. Tolkien refers to the compound *barrow-wight* as 'an invention', but the *OED* has an earlier example of it. Andrew Lang, in his *Essays in Little* (1891), page 146, writes: 'In the graves where treasures were hoarded the Barrowwights dwelt, ghosts that were sentinels over the gold.' This essay is a review of English translations of Norse sagas; the passage outlines the pagan beliefs that persisted after the conversion of the North to Christianity. It probably refers to an incident in *Grettis Saga: the Story of Grettir the Strong*, translated by Eiríkr Magnússon and William Morris and published in

1869. In chapter xviii, Grettir digs into a burial mound in order to steal the treasure in it, but meets powerful resistance from the dead occupant: 'Everything in their way was kicked out of place, the barrow-wight setting on with hideous eagerness; Grettir gave back before him for a long time, till at last it came to this, that he saw it would not do to hoard his strength any more.' Morris and Magnússon also use *barrow-bider* and *barrow-dweller* in the same passage, which shows that the compound at this stage was an occasional formation, not the established name for a species of being as Tolkien has made it.

Tolkien surely invented the adjective *barrow-wightish*, which Merry uses of an avenue of ancient stones: 'I am not sure that I like it: it has a—well, rather a barrow-wightish look' (*LR* i. xi).

✦ Wilderland and Wold ✦

Long after…there lived by the banks of the Great River on the edge of Wilderland a clever-handed and quiet-footed little people.
(*LR* i. ii)

The map provided in *The Hobbit* shows 'Wilderland' as a region lying east of a double red line running north–south just to the west of Rivendell and labelled 'Edge of the Wild'; in *The Lord of the Rings*, the map has 'Wilderland' labelling the region to the east of the Great River.

Tolkien says that the word is 'An invention (not actually found in English), based on *wilderness* (originally meaning country of wild creatures, not inhabited by Men), but with a side-reference to the verbs *wilder* "wander astray" and *bewilder*. It is supposed to be the Common Speech name of *Rhovanion* (on the map, not in the text), the lands east of the Misty Mountains (including Mirkwood) as far as the River Running' ('Guide to the Names in *LR*').

This word is an invention of Tolkien's, but most readers probably deduce correctly that it is based on the element *wilder-* appearing in the word *wilderness*. This word is related to *wild*, though its exact origin is uncertain; it is probably from an adjective *wildern* 'wild, desert', in Old English *wilddeoren* 'savage' or, literally, 'having to do with wild beasts' (*wilddeor*, 'wild beast', comes from *wild* 'wild' and *deor* 'animal': *deer* in modern English).

The origin of the word *wild* is itself something of an enigma, and the *OED* mentions two possible theories (*OED*: WILD *a.* and *n.*). The one which the editors preferred connects it to an ancient pre-Germanic root shared with the Celtic languages (and surviving in certain words in Welsh and Irish). However, they do mention another theory, based on a parallel with the Latin words *silvestris* and *silvaticus*. These also mean 'wild' (the second of them is the ancestor of French *sauvage* and English *savage*), but they are actually formed from the Latin word *silva* 'wood'; this has suggested that *wild* might be connected with the Germanic word meaning 'forest' (in German *Wald*, in Old English *weald* or *wald*, in modern English *wold*). Tolkien, who worked on the etymologies of WILD and WOLD when he was on the staff of the *OED*, is known to have preferred this etymology, and criticized the *OED*'s treatment of WILD in a review written after he had left the staff (see p. 39). Certainly, a large part of Wilderland is occupied by the great forest of Mirkwood. *(165)*

The word **Wold** itself appears on the map of Middle-earth as the name of a region to the east of Fangorn Forest ('the windy uplands of the Wold of Rohan': *LR* III. ii). Here the word is applied not in the original sense of 'forest' but in the modern sense, 'a hilly tract of country, as it occurs in the names of various parts of England such as the Yorkshire Wolds and the Cotswolds' (*OED*: WOLD *n.*, sense 4). 'The Hunters' Wold', or 'the Wold of Hunters', is also mentioned in 'The Lay of the Children of Húrin' (*HME* III).

✤ Withywindle ✤

It was a winding river bordered by willows (withies). *Withy-* is not uncommon in English place-names, but *-windle* does not actually occur (*Withywindle* was modelled on *withywind*, a name of the convolvulus or bindweed). ('Guide to the Names in *LR*')

The name *withywind* for the convolvulus or bindweed can ultimately be traced back to Old English *wiþewinde* (*OED*: WITHWIND *n.* and WITHYWIND *n.*). The first part of the word is related to *withy* 'willow' (which has influenced the later spelling), and its oldest meaning in English is 'a band, tie, or shackle consisting of a tough flexible twig or branch...as of willow or osier' (*OED*: WITHE, WITH *n.*). The second part, *-wind*, means simply 'something that winds'. As Tolkien implies, *withywindle* does not occur as an English word, but a verb *windle* does exist, meaning, among other things, 'to move sinuously, to meander' (*OED*: WINDLE *v.*[1]). On the basis of a real word, the name of a winding plant that strangles and smothers other plants, Tolkien has created a name for the Old Forest river with elements that exactly fit its character: 'willow' and 'wind sinuously'. He may also have been influenced by an Old Norse word *viðvindill*—not because of its precise meaning, which is 'ivy', but because in Cleasby and Vigfusson's *Icelandic–English Dictionary* it is suggestively and poetically translated as 'wood-windle'.

Tolkien also played with both components of the river-name in the poem 'Bombadil Goes Boating' (published in *The Adventures of Tom Bombadil*), in which Tom journeys 'west down the withy-stream', coming in due course to 'Withy-weir' and 'Windle-reach'.

❧ wolf-rider ❧

He [Saruman] has taken Orcs into his service, and Wolf-riders, and evil Men. (*LR* ii. ii)

Swiftly, a scout rode back and reported that wolf-riders were abroad in the valley. (*LR* ii. vii)

Orcs riding on the backs of wolves first appear in Tolkien's manuscripts in the second version of the 'Tale of Tinúviel' (*HME* II. 44). They are quite often mentioned in early accounts of the battles of the First Age (for example, in 'The Fall of Gondolin': *HME* II. 190). In *The Hobbit* (chapter vi) we learn: 'They [the goblins] often got the Wargs to help and shared the plunder with them. Sometimes they rode on wolves like men do on horses.' Tolkien may have had plans to depict a pitched battle between the Rohirrim and wolf-riders (*HME* VII. 412), but they were not realized. However, wolf-riders are memorably portrayed in the film version of *The Two Towers* (2002).

References to the riding of wolves surface occasionally in Germanic mythology, though there they seem to be associated with female figures of magic power. A notable instance occurs in the tale of the death of Balder in the Norse Prose Edda: unable to launch the ship on which Balder's body is borne, the gods send for the giantess

Hyrrokken, who arrives riding a wolf with serpents for reins. Another (or perhaps the same) figure appears in *The Lay of Helgi Hjörvarðsson* in the Poetic Edda, in which we are told that Heðinn, travelling in the forest, met a troll-woman riding on a wolf, with a rein made of serpents.

However, neither Old English nor Old Norse seems to have had a word directly equivalent to *wolf-rider*. The earliest example known to the *OED*'s editors (*OED*: WOLF *n.*, sense 11b) dates only from 1848, in Edward Bulwer-Lytton's novel *Harold, the Last of the Saxon Kings* (where the image is probably taken from the Edda):

> 'Githa,' she said, slowly, 'doubtless thou rememberest in thy young days to have seen or heard of the terrible hell-maid Belsta?' 'Ay, ay,' answered Githa shuddering; 'I saw her once in gloomy weather, driving before her herds of dark grey cattle. Ay, ay; and my father beheld her ere his death, riding the air on a wolf, with a snake for a bridle... Belsta, and Heidr, and Hulla of old, the wolf-riders, the men-devourers, could win to the uttermost secrets of galdra [i.e. magic spells: see **sigaldry**], though applied only to purposes the direst and fellest to man.' (*Harold*, part v, chapter i)

❖ worm ❖

Every worm has his weak spot. (*Hobbit*, ch. xii)

More often than not in *The Hobbit*, Smaug is referred to by the familiar term 'dragon', but on a few occasions the ancient Germanic word 'worm' is used. Éowyn says of the horn she gives to Merry at their parting that it 'came from the hoard of Scatha the Worm' (*LR* VI. vi). In *The Silmarillion* the dragon Glaurung is also called the Great Worm, and Túrin addresses him as 'Worm of Morgoth'. In

Farmer Giles of Ham the dragon Chrysophylax is frequently referred to, and even addressed, as a 'worm', and Tolkien playfully derives the Buckinghamshire village-name *Worminghall* from the fact of its being where Giles and Chrysophylax first met. Although the use of this word has belittling overtones for the modern reader, it need not be taken as ironic at all. In Old English, the word *worm* was applied to various kinds of animal that creep or crawl, including reptiles and caterpillars as well as what we now call 'worms', and one of its specific uses was for 'a serpent, snake, dragon' (*OED*: WORM *n*, sense 1). This particular use of the word is an ancient Germanic one, found also in related languages. In Old Norse, for example, *ormr* is prominent in heroic poetry as the word for a dragon, just as Old English *wyrm* is in *Beowulf*.

A dragon's power lies not only in fiery breath and bodily strength, but also in the ability to trap a victim into suspicion and delusion *deceit* with cunning words. This characteristic is displayed both by Glaurung, entrapping Túrin in a web of lies (*Silmarillion*, ch. xxi), and by Smaug, who raises suspicions in Bilbo's mind about his companions the dwarves (*Hobbit*, ch. xii). This meaning also underlies the significance of the Gríma's nickname *Wormtongue*, which is intended to liken the evil counsellor not to a paltry earth-worm, but to a deceitful reptile. Tolkien explains it as a 'modernized' form of the Rohan word *wyrmtunga* 'snake-tongue', which is clearly Old English in form ('Guide to the Names in *LR*'). Although *wyrmtunga* is not attested in the Old English manuscripts, it can hardly be a coincidence that Old Norse *Ormstunga* 'Worm's tongue' is found as a nickname—in particular as the nickname of the subject of *Gunnlaugssaga Ormstungu* (The Saga of Gunnlaugr Wormstongue), one of the sagas translated by William Morris in his *Three Northern Love-Stories* (1875).

❖ wose ❖

> You hear the Woses, the Wild Men of the Woods: thus they talk
> together from afar. They still haunt Drúadan Forest, it is said.
> Remnants of an older time they be, living few and secretly, wild and
> wary as the beasts. (Elfhelm of Rohan, in *LR* v. v)

Tolkien did not invent this word, but borrowed it from the Old
English *wudewasa* 'a wild man of the woods; a savage; a satyr, faun'
(*OED*: WOODWOSE). This word had continued in use through the
medieval period: Capgrave, in his *Chronicle* of 1460, records that
'the Kyng of Frauns daunsed in his halle with IIII knites, and was
arayed lich a wodwous'. Even in the 16th century, it was still familiar
enough to be applied to someone dressed as a savage or satyr in a
pageant, though the meaning of -*wose* was long forgotten and the
spelling had often become altered to *woodhouse*. There are numerous other late spellings, but *woodwose* represents the most regular
development from the Old English form, and both the *OED* editors
and Tolkien take this as the most appropriate form to give the word
in a modern context. As Tolkien notes,

> the *wāsa* element meant originally a forlorn or abandoned person,
> and now—for instance in German *Waise* and Dutch *wees*—means
> 'orphan'. The origin of this idea was no doubt the actual existence of
> wild folk, remnants of former peoples driven out by invaders, or of
> outlaws, living a debased and savage life in forests and mountains.
> ('Guide to the Names in *LR*')

Tolkien presumes that the element *wāsa* existed on its own in the
language of Rohan, *wose* being the form that this would have taken if
it had survived in modern English. The full form *woodwose* appears
in Saeros's taunting of Túrin: 'How long shall we harbour this

woodwose?'; 'Outside the hall I could answer you, Woodwose!' ('Narn i Hîn Húrin' in *Unfinished Tales* 80).

Tolkien is not the only 20th-century author to have 'reclaimed' old spellings of this word. Charles Doughty, a poet whose fondness for archaisms makes much of his work almost unreadable, mentions 'woodwoses' in his epic *Mansoul* (1923). And a wild creature called a *wodwo* features in Ted Hughes's 1967 poem (and anthology) of the same name—this being a supposed singular form derived from the apparent plural *wodwos*, which occurs in *Sir Gawain and the Green Knight* (and which Tolkien and E. V. Gordon discuss in their edition of the poem).

✢ wraith ✢

1. An apparition or spectre of a dead person; a phantom or ghost…
2. An immaterial or spectral appearance of a living being, frequently regarded as portending that person's death; a fetch.
(*OED*: WRAITH *n.*)

The word is of Scottish origin, both meanings being traced back by the *OED* to a verse-translation of Virgil's *Aeneid* made in 1513 by the Scottish poet and bishop Gavin Douglas. Tolkien has taken the first sense and given it a particular twist: the *Ringwraiths* are a kind of living dead, invisible and completely controlled by Sauron by means of the rings they once wore.

Long ago they fell under the dominion of the One, and they became Ringwraiths, shadows under his great Shadow. (*LR* I. ii)

Ringwraith is the commonest term, but we also find *Wraith-lord* and *Wraith-king* (*LR* IV. viii). And Frodo speaks with dramatic irony in *LR* I. xi when he jokes: 'I hope the thinning process will not go on indefinitely, or I shall become a wraith.' In early drafts of *The Lord of the Rings*, before the scope of the various rings of power was more precisely determined, there are references to *men-*, *elf-*, *dwarf-*, and *goblin-wraiths* (*HME* VI. 78). Also in the drafts of Appendix A we read of 'a way beneath the White Mountains of Gondor that no man dared to tread, because of the fell wraiths of the Forgotten Men that guarded it' (*HME* XII. 267).

The earlier history and derivation of the word *wraith* is not known. However, there is an etymological possibility which Tolkien favoured, though it is not mentioned by the *OED*. It is conceivable that *wraith* might be descended from an unrecorded noun related to the verb *writhe*, the original meanings of which are 'to coil (something)' or 'to envelop or swathe (something)'. *Writhe* was at one time inflected on the same pattern as *ride*, with past tense *wrothe* and the past participle *writhen* (used by Tolkien to describe the hills behind Mindolluin: *LR* v. v). Just as the verb *ride*, past tense *rode*, is related to the noun *raid*, which is the Scots form of *road*, so *writhe* could be related to *wraith*.

Epilogue

Tolkien's influence on the English language

We have seen how Tolkien's lifelong engagement with the English language led to his coining many words, and using many others in distinctive ways. But that is not the end of the story: when an author's works are read, any distinctive usages may be absorbed into the reader's own vocabulary; the reader may in due course reproduce the usage, and other readers may take it up; and eventually it may become part of the language. To what extent has this happened with Tolkien? Can we find evidence of Tolkien's words having been taken up by other writers?

This is a risky business: when a word used by one author turns up in the work of another, we cannot simply assume that the word has been directly borrowed. The fact that entries in the *OED* include only a selection of the quotations they could contain has made them liable to misinterpretation of this kind; but it would almost certainly be wrong to attribute, for example, Tolkien's use of the word *hill-brow* to his having encountered D. H. Lawrence's use of the same word in a poem of 1913, even though the *OED* records Lawrence's use of it as the first known example (followed by Tolkien's use of it in *The Fellowship of the Ring*). The risk of misattribution is particularly high in the case of words which have been constructed from elements which are freely available to all writers: compounds like *hill-brow*, for example, and prefixed or suffixed forms like ***unlight***. Even a more unusual mode of word-formation, such as the jocular antonymy of *malefit*, can be re-invoked independently by a succession of writers. Even where words have genuinely been borrowed, the borrower rarely acknowledges the fact. Tom Shippey comments on this in a discussion of the influence of Tolkien on the fantasy writer Stephen Donaldson: 'people often do not remember where or when they learned particular words, nor do they regard them as a debt' (*Tolkien: Author of the Century*, p. 322). But Shippey is in no doubt that when Donaldson uses the words *gangrel*, *eyot*, and *dour-handed* he is, consciously or unconsciously, borrowing from Tolkien. (Another clear borrowing is *wilderland*, which Donaldson uses in *Lord Foul's Bane* (1977), and which various other fantasy writers have used subsequently.)

Of course, writers have been borrowing words from their predecessors for centuries. The conscious use of archaisms by historical writers has already been noted (see p. 65); there is a similar tradition in the very different world of science fiction, where if a writer comes up with a new concept which other authors wish to borrow, they may well borrow the word too. By borrowing within the genre, science fiction authors have created a sizeable shared vocabulary, which has proved of such historical interest to some SF readers that there is now a website devoted to the collection of examples for possible use in the preparation or revision of *OED* entries (see http://www.jessesword.com/sf). A similar shared vocabulary can be found among fantasy writers, who are often interested both in creating an archaic atmosphere and in featuring novel concepts. The world of fantasy role-playing games is even more of a lexical melting pot in this respect: players of such games have responded to the need for ad hoc milieux in which to set their adventures by plundering elements from all of their favourite reading. Thus we find 'Lewis

Carrollisms' like *vorpal* (a rare example of a borrowed adjective) alongside coinages by Lord Dunsany (*gnoll*, a cross between a gnome and a troll—although Dunsany's original spelling was *gnole*). Unsurprisingly, Tolkien's word-hoard has from the start been a prominent component of the mixture. His creatures—*halflings* and *orcs*, and even the occasional *warg* or *Balrog*—are ubiquitous, and the adoption of *dweomer* may also originate in Tolkien's use.

Within fantasy literature, Tolkien's coinages and distinctive uses can be found everywhere. A particularly interesting example is the word *lore-master*. Boromir calls Elrond 'greatest of lore-masters' (*LR* ii. ii), and the word recurs elsewhere in *The Lord of the Rings*. Tolkien seems to have been the first to use the word in modern English, although the Middle English form *lore maistir* occurs once in the 15th-century poem *Cursor Mundi*. It has been gratefully taken up by authors looking for a word with a more archaic flavour than, say, *expert*, *sage*, or *storyteller*, among whom one of the earliest was Alan Garner, whose successful children's fantasy novel *The Weirdstone of Brisingamen* (1960) contains a number of thematic echoes of Tolkien (as discussed by Shippey). Curiously, Garner claims never to have read *The Lord of the Rings*, as part of a policy of not reading fiction for fear of being subconsciously influenced by other writers' ideas; and yet, unless Garner had also read *Cursor Mundi*, there is no other obvious source for his description of the evil wizard Grimnir as 'a great lore-master'. The word now occurs frequently in fantasy writing, e.g. in the name of a whole cycle of novels (1986–98) by Mike Jefferies, 'Loremasters of Elundium'. (It has also been used of Tolkien himself: one reviewer of his posthumously published translation of *Sir Gawain and the Green Knight*, *Pearl*, and *Sir Orfeo* said it could be seen as 'the great lore-master's own farewell'.) However, examples in the *OED*'s files show that the word has also been widely used in discussions of medieval scholarship, oral culture, and even ethnobotany. It evidently fills a gap, and has apparently made its way out beyond the restricted context of fantasy into more general use.

There is some evidence that something similar has happened with *mathom*. When James Blish allowed a character in his 1970 Star Trek novel *Spock Must Die!* to refer to his 'collection of duplicate mathoms' (the quotation appears in the *OED Online* entry for *mathom*), he could use the word without explanation, knowing that the popularity of *The Lord of the Rings* among SF readers at that time was such that the word would be understood. But outside the SF/fantasy context, Keri Hulme has used *mathom* in her Booker Prize-winning novel *The Bone People* (1983), and the *OED Online* entry for the word also includes a 1998 quotation from the computing magazine *Byte*.

Other items from the Tolkien word-hoard have achieved currency within the more limited world of fantasy (and science fiction). *Pipe-weed*, for example, is now frequently used in fantasy contexts as a more striking word for 'tobacco' (e.g. by Terry Pratchett in *Equal Rites*, 1987). Similarly, Ursula Le Guin includes a reference to *way-bread* in her 1966 novel *Rocannon's World*, and other writers have also taken it up. (Le Guin's use of *kingsfoil* in *A Wizard of Earthsea* (1968) is another Tolkien borrowing, but in this case the word has not caught on very widely.)

The names of the creatures which populate Middle-earth are something of a special case. Words like *dwarf* and *elf* already had a strong presence in the language before Tolkien used them; within the fantasy context his distinctive conception of what these words denoted, particularly *elf,* has had a powerful influence on how other writers use them. The creature-names which owe their origin to forgotten words from earlier periods of English have now been given a new lease of life—but only on Tolkien's terms. Whatever an *ent* or an *orc*—or a *warg* or a *wose*—was in Old English, the modern conception of them owes almost everything to how Tolkien conceived them.

Many other words from Tolkien's writings, while not bound up with Middle-earth in a way that would make them unusable outside a comparable fantasy milieu, have remained so rare that when another author uses them a link (conscious or unconscious) with Tolkien may safely be assumed—especially when the new context is also a fantasy one. Thus the occurrences of ***confusticate*** in Diana Wynne Jones's *Chrestomanci* books (starting with *Charmed Life*, 1977) and *hagling* in Jan Siegel's *The Dragon Charmer* (2000) are surely borrowings from Tolkien. ***Staggerment*** may be slightly better established but it is still extremely rare, so that Alison Baird's use of it in *The Stone of the Stars* (2004) is most likely to be a direct borrowing from Tolkien.

In short, the English language has begun the process of assimilating Tolkien's personal word-hoard. And the *OED* will continue to record this process.

Bibliography

Works by Tolkien (mentioned in this book):

A Middle English Vocabulary. Oxford: Clarendon Press, 1922.

'Enigmata Saxonica Nuper Inventa Duo', in *A Northern Venture: Verses by members of the University of Leeds University English School Association*, p. 20. Leeds: Swan Press, 1923.

'Henry Bradley: 3 Dec., 1845–23 May, 1923', in *Bulletin of the Modern Humanities Research Association*, No. 20 (October), pp. 4–5. London: 1923.

Sir Gawain and the Green Knight. Edited by J. R. R. Tolkien and E. V. Gordon. London: Oxford University Press, 1925.

'Philology: General works' in *The Year's Work in English Studies* vol. VI (for 1925), pp. 32–66. London: 1927. (Tolkien also provided this review essay in the volumes for 1923 and 1924.)

'Adventures in Unnatural History and Medieval Metres: being the Freaks of Fisiologus. (i) Fastitocalon. (ii) Iumbo, or Ye Kind of Ye Oliphaunt', in *Stapeldon Magazine*, vol. 7, no. 40 (June), pp. 123–7. Oxford: 1927. (Revised version of 'Fastitocalon' published in *The Adventures of Tom Bombadil.*)

'Sigelwara Land [Part I]'. In *Medium Aevum*, Vol. 1, no. 3 (December), pp. 183–196. Oxford: 1932.

'Errantry'. In *The Oxford Magazine*, Vol. 52, no. 5 (9 November), p. 180. Oxford: 1933. Reprinted in *The Adventures of Tom Bombadil*.

'Sigelwara Land (continued from I 196)'. In *Medium Aevum*, Vol. 3, no. 2 (June), pp. 95–111. Oxford: 1934.

The Hobbit, or There and Back Again. London: George Allen & Unwin, 1937; second edition, 1951; (Puffin paperback edition, 1961); third edition, 1966.

Notes on the various editions, and commentary, can be found in *The Annotated Hobbit*, with introduction and notes by Douglas A. Anderson (London: Unwin Hyman, and Boston: Houghton Mifflin, 1988).

'Leaf by Niggle', in *Dublin Review* (January 1945), pp. 46–61. Reprinted in *Tree and Leaf* (London, 1964) and later collections.

'On Fairy-Stories', in *Essays presented to Charles Williams*, London: Oxford University Press, 1947; pp. 38–89. Originally given as a lecture in 1939. A revised version appears in *Tree and Leaf* (London, 1964) and later collections.

Farmer Giles of Ham. London: George Allen & Unwin, 1949.

The Lord of the Rings. Originally three volumes; London: George Allen & Unwin, 1954–5.

> *The Fellowship of the Ring: being the First Part of The Lord of the Rings*. 1954.
> *The Two Towers: being the Second Part of The Lord of the Rings*. 1954.
> *The Return of the King: being the Third Part of The Lord of the Rings*. 1955.

Major revised editions 1965 (New York: Ballantine Books), 1966 (London: George Allen & Unwin), 1987 (Boston: Houghton Mifflin), 1994 (London: HarperCollins), 2004 (London: HarperCollins and Boston: Houghton Mifflin).

The Adventures of Tom Bombadil. London: George Allen & Unwin, 1962.

Smith of Wootton Major. London: George Allen & Unwin, 1967. Reprinted with additional material edited by V. Flieger (London: HarperCollins, 2005).

The Homecoming of Beorhtnoth, in *Essays and Studies by members of the English Association*, N.S. vol. 6 (1953), pp. 1-18. Reprinted in *The Tolkien Reader* (New York, 1966) and later collections.

'The Lay of Aotrou and Itroun' in *The Welsh Review*, vol. 4, no. 4 (December 1945), pp. 254–266.

'Guide to the Names in *The Lord of the Rings*', edited by Christopher Tolkien, in *A Tolkien Compass*, edited by Jared Lobdell. La Salle, Ill.: Open Court, 1975. Cited from the edition by Ballantine Books (New

York, 1980). Reprinted in *The Lord of the Rings: A Reader's Companion* (2005).

The Father Christmas Letters. Edited by Baillie Tolkien. London: George Allen & Unwin, 1976.

The Silmarillion. Edited by Christopher Tolkien. London: George Allen & Unwin, 1977.

Unfinished Tales of Númenor and of Middle-earth. Edited by Christopher Tolkien. London: George Allen & Unwin, 1980.

Letters of J. R. R. Tolkien: a selection. Edited by Humphrey Carpenter, with the assistance of Christopher Tolkien. London: George Allen & Unwin, 1981.

Finn and Hengest: the Fragment and the Episode. Edited by Alan Bliss. London: George Allen & Unwin, 1982. (Based on lectures given in the 1930s.)

The Monsters and the Critics and Other Essays. Edited by Christopher Tolkien. London: George Allen & Unwin, 1983. Includes 'Beowulf: the Monsters and the Critics', 'On Translating Beowulf', 'Sir Gawain and the Green Knight', 'On Fairy-Stories', 'English and Welsh', 'A Secret Vice', and 'Valedictory Address to the University of Oxford'.

The History of Middle-earth. Edited by Christopher Tolkien. Twelve volumes, 1983–96 (short titles as follows):

The Book of Lost Tales, Part I. London: George Allen & Unwin, 1983. (*HME* I)

The Book of Lost Tales, Part II. London: George Allen & Unwin, 1984. (*HME* II)

The Lays of Beleriand. London: George Allen & Unwin, 1985. (*HME* III)

The Shaping of Middle-earth. London: George Allen & Unwin, 1986. (*HME* IV)

The Lost Road and other Writings. London: George Allen & Unwin, 1987. (*HME* V)

The Return of the Shadow. London: Unwin Hyman, 1988. (*HME* VI)

The Treason of Isengard. London: Unwin Hyman, 1989. (*HME* VII)

The War of the Ring. London: Unwin Hyman, 1990. (*HME* VIII)

Sauron Defeated. London: HarperCollins, 1992. (*HME* IX)

Morgoth's Ring. London: HarperCollins, 1993. (*HME* X)

The War of the Jewels. London: HarperCollins, 1994. (*HME* XI)

The Peoples of Middle-earth. London: HarperCollins, 1996. (*HME* XII)

All published in the U.S. by Houghton Mifflin (Boston).

'Qenya Lexicon'. In the journal *Parma Eldalamberon*, no. 12, 1998.

Versions of the *Oxford English Dictionary*:

'*OED*' = *The Oxford English Dictionary*, First Edition (1884–1928), published in parts and reissued in 10 (later 12) volumes; also with a supplement volume published in 1933.

The abbreviation '*OED*' is also used to refer to the dictionary in all its editions, collectively considered as a single work.

'*Supplement to the OED*' = *A Supplement to the Oxford English Dictionary* (1972–86), 4 volumes.

'*OED* (Second Edition)' = *The Oxford English Dictionary*, Second Edition (1989), 20 volumes, incorporating the text of the First Edition and the *Supplement to the OED*, with some additional material.

'*OED Online*' = *Oxford English Dictionary Online* (2000–), an electronic resource incorporating the text of the *OED* (Second Edition) together with draft revised entries for the Third Edition, additional revised material being released quarterly to subscribing individuals and institutions.

Secondary sources and further reading:

Humphrey Carpenter, *J. R. R. Tolkien: A Biography* (London: George Allen & Unwin, 1977).

Humphrey Carpenter, *The Inklings: C. S. Lewis, J. R. R. Tolkien, Charles Williams, and their friends* (London: George Allen & Unwin, 1978).

Verlyn Flieger, *Splintered Light: Logos and Language in Tolkien's World* (Grand Rapids, Mich.: Eerdmans, 1983; revised edition 2002).

Verlyn Flieger & Carl F. Hostetter, eds., *Tolkien's Legendarium: essays on The History of Middle-earth* (London & Westport, Conn.: Greenwood, 2000).

John Garth, *Tolkien and the Great War* (London: HarperCollins, 2003).

Wayne G. Hammond & Christina Scull, *J. R. R. Tolkien: Artist & Illustrator* (London: HarperCollins, 1995).

Wayne G. Hammond & Christina Scull, *The Lord of the Rings: A Reader's Companion* (London: HarperCollins, 2005).

Paul H. Kocher, *Master of Middle-earth: the achievement of J. R. R. Tolkien* (Boston: Houghton Mifflin, 1972).

K. M. Elisabeth Murray, *Caught in the Web of Words: James Murray and the Oxford English Dictionary* (Oxford: Oxford University Press, 1977).

T. A. Shippey, *The Road to Middle-earth* (London: George Allen & Unwin, 1982; second edition, London: Grafton, 1992; references in the text are to the revised and expanded paperback edition, London: HarperCollins, 2005).

T. A. Shippey, *J. R. R. Tolkien: author of the century* (London: HarperCollins, 2000).

Simon Winchester, *The Meaning of Everything: the story of the Oxford English Dictionary* (Oxford: Oxford University Press, 2003).

Index

Index